Photoshop® CS4
Top 100

Simplified®

TIPS & TRICKS

by Lynette Kent

Visual

WILEY

Photoshop® CS4: Top 100 Simplified® Tips & Tricks

Published by
Wiley Publishing, Inc.
10475 Crosspoint Boulevard
Indianapolis, IN 46256
www.wiley.com

Published simultaneously in Canada

Copyright © 2009 by Wiley Publishing, Inc., Indianapolis, Indiana

Library of Congress Control Number: 2008942307

ISBN: 978-0-470-44254-8

Manufactured in the United States of America

10 9 8 7 6 5 4 3 2 1

Trademark Acknowledgments

Contact Us

For general information on our other products and services contact our Customer Care Department within the U.S. at 877-762-2974, outside the U.S. at 317-572-3993, or fax 317-572-4002.

For technical support please visit www.wiley.com/techsupport.

Permissions

Corbis Digital Stock
PhotoDisc, Inc.
Photospin
Purestoc

WILEY

Wiley Publishing, Inc.

U.S. Sales

Contact Wiley at
(800) 762-2974 or
fax (317) 572-4002.

PRAISE FOR VISUAL BOOKS

"I have to praise you and your company on the fine products you turn out. I have twelve Visual books in my house. They were instrumental in helping me pass a difficult computer course. Thank you for creating books that are easy to follow. Keep turning out those quality books."

Gordon Justin (Brielle, NJ)

"What fantastic teaching books you have produced! Congratulations to you and your staff. You deserve the Nobel prize in Education. Thanks for helping me understand computers."

Bruno Tonon (Melbourne, Australia)

"A Picture Is Worth A Thousand Words! If your learning method is by observing or hands-on training, this is the book for you!"

Lorri Pegan-Durastante (Wickliffe, OH)

"Over time, I have bought a number of your 'Read Less - Learn More' books. For me, they are THE way to learn anything easily. I learn easiest using your method of teaching."

José A. Mazón (Cuba, NY)

"You've got a fan for life!! Thanks so much!!"

Kevin P. Quinn (Oakland, CA)

"I have several books from the Visual series and have always found them to be valuable resources."

Stephen P. Miller (Ballston Spa, NY)

"I have several of your Visual books and they are the best I have ever used."

Stanley Clark (Crawfordville, FL)

"Like a lot of other people, I understand things best when I see them visually. Your books really make learning easy and life more fun."

John T. Frey (Cadillac, MI)

"I have quite a few of your Visual books and have been very pleased with all of them. I love the way the lessons are presented!"

Mary Jane Newman (Yorba Linda, CA)

"Thank you, thank you, thank you...for making it so easy for me to break into this high-tech world."

Gay O'Donnell (Calgary, Alberta,Canada)

"I write to extend my thanks and appreciation for your books. They are clear, easy to follow, and straight to the point. Keep up the good work! I bought several of your books and they are just right! No regrets! I will always buy your books because they are the best."

Seward Kollie (Dakar, Senegal)

"I would like to take this time to thank you and your company for producing great and easy-to-learn products. I bought two of your books from a local bookstore, and it was the best investment I've ever made! Thank you for thinking of us ordinary people."

Jeff Eastman (West Des Moines, IA)

"Compliments to the chef!! Your books are extraordinary! Or, simply put, extra-ordinary, meaning way above the rest! THANKYOU THANKYOU THANKYOU! I buy them for friends, family, and colleagues."

Christine J. Manfrin (Castle Rock, CO)

CREDITS

Sr. Acquisitions Editor
Jody Lefevere

Project Editor
Sarah Hellert

Technical Editor
Dennis R. Cohen

Copy Editor
Scott Tullis

Editorial Manager
Robyn Siesky

Business Manager
Amy Knies

Sr. Marketing Manager
Sandy Smith

Project Coordinator
Erin Smith

**Media Development Project
Manager**
Laura Moss

**Media Development Associate
Producer**
Josh Frank

Layout
Andrea Hornberger
Jennifer Mayberry

Graphics
Ana Carrillo
Ronda David-Burroughs
Jill A. Proll

Quality Control Technician
John Greenough

Proofreader
Cynthia Fields

Indexer
Broccoli Information Mgt.

**Media Development Assistant
Project Manager**
Jenny Swisher

**Vice President and Executive
Group Publisher**
Richard Swadley

**Vice President and Executive
Publisher**
Barry Pruett

Composition Director
Debbie Stailey

ABOUT THE AUTHOR

Lynette Kent (Huntington Beach, CA) studied art and French at Stanford University, where she received a Master's degree. A photographer and artist, Lynette writes books and magazine articles on digital imaging and photography. She enjoys traditional and digital painting and often blends these techniques with her photographs. Her photos and those permitted per agreement can be found at www.wiley.com/go/photoshopcs4top100. In addition to the *Top 100 Simplified Tips & Tricks* titles for Photoshop CS2, CS3, and CS4, her latest book is *Teach Yourself VISUALLY Adobe Photoshop Lightroom 2*. She has also written *Teach Yourself VISUALLY Mac OS X Leopard* and *Teach Yourself VISUALLY Digital Photography*, 3rd edition. Lynette helps run the Adobe Technology Exchange of Southern California, a professional organization for photographers, graphic designers, and fine artists.

HOW TO USE THIS BOOK

Photoshop® CS4: Top 100 Simplified® Tips & Tricks includes 100 tasks that reveal cool secrets, teach timesaving tricks, and explain great tips guaranteed to make you more productive with Photoshop. The easy-to-use layout lets you work through all the tasks from beginning to end or jump in at random.

Who is this book for?

You already know Photoshop basics. Now you'd like to go beyond, with shortcuts, tricks and tips that let you work smarter and faster. And because you learn more easily when someone *shows* you how, this is the book for you.

Conventions Used In This Book

❶ Steps

This book uses step-by-step instructions to guide you easily through each task. Numbered callouts on every screen shot show you exactly how to perform each task, step by step.

❷ Tips

Practical tips provide insights to save you time and trouble, caution you about hazards to avoid, and reveal how to do things in Photoshop that you never thought possible!

❸ Task Numbers

Task numbers from 1 to 100 indicate which lesson you are working on.

❹ Difficulty Levels

For quick reference, the symbols below mark the difficulty level of each task.

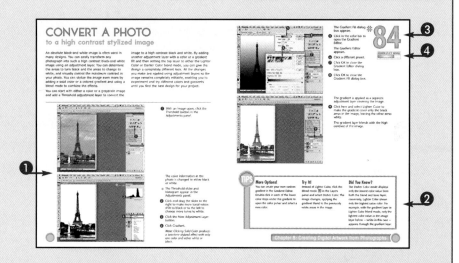

DIFFICULTY LEVEL	Demonstrates a new spin on a common task
DIFFICULTY LEVEL	Introduces a new skill or a new task
DIFFICULTY LEVEL	Combines multiple skills requiring in-depth knowledge
DIFFICULTY LEVEL	Requires extensive skill and may involve other technologies

Table of Contents

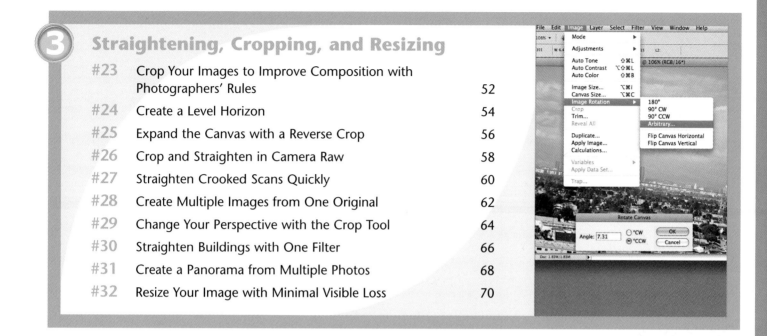

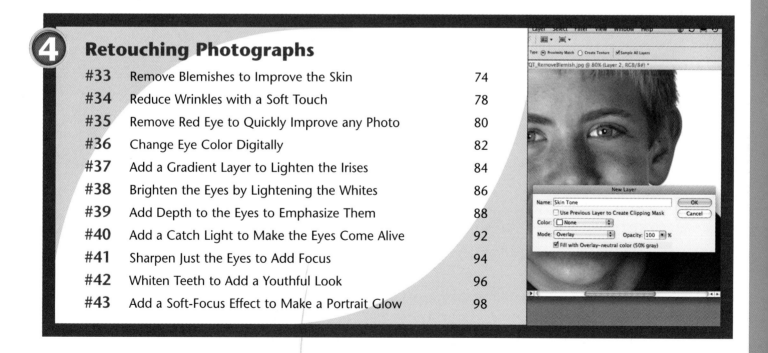

Table of Contents

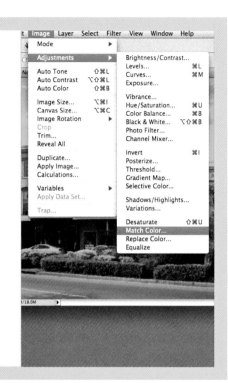

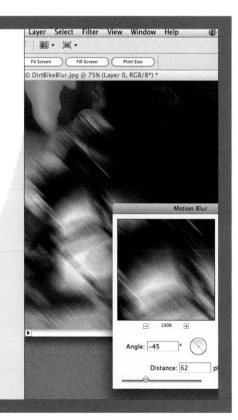

Table of Contents

Customizing Photoshop for Your Projects

Photoshop is an incredibly powerful program. Not only can you perform many different tasks with Photoshop, but you can also choose from a number of ways to complete each project.

By setting up Photoshop to work for you, you can develop your own techniques and find ways to adapt the standard tools so you can be more creative.

When you work on an image, you may prefer to see some panels and not others. You may also prefer certain tool settings to others. Customizing Photoshop to work your way makes you more productive, the program more useful, and everything you do with Photoshop much more fun.

With Photoshop CS4, Adobe has changed the look of the interface and taken customization to a new level. You can modify your settings and preferences by adjusting the workspace, the panels, and the tools to fit the requirements of specific projects. You can close some panels and open others to simplify your screen and keep only the tools you need available. You can make your own gradients, customize shortcuts, and design your own brushes. These may seem like boring steps, yet by learning to customize Photoshop you gain familiarity with the program and become more efficient as you try different projects.

Top 100

SELECT THE COLOR SETTINGS
for your projects

Using Photoshop CS4 is an image-altering experience! You can improve photographs, repurpose them, or create original designs. Because printed images and Web images have different limits on the range of colors that they can represent, you need to set the working color space for your project.

Photoshop's default color space is set to sRGB, a limited color space intended for Web images to be viewable on even the lowest-quality monitor. sRGB is a much smaller color space than what better monitors can show and what printers can actually produce. Designers and photographers generally prefer the larger color space called Adobe RGB (1998) for working with projects intended for print.

In Photoshop CS4, you can easily choose your working color space and save it. Set your color space to the North America Prepress 2 settings and Adobe RGB (1998) to make your printed colors look much better.

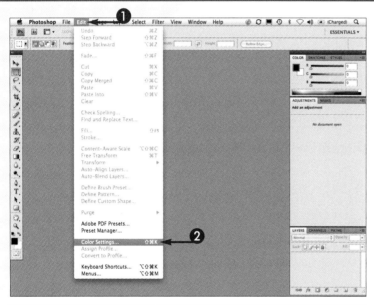

❶ Click Edit.

❷ Click Color Settings.

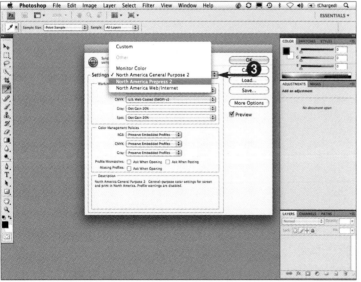

The Color Settings dialog box appears.

❸ Click here and select North America Prepress 2.

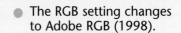

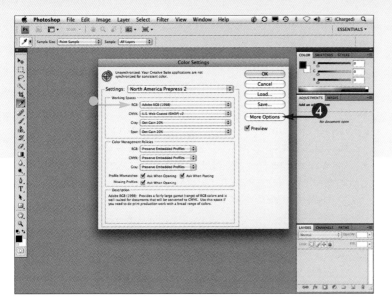

The RGB setting changes to Adobe RGB (1998).

Note: *ProPhoto RGB is an even larger color space often preferred by professional photographers because it includes a wider range of tones and allows for fine detail editing.*

The rest of the Color Settings dialog box changes to reflect the preferred working space for images that you print.

④ Click More Options.

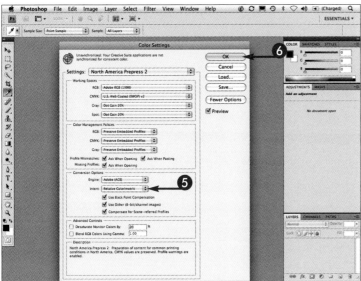

The dialog box expands.

⑤ Click here and select Relative Colorimetric for a graphic design project or Perceptual for most photographic projects.

⑥ Click OK.

Your color settings are saved until you reset your preferences.

TIPS

Customize It!

You can save your own Color Settings preset. The name of the preset changes to Custom when you deselect any check box or make any other changes. Click Save after customizing your settings. Type a name in the Save dialog box and click Save. Your customized preset appears in the Settings pop-up menu, ready for you to choose.

Try This!

You can synchronize the color settings in other Creative Suite CS4 applications to match your saved custom Photoshop CS4 color settings. In Photoshop, click File and select Browse in Bridge. In Bridge, click Edit and select Creative Suite Color Settings. Click North America Prepress 2 and click Apply.

SET THE PREFERENCES
for the way you work

The Preferences menu option includes ten options for Photoshop and one for Camera Raw. All the Photoshop-specific preferences are accessed through different panes in the main Preferences dialog box. Although you can work with the default settings, changing some of these can make your computer run more efficiently or make working with your projects easier. For example, by default, Photoshop is set to use more than half of the available RAM. You can lower this setting to fit the amount of RAM installed in the computer and the number of applications you run at the same time. You can change the default colors for the guides and grid when they are similar to those in your image. Designating an additional plug-ins folder keeps third-party items separate from those included with Photoshop. You can set a separate scratch disk to speed up your work on large files and set Photoshop to automatically launch Bridge.

Read through each Preferences pane and select the settings to make Photoshop work for you.

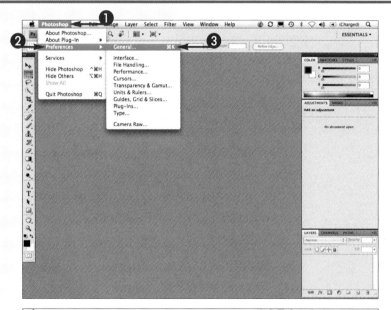

1 Click Photoshop (Edit).

2 Click Preferences.

3 Click General.

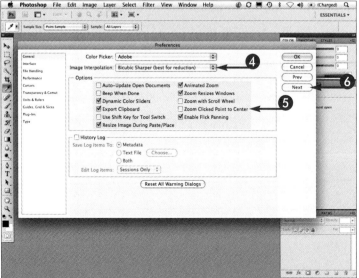

The General Preferences dialog box appears.

4 Click any arrows to change your settings.

5 Click to select the options you want or to deselect those you do not want.

6 Click Next to continue customizing Preferences.

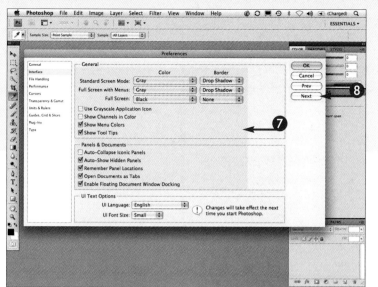

The dialog box changes to the Interface Preferences.

⑦ Click to select the interface options you want or deselect those you do not want.

⑧ Click Next.

DIFFICULTY LEVEL

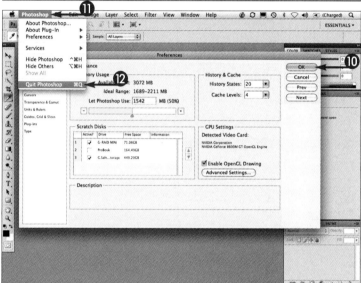

⑨ Make any other changes that you prefer in the other Preferences panes.

⑩ Click OK when you have cycled through all the Preferences panes.

⑪ Click Photoshop (File).

⑫ Click Quit Photoshop (Exit).

The next time you start the application, your own settings take effect.

TIPS

Did You Know?
You can use keyboard shortcuts to set the Preferences. Press ⌘+K (Ctrl+K). Set your options for the General Preferences. Press ⌘+2 (Ctrl+2), and so on, for each of the Preferences panes.

Try This!
You can change the default Preferences so that just pressing the appropriate letter toggles each tool. In the General Preferences pane, deselect the Use Shift Key for Tool Switch check box.

Did You Know?
You can restore the Preferences any time by holding the ⌘+Option+Shift (Ctrl+Alt+Shift) keys as you launch the application. Click Yes in the dialog box that appears, and the Preferences are reset to the defaults.

Move the panels and tools to
CUSTOMIZE YOUR WORKSPACE

The workspace in Photoshop refers to the layout of the different panels and tools on your screen. Photoshop CS4 enables you to design your workspace to fit your needs. You can then save your custom workspace to reuse it with other images.

You can open the panels that you use most and collapse others into buttons. You can move and resize individual panels and docks. You can move the single-column toolbox, dock it, or change it to a two-column toolbox. When you select Full Screen Mode

With Menu Bar from the View menu, your image appears as large as possible with all the tool panels available. You can save the layout with your preferred tools and panel locations.

Photoshop CS4 also includes some preconfigured workspaces, which you can use or modify to accommodate different tasks, such as one for color-correcting photographs and one for working with type.

① With an image open, click View.

② Click Screen Mode.

③ Click Full Screen Mode With Menu Bar.

The image on-screen maximizes to fill the space.

④ Click here to reduce the panel groups to buttons with names.

⑤ Click here and drag to the right to shrink the docks to buttons only.

⑥ Click here to change the width of the toolbar.

⑦ Click here and drag to move the Options bar.

Note: You can make any changes you prefer for your custom workspace.

⑧ Click here to open the Workspace menu.

Note: Optionally, click Window and click Workspace.

⑨ Click Save Workspace.

The Save Workspace dialog box appears.

⑩ Type a name for your workspace.

⑪ Make sure that the Panel Locations check box is selected.

● You can also save custom keyboard shortcuts and menus by selecting these check boxes.

⑫ Click Save.

Your custom workspace is saved.

TIPS

Did You Know?

You can return to the original default workspace any time by clicking Window, Workspace, and Essentials (Default) or by clicking Essentials in the Workspace pop-up menu on the top toolbar. You can also delete unused custom workspaces by clicking Window, Workspace, and Delete Workspace and selecting the one that you want to delete.

More Options!

You can also change workspaces by clicking the name of the current workspace on the menu bar and then clicking another workspace from the pop-up menu.

Try This!

Photoshop CS4 includes a number of predesigned workspaces for particular projects, such as Color and Tone or Painting. You can select a Photoshop CS4 predesigned workspace by clicking Window, selecting Workspace, and then clicking a specific workspace from the menu.

PERSONALIZE YOUR VIEW
of Bridge

Bridge, which ships with Photoshop CS4, acts as a power browser and central hub for all the Creative Suite 4 applications and shows all types of files and folders that are available. You can even see thumbnails of documents and files from other applications, such as Word or Acrobat files. When you double-click a thumbnail from Bridge, the other application launches. You can open Bridge from within Photoshop or as a separate application.

Bridge offers different ways to search, categorize,

and view your files, options for adding information, and automation for various repetitive tasks. By customizing and saving your own Bridge workspace, you can review and compare images more efficiently and have more fun doing so.

To launch Bridge from within Photoshop, click File and Browse in Bridge. You can also click the Bridge button in the Options bar, or press the keyboard shortcut ⌘+Option+O (Ctrl+Alt+O).

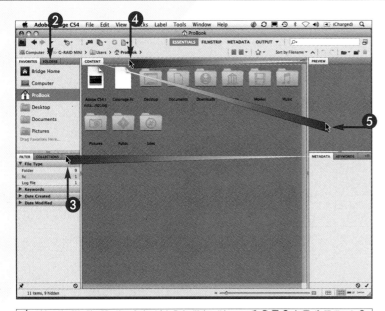

① Launch Bridge.

   Note: You can make any changes you prefer for your custom workspace.

② Click the Folders tab to navigate to a folder of images.

③ Click and drag the Metadata and Keywords tabs to the left panel between the Folders and the Filter tab.

④ Click and drag the Preview tab to the center pane.

⑤ Click and drag the Content tab to the right pane.

   The Content images align vertically on the right.

⑥ Click an image to see it in the Preview tab.

⑦ Click here and drag to the right.

   The Preview tab enlarges and the Content tab narrows.

● You can also click the left separator bar and drag to the left to enlarge the Preview tab more.

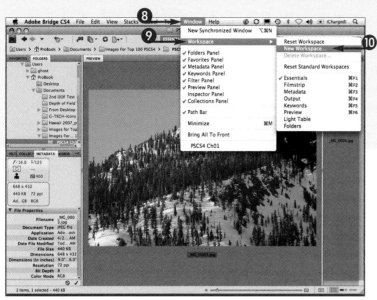

8 Click Window.

9 Click Workspace.

10 Click New Workspace.

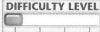

DIFFICULTY LEVEL

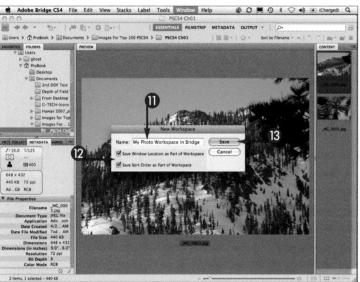

The New Workspace dialog box appears.

11 Type a name for the workspace.

12 Make sure that both check boxes are checked.

13 Click Save.

Your custom workspace is saved and listed in the top panel.

 TIPS

More Options!

You can sort files using the Filter panel. For example, you can view only the portrait-orientation images or all the images created on a specific date. You can also compare images in the Preview panel by pressing Shift and clicking multiple images in the Content panel.

Enlarge It!

Press Tab and the Preview window fills the screen as the other panels slide away on the sides. Press Tab again to return to your custom Bridge workspace.

Try This!

Press ⌘ (Ctrl) and click multiple images in the Content panel to compare them in the Preview panel. You can also stack the selected images by clicking Stacks and then Group or by pressing ⌘+G (Ctrl+G).

ADD A KEYBOARD SHORTCUT
for a favorite filter

Photoshop includes keyboard shortcuts for the tools that you use most often. Many of the tools already have keyboard shortcuts assigned. Still, you may find yourself going to the menu to select an item, such as the Gaussian Blur filter, so often that a personalized keyboard shortcut becomes a huge timesaver.

You can create your own custom keyboard shortcuts or even change some Photoshop keystrokes to something that you can remember better. If the keyboard shortcut that you choose is already

assigned by Photoshop for another function, a warning appears. Although you should generally avoid keyboard shortcuts that are used by your operating system, you can change Photoshop's default shortcuts, or you can apply a different set of keystrokes that are not already assigned.

Learning and using custom keyboard shortcuts can streamline your workflow, leaving you more time for designing and photo-editing.

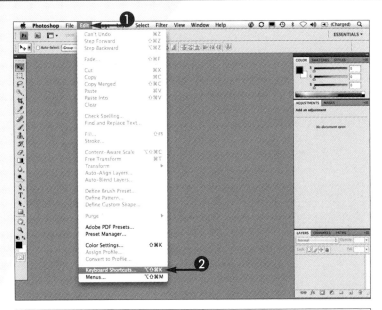

1 Click Edit.

2 Click Keyboard Shortcuts.

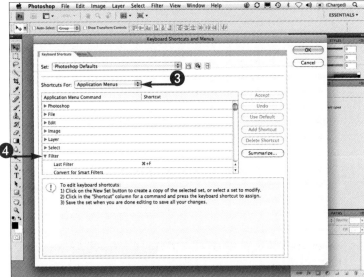

The Keyboard Shortcuts and Menus dialog box appears with the Keyboard Shortcuts tab preselected.

3 Click here and select Application Menus.

4 Click the Filter disclosure triangle.

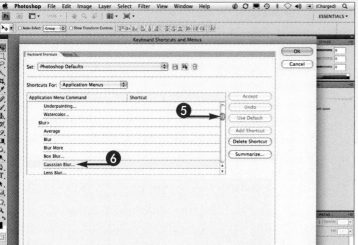

The filters are listed along with any existing keyboard shortcuts.

5 Scroll down to the filter for which you want to add a shortcut.

6 Click the filter.

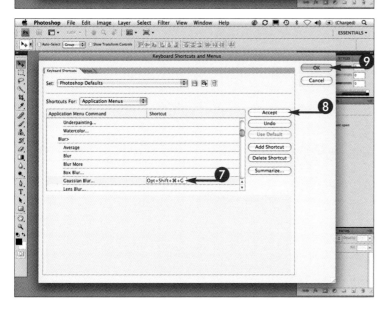

The filter is highlighted, and an empty data field appears under the Shortcut column.

7 Press ⌘ (Ctrl) and type your shortcut in the data field.

Note: *A shortcut must contain either ⌘ (Ctrl) or an F key (function key) in the name.*

8 Click Accept.

The Photoshop Defaults set is modified to include your shortcut.

9 Click OK to finish adding your custom keyboard shortcut.

Did You Know?

You can access the Keyboard Shortcuts and Menus dialog box by using the keyboard shortcut ⌘+Shift+ Option+K (Ctrl+Shift+Alt+K).

Try This!

You can save and print a list of all keyboard shortcuts. Click Summarize in the Keyboard Shortcuts and Menus dialog box and save the file as Photoshop Defaults.htm. Open the file and print the list for reference.

CREATE A CUSTOM ACTION
to increase your efficiency

Actions help you perform repeated steps quickly. An *action* is a series of commands that you can apply to an image with one click of the mouse. Unlike a keyboard shortcut, which can only invoke a command, an action can open a command, apply changes to an image, step through another command, apply it, and even save a file in a particular way. You can create your own actions for steps that you do over and over and add them to the Actions panel.

Using the Actions panel, you record a sequence of steps and save your new action. When you need to apply the same steps to a different image, even to an entire folder of files, you play the action, and Photoshop automatically applies the steps.

Actions can help you automate your work for repetitive tasks, leaving you more time to work on creative projects.

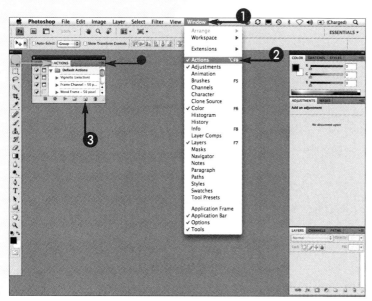

Note: As an example, the following steps show creating an action of opening a new 7- x-5- inch document at 300 pixels/inch for a greeting card.

To create an action for changing an image, start by opening an image.

1 Click Window.

2 Click Actions.

● The Actions panel appears.

3 Click the New Action button.

● Alternatively, you can click here and select New Action from the menu.

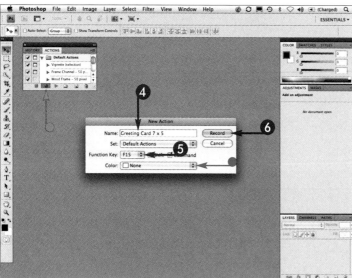

The New Action dialog box appears.

4 Type the name of your action.

5 Click here and select a function key for a keyboard shortcut.

● You can click here and select a color for the action.

6 Click Record.

● The Record button in the Actions panel turns red.

7 Perform the steps that you want to record as an action.

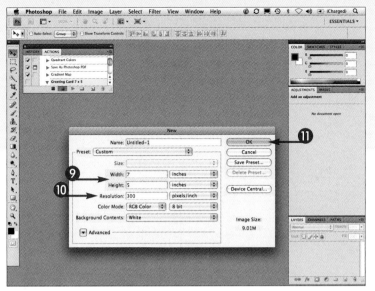

 # 6

DIFFICULTY LEVEL

⑧ Press ⌘+N (Ctrl+N) to open a new file.

The New file dialog box appears.

⑨ Type your specific dimensions in the Width and Height fields.

⑩ Type **300**, or your desired resolution, in the Resolution field.

⑪ Click OK.

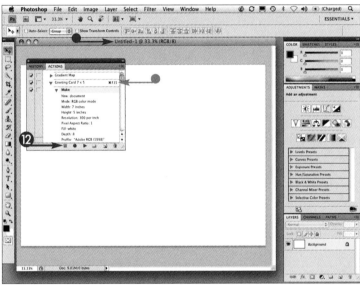

● A new untitled document appears.

⑫ After you perform the last step of your action, click the Stop Recording button.

● Your custom action is now recorded and is listed in the Actions panel.

You can test your action by pressing the keyboard shortcut that you assigned.

TIPS

More Options!

You can apply an action to a folder of files by clicking File, Automate, and Batch and selecting the action and a source folder. Or you can apply an action to a group of images from Bridge by clicking Tools, Photoshop, and Batch.

Try This!

You can make the actions easier to find by selecting Button Mode in the Actions panel's pop-up menu. Your actions change to color-coded buttons.

Did You Know?

You can load other prerecorded actions included with Photoshop CS4 such as Frames or Image Effects by clicking the Actions panel's pop-up menu and clicking a set in the bottom section of the menu.

DESIGN A CUSTOMIZED BRUSH
with your settings

Whether you retouch photographs, design brochures, or paint from scratch, you will use many different variations of the Brush tool.

The pop-up menu on the Options bar includes a variety of brushes, and you can modify the attributes of any of the existing brushes to suit your drawing style or your image. You can then save the modified brush as your own custom brush so that it is ready to use for your next design.

A number of other tools also have modifiable brush options, including the Pencil tool, the Eraser tool, the Clone Stamp tool, the Pattern Stamp tool, the History Brush, the Art History Brush, the Blur tool, the Sharpen tool, the Smudge tool, the Dodge tool, the Burn tool, and the Sponge tool.

Customizing Brush tools for your projects is a timesaving technique, and it is fun.

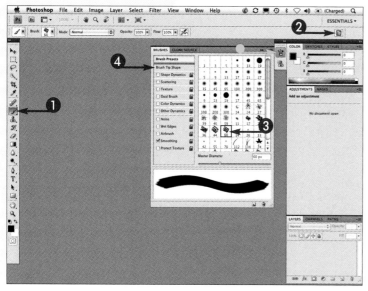

1 Click the Brush tool.

2 Click the Brushes panel toggle button.

● You can also click the Brushes panel button if it is visible.

The Brushes panel opens.

3 Click the preset brush that you want to modify into a custom brush.

4 Click Brush Tip Shape.

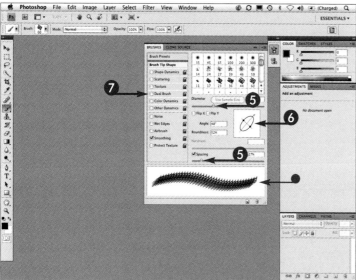

The controls for the brush shape are now visible.

5 Click and drag any of the sliders to change the size and look.

6 Drag the black handles and gray arrow to alter the roundness and brush angle.

● The Preview window displays the changed brushstroke.

7 Click another attribute that you want to change, such as Dual Brush (☐ changes to ☑).

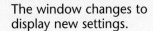

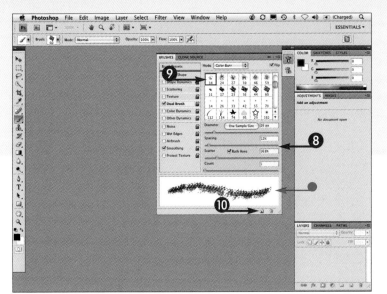

The window changes to display new settings.

⑧ Click and drag any of the sliders to change the size and look.

⑨ Click another selection in the window.

● The Preview window displays the changed brushstroke.

⑩ Click the New Brush button at the bottom of the panel.

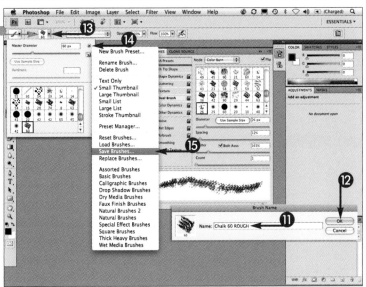

The Brush Name dialog box appears.

⑪ Type a name for your brush.

⑫ Click OK.

● Your customized brush is now available in the Brushes panel and stored with your Photoshop CS4 Preferences.

⑬ Click here to open the brush picker.

⑭ Click here to open the menu.

⑮ Click Save Brushes.

When the Save dialog box appears, type a name for this brush set and click Save.

Your brushes, including your new custom brush, are now saved in Photoshop CS4 Brushes folder in the Presets folder.

TIPS

Important!

You can save your brushes folder to another location on your hard drive, such as the Documents folder, rather than the Photoshop folder. Your custom brush set can then be transferred to another computer or reloaded if you have to reinstall Photoshop.

More Options!

Photoshop CS4 includes many different brush files listed both at the bottom of the submenus on the Brushes panel and the Brush options menu in the Options bar. You can load any set by clicking its name and then clicking Append in the dialog box to add this set to the existing brushes.

Did You Know?

You can view the brushes by name or as a list rather than by the stroke thumbnails. Click the pop-up menu on the Brushes Preset Picker or the Brushes panel. Click Text Only or click a list view or even a different-sized thumbnail.

MAKE A SPECIAL GRADIENT
to suit your design

You can use the Gradient tool to blend colors to fill text with soft gradations of color, to fill backgrounds with a colored gradient, to work with layers and masks, and for making composite images. You can find more gradient color sets in the pop-up menu in the Options bar. You can also create your own gradient by sampling colors from areas in your image or choosing different colors altogether.

You can add intermediate colors and design a blend among multiple colors in any order that you want.

You can even design gradients that fade from any color to transparent.

You can also choose a style for the gradient, such as linear, radial, angled, reflected, or diamond. You customize the gradients from the Gradient Editor. Start with an existing gradient and modify the colors, the color stops, and other variations in the dialog box. The possibilities are almost endless!

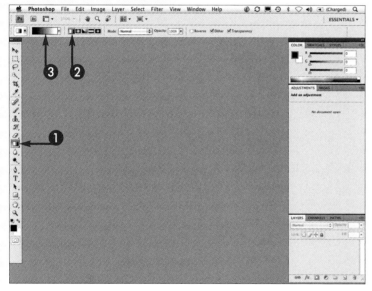

❶ Click the Gradient tool.

❷ Click a gradient type in the Options bar, a linear gradient in this example.

❸ Click inside the gradient thumbnail in the Options bar.

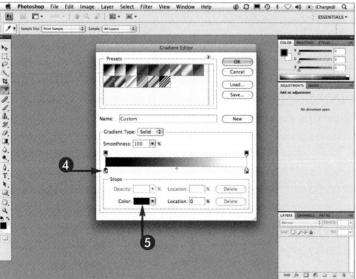

The Gradient Editor dialog box appears.

❹ Click the left color stop under the gradient bar to select it.

❺ Click the Color thumbnail to choose a new color.

The Color Picker dialog box appears.

⑥ Select a color from the dialog box.

Note: If you have an image open, you can move the cursor over the image to select a color.

⑦ Click OK.

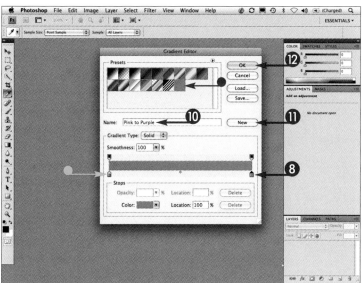

● The selected color fills the left color stop in the Gradient Editor.

⑧ Click the right color stop under the gradient bar to select it.

⑨ Repeat steps 5 to 7 to select the colors for the right color stop.

⑩ Type a name for your new gradient in the Name field.

⑪ Click New.

● The custom gradient appears in the presets.

⑫ Click OK.

Your custom gradient remains in the gradient presets so you can apply it again to other projects.

TIPS

Caution!

You must save your custom gradients in a preset library to avoid losing them when you reset Photoshop's preferences. Click Save in the Gradient Editor dialog box or choose Save Gradients from the pop-up menu in the Gradient picker. Type a name for your gradient library with the suffix .grd. Click Save, and your gradients are saved in Photoshop's presets.

More Options!

Vary your custom gradient by adding color stops. Press Option (Alt) and drag the first color stop to another location or drag a new color stop over other color stops. To remove a color stop, click the color stop and drag straight down.

CALIBRATE AND PROFILE
your monitor for better editing

You adjust colors in Photoshop based on what you see on the screen. Because each monitor displays color differently and because a monitor's characteristics change over time, you should calibrate and profile your monitor regularly to make sure that you are viewing the colors that are actually in your files.

Calibration is the process of setting your monitor to an established color standard. Profiling is the process of creating a data file describing how your monitor reproduces color or an International Color Consortium (ICC) profile.

You need to use a hardware calibration device called a colorimeter or spectrophotometer to accurately adjust your monitor. The software-only methods included with the operating system are too subjective. Both X-Rite and DataColor make affordable devices. A colorimeter can only correct the colors on your screen. A spectrophotometer can also measure and adjust color for your printer.

Please note that the following steps are those used with an X-Rite i1 Display LT. You can follow similar steps for an X-Rite Pantone Huey, ColorMunki, or other device.

① Install and launch the software included with the device, and plug the device into a USB port.

Note: Macintosh users should be logged in as an Admin account.

② Click the monitor image.

③ Click Easy.

④ Click the Forward button.

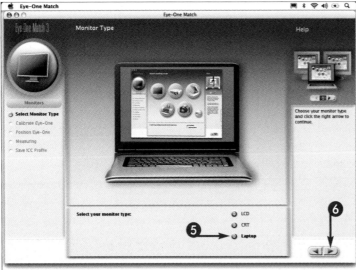

The Monitor Type screen appears.

⑤ Click to select your monitor type.

⑥ Click the Forward button.

⑦ Place your i1 Display on a black surface or place the i1 Pro in its cradle and click Calibrate.

⑧ Click the Forward button to continue.

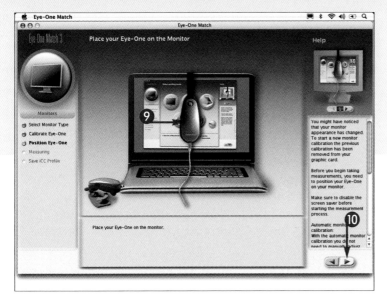

The Place Your Eye-One on the Monitor screen appears.

9 Place the unit on the monitor as the image shows.

10 Click the Forward button.

The screen goes black, and then a box appears under the colorimeter on the screen.

The box fills with white, then black, and then colors as the device automatically measures the color presentation capabilities of your monitor.

● A new screen appears, showing the name of the monitor profile created by the device.

11 Click here to select a reminder for the next calibration.

12 Click the Forward button.

A dialog box appears, telling you where the profile was saved on your computer's hard drive.

13 Click OK.

14 Quit the i1 Match software application and disconnect the i1 Colorimeter or Spectrophotometer.

TIPS

Did You Know?

As monitors age, they lose their color accuracy more quickly. Calibrate and profile regularly — monthly if your monitor is new or weekly if your monitor is over two years old. CRT monitors need to warm up for 30 minutes before you calibrate and create a profile.

Important!

The brightness level of LCD monitors is often set to the maximum at the factory. When you first calibrate and profile an LCD, it may appear dark by comparison. However, after calibrating and profiling, the monitor displays a more accurate representation of the colors in your images.

More Options!

X-Rite's i1 Match software keeps a Help file open in a column along the right side of the screen explaining each step as you proceed. You can increase your understanding of color calibration by reading the explanations as you proceed.

Turn on the full power of Photoshop with a
PEN TABLET

Using a mouse as an input device may work for placing insertion points in text or dragging a rectangular selection in Photoshop, but using a Brush tool or selecting specific areas with a mouse is similar to writing your name with a bar of soap — clunky and inaccurate. You can edit images with greater comfort and control using a pressure-sensitive tablet and pen, such as the Wacom Intuos or Cintiq. More than 20 Photoshop tools, such as the Brushes, the Eraser, the Quick Selection tool, the Clone Stamp, the Dodge and Burn tools, and others can be customized only when a tablet is connected to

the computer. You can then change brush size, roundness, flow, or opacity by applying more or less pressure with the pen.

Instead of scooting the mouse around, you use the pen to place the cursor exactly where you want, and make precise selections or paint digitally as with a traditional paintbrush on paper.

The key to using a tablet and pen and turning on the full power of Photoshop is to start by setting the Tablet Preferences located in the System Preferences or Control Panel.

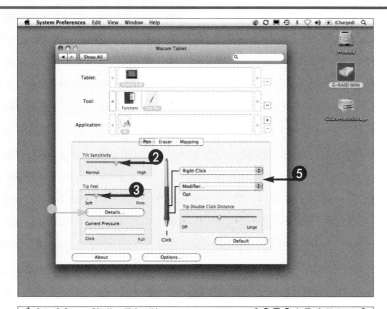

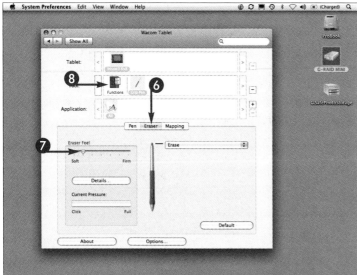

① With a Wacom tablet plugged into a USB port and the Wacom driver installed, open the Tablet preferences.

The Tablet preferences open to the Pen tab.

② Click and drag the Tilt Sensitivity slider to the right for greater tilt response.

③ Click and drag the Tip Feel slider for a softer or firmer touch.

● You can click Details instead of using the slider.

④ When a window drops down, test your settings by drawing in the Try Here box. Click and drag the Sensitivity slider toward Firm or Soft, and then draw in the Try Here box again. You can also click the Try Here box and then move the Click Threshold slider toward Low or High and test again.

⑤ Click different rocker switch settings.

⑥ Click the Eraser tab.

The Eraser preferences appear.

⑦ Click and drag the Eraser Feel slider for softer or firmer eraser pressure.

⑧ Click the Functions tool to customize the tablet keys.

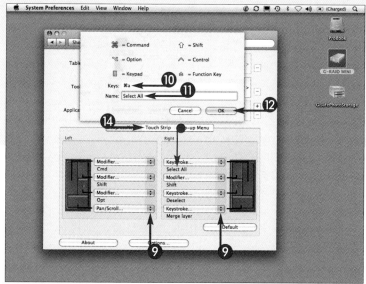

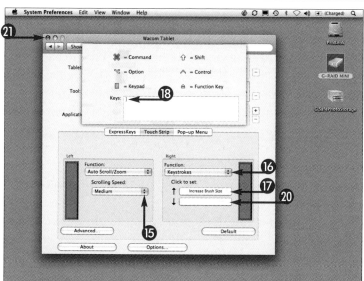

The ExpressKeys preferences appear.

#10

⑨ Click any of the options to change the settings for this ExpressKey.

⑩ Type the keystrokes in the window that drops down and click OK.

⑪ Type a name for the Keystroke in the next window that drops down.

⑫ Click OK to apply the keystroke and name to the ExpressKey.

⑬ Repeat steps 8 to 12 for any other ExpressKey you want to change.

● The ExpressKeys display the names you typed.

⑭ Click the Touch Strip tab.

The Touch Strip preferences appear.

⑮ Click here to change the scrolling speed.

⑯ Click here and select Keystrokes.

⑰ Click in the first Click to Set box.

⑱ Type your keystroke preferences in the dialog box that appears and click OK.

⑲ Type a name for the Keystroke in the next window that drops down and click OK.

⑳ Repeat steps 16 to 18 for the other Click to Set box.

㉑ Click the Close button.

Your custom settings are saved in the Preferences.

TIPS

Try This!

You can save different settings for each option depending on the application. Click the plus sign (⊞) to the right of the Application section and select an application. Then set the Pen, Eraser, ExpressKeys, and Touch Strip options for the tools you use most in that particular application and close the Tablet Preferences. Your pen tablet will respond differently depending on the application.

Important!

There are three basic types of Wacom pen tablets: the Bamboo, the Intuos, and the Cintiq, and each comes in multiple sizes. The Preferences dialog box varies slightly depending on the type of Wacom tablet you have connected.

Did You Know?

More than 20 Photoshop tools are specifically designed for use with a pressure-sensitive tablet and pen. For example, using a mouse, you can only select Off or Fade for Brush opacity. With a tablet attached to the computer, you can also select Pen Pressure, Pen Tilt and Stylus Wheel, giving you more natural and responsive control when painting or editing photos.

Change your
WINDOW VIEWS

Photoshop CS4 enables you to open and view your images in various configurations on the screen. You can open multiple similar photographs at the same time to see which one is the best of the group. You can also have two windows of the same image open.

Photoshop automatically opens multiple images as separate tabs in one window. You can quickly change from one image to the next by clicking the tabs, and you can close any images you do not need by clicking X on the image tab. You can select one image and open it in a separate window while leaving

all the others as tabs in the group or view all the images as cascading individual windows. You can also tile multiple windows so they all fit on the screen at once. You can open a second window of one image and view an enlarged version in one window and the full photo in the other, so you can edit a particular area while still viewing the overall effect on the entire image. Comparing specific areas on similar photos is easy because you can match the areas displayed in each of the images and even match a zoomed-in location.

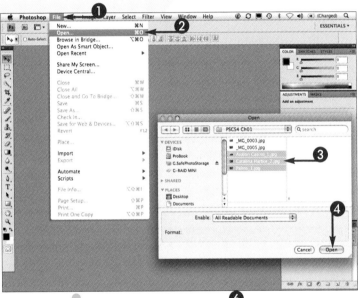

① Click File.

② Click Open.

The Open dialog box appears.

③ Shift+click multiple images to select them.

④ Click Open.

● The images open in the default tabbed mode.

⑤ Click any tab to view a different image.

⑥ Click Window.

⑦ Click Arrange.

⑧ Click Float All in Windows.

● The images open in separate windows cascading down the screen.

9 Click Window.

10 Click Arrange.

11 Click Tile.

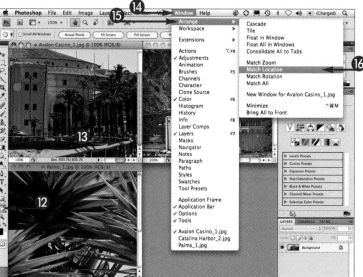

● The images tile across the screen.

12 Click the Hand tool.

13 Click and drag in one image to move it to the bottom right corner.

14 Click Window.

15 Click Arrange.

16 Click Match Location.

All the windows move their contents to display the bottom right corner of each image.

TIPS

Did You Know?
If you zoom in on one image and then tile the windows, you can click Window, Arrange, and Match Zoom to zoom the same amount on all the windows.

More Options!
You can drag one or more windows to a second monitor. You can then have all your tools and panels on one monitor and all your images on the other, or one version of an image on one monitor and an edited version on the other.

Try This!
Click the Arrange Documents button (▦) in the Photoshop bar and click any of the buttons to select a different tiling arrangement, or click Match Zoom, Match Location, or Match Zoom and Location to quickly change your window views.

Working with Layers, Selections, and Masks

Unless you use Photoshop only to resize and print photographs, you will use layers, selections, and masks for most projects. You may simply duplicate a layer as a safety step or build a complex multilayered image combining layers and layer effects with selections and masks.

A *layer* is a similar to a transparency sheet with an image on it. You can edit, transform, or add filters to a layer independently from other layers. You can make one layer alter the look of a layer above or below it. You can flatten all the layers to finalize an image or save a file with the layers for future editing. You can also drag a layer from one document to another.

Selections enable you to isolate areas in your image and apply different effects or filters without affecting the rest of the image. You can even select areas on one layer and create a new layer with that selection. You can make selections with many Photoshop tools depending on the type of area that you need to isolate or remove. You can copy, move, paste, and save selections.

A *mask* is a selection shown as a grayscale image: The white areas are selected; the black areas are not. You can use masks to block out areas of an image or to prevent edits. You can create bitmap layer masks with painting tools or resolution-independent vector masks with a shape tool.

Top 100

NAME AND COLOR-CODE LAYERS
to organize the Layers panel

Layers are one of Photoshop's most powerful features and the key to editing any image. You can name individual layers to help you remember which one applied a specific adjustment to an image. You can also color-code your layers to help you visually organize the Layers panel. You can view all the layers by scrolling or you can expand the Layers panel to view all the layers at once by clicking and dragging the Layers panel tab to separate it from the other panels on the screen. You can also close any panel

tab groups you are not using so the Layers panel expands automatically to fill the space.

Although the tasks in this chapter add only a few layers to each image, you will accumulate many more layers in the Layers panel as you work, depending on the complexity of the project. Whether you work alone or with a group of designers and share projects, naming layers and color-coding them helps you maintain an organized Layers panel and streamlines your workflow and the entire editing process.

CLOSE LAYER TABS

① Click here on any unused tab group.

② Click Close Tab Group.

The tabbed group disappears and the other tabbed groups expand to fill the space.

Note: Optionally, repeat steps 1 and 2 for other unused groups.

Note: You can also click and drag a panel out of a group to maintain it on the screen before closing the other tabs in the tabbed group.

RENAME LAYERS

① Double-click the name of a layer.

② Type a new name in the box.

③ Repeat for any other layers to give each layer a distinctive name.

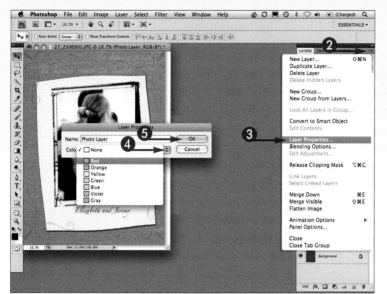

COLOR-CODE LAYERS

1. Start by clicking one layer, such as the Photo Layer, to select it.

2. Click here on the Layers tab.

3. Click Layer Properties.

   The Layer Properties dialog box appears.

4. Click here and select a different color.

5. Click OK to apply the color to the layer.

- The layer's visibility button box changes color.

6. Repeat steps 1 to 4 to color other layers.

TIPS

Try This!

You can group multiple layers into one layer group by selecting the layers and then clicking the New Group button (⬜) on the bottom of the Layers panel, or by clicking Layer and selecting Group Layers from the main menu. Layer groups can be opened for editing purposes and then collapsed to display a single folder. You can also move layers in a group all at once.

More Options!

You can merge any layers that do not need to remain separately editable. Make sure the two layers are one above the other in the Layers panel by clicking and dragging them if necessary. Click the top layer to select it. Click the pop-up panel menu button (▼≡) on the Layers panel and select Merge Down, or press ⌘+E (Ctrl+E). You can also merge layers by ⌘+clicking (Ctrl+clicking) two or more layers and then click Layers and Merge Selected.

DUPLICATE AND CHANGE
the Background layer for more options

The Background layer is generally the bottommost image in the Layers panel — and the only layer in the file when you first open a new photograph. You can duplicate the Background layer and use it to edit the photo or simply work on the duplicated layer to protect the original. Layers are the key to *nondestructive image editing* — that is, working on your images without damaging existing pixels.

Although it does increase the file size, working on a duplicated layer works well for simple changes and can be used as a safety step in most workflows. With a duplicate Background layer, you can quickly

compare your modified image with the original by clicking the visibility button, the leftmost box next to the layer thumbnail in the Layers panel, to toggle the duplicated layer on and off to see the changes you made.

You can add layers above the original Background layer to edit the image. You can also convert the original Background layer to a regular unlocked layer so you can apply special layer effects directly to this layer, change its fill or opacity settings, or move it to another position in the Layers panel.

① Open an image in Photoshop.

Note: In this example, the exposure in an overexposed image is adjusted by duplicating the Background layer and changing the layer blend mode.

② Click and drag the Background layer thumbnail over the New Layer button and release the mouse button.

Photoshop places a duplicated Background layer above the original.

③ Double-click the Background copy's name in the Layers panel to highlight it.

④ Type a different name for the copy.

⑤ Click here and change the blend mode to Multiply.

The photo appears darker.

Note: *If the photo is still overexposed, follow steps 6 and 7. If it appears too dark, go directly to step 8.*

⑥ Click and drag the copied layer over the New Layer button and release the mouse button.

⑦ Repeat step 6 until the photo appears slightly dark.

⑧ Click and drag to the left directly on the word *Opacity* to lower the opacity of the top layer until the photo appears properly exposed.

TIPS

Try This!
You can duplicate the Background layer or any other layer with a keyboard shortcut. Click the layer to be duplicated in the Layers panel to select it and make it the active layer. Press ⌘+J (Ctrl+J).

More Options!
To move the Background layer, you must unlock it by double-clicking its name, typing a new name in the dialog box that appears, and clicking OK.

Did You Know?
The selected layer is called the *active layer*. You can select multiple layers by pressing ⌘ (Ctrl) and clicking them. You can then move them together or add effects to them all at the same time.

Adjust a photo with an
ADJUSTMENT LAYER

You can make a variety of adjustments to an image using the Adjustments option on the Image menu. However, each time you change the pixels in an image, you lose some data. If you combine adjustments, you lose even more pixel information. By applying an adjustment layer instead, you can make color and tonal changes to your image without changing any pixel values.

With adjustment layers, you can edit the adjustment at a later time. You can reduce or vary the effect of the adjustment by using the Opacity or Fill sliders. You can also combine various adjustment layers.

You can access the adjustment layers from either the Layer menu in the Layers panel, or in the Adjustments panel, which provides more options. With the Adjustments panel open, you can quickly add adjustment layers and access the adjustment tools without opening menus or dialog boxes to block your view of the image. Using the options in the Adjustments panel, you can make the adjustment affect all the layers below, or just the top layer.

1 Open an image in Photoshop.

> *Note: In this example, an overexposed image is edited using an adjustment layer.*

2 Click one of the adjustment layer buttons such as Brightness and Contrast.

● An adjustment layer appears above the Background layer in the Layers panel, and the Brightness/Contrast adjustments appear.

3 Click and drag the sliders to adjust the photo.

The adjustment layer's changes are applied to the image.

4 Click the Return to Adjustment List arrow.

The Adjustments panel returns to the Adjustment layer list.

⑤ Click another adjustment such as Black & White.

● Another adjustment layer appears in the Layers panel and the Black & White adjustment options appear.

⑥ Click the Click and Drag button and then click and drag directly on areas of the photo to change the values.

⑦ Click the View Previous State button to temporarily view the adjustment prior to the slider changes you made in step 3.

⑧ Click the visibility button to toggle the visibility of the adjustment layer on and off.

⑨ Click the Reset button to reset the adjustment layer to the default settings.

⑩ Click the trash button to delete the adjustment layer.

TIPS

More Options!

All adjustment layers include a layer mask, represented by a white thumbnail in the Layers panel. You can click the layer mask thumbnail and paint with black in the image to limit where the adjustment affects the underlying photo. If you accidentally reveal too much of the underlying image, you can change the foreground color to white and paint in the mask to reapply more of the adjustment.

Did You Know?

You can use an empty adjustment layer and change the layer blending mode to get the same effect as duplicating a layer and changing the blending mode. Simply click an Adjustment Layer button in the panel but do not make any changes. Then select a different blending mode for the empty adjustment layer in the Layers panel.

BLEND TWO PHOTOS TOGETHER
with a layer mask

Layer masks open a world of imaging possibilities that you just cannot create with traditional tools. Using a layer mask to hide parts of an image, you can easily blend one photograph into another and create designs that are sure to grab a viewer's attention. For example, you can blend a photograph of a wedding couple into a photo of the bride's bouquet or blend a photo of a potato with a photo of a person lying on a couch.

You can blend with a black to white gradient on the layer mask for a smooth transition, or simply use a

brush to paint away parts of the image. As you paint with black on a white layer mask, the images blend. If you paint away too much, simply reverse the colors and paint with white.

This technique is especially effective using a pen tablet. You can easily control how much of the image you reveal with each brush stroke by setting the brush opacity to respond to pen pressure.

1 With the two photographs you want to blend open, click the Move tool.

2 Click and drag the photo you want to blend on top of the photo you want for the base.

3 Close the original top photo.

Note: If the images are the same size and resolution, the top image hides the base image.

4 Click the Layer Mask button in the Layers panel.

● A white layer mask thumbnail appears in the Layers panel.

5 Click the Default Colors icon to set the foreground and background colors.

6 Click the Switch Colors icon to make the foreground color black.

7 Click the Brush tool.

8 Click here to open the brush picker.

9 Click a soft-edged brush.

10 Click the layer mask in the Layers panel to make sure it is still selected.

11 Paint over areas to hide parts of the top image and reveal more of the background photo.

12 Click the Switch Colors icon to reverse the foreground and background colors.

13 Paint with white to fill in areas where you have painted away too much of the top image.

The white paint strokes bring some edge details of the top image back.

TIPS

Try This!

Using a pen tablet, you can vary your paint strokes with pen pressure. Click the Brushes thumbnail to open the Brushes Presets. Click Shape Dynamics and set Size Jitter Control to Pen Pressure.

Customize It!

Double-click the Foreground Color button in the toolbox and select a gray in the color picker. Paint some areas of the layer mask with gray to make them only partially visible.

More Options!

Type some text in an image using the Type tool (T) and click the Layer mask in the Layers panel. Paint over some areas of the letters with black to hide them to make the text appear from behind parts of an image.

Add a design with a
CUSTOM SHAPE LAYER

Custom shapes are resolution-independent vector shapes, meaning that they maintain crisp edges when resized or saved in a PDF file. You can select any of Photoshop CS4's predesigned custom shapes or create your own shape with the Pen tools. You can also load custom shapes you purchase from third party vendors. You can add shapes to any image as a design element or to alter the shape of a photo.

Shapes are applied as separate layers, and each shape layer has two parts: the fill layer and a linked vector mask. The mask is the shape's outline. You can choose the fill layer's color in the Options bar before you draw the shape or you can click in the fill box for the shape layer in the Layers panel and select a different color for the shape. You can also set the fill color to a zero opacity fill.

You can add special effects such as a drop shadow or a stroke to a shape layer by clicking the Layer Style button (fx) at the bottom of the Layers panel.

1 Duplicate the Background layer of an image.

2 Click the Shape tool.

3 Click the Custom Shape tool in the options bar.

4 Click here and double-click a shape in the menu.

5 Click here.

6 Double-click a style button in the menu.

7 Click and drag in your image to draw the shape.

8 ⌘+click (Ctrl+click) the shape thumbnail.

The shape changes to a selection.

9 Click the layer thumbnail and drag it to the trash.

The selection remains on the image.

10 Press D to reset the foreground and background colors.

11 Press X to make the foreground color white.

⑫ Press ⌘+J (Ctrl+J) to duplicate the selection onto its own layer.

⑬ Click the Background copy layer to select it.

⑭ Click the Adjustment Layer button in the Layers panel.

⑮ Click Gradient.

16

DIFFICULTY LEVEL

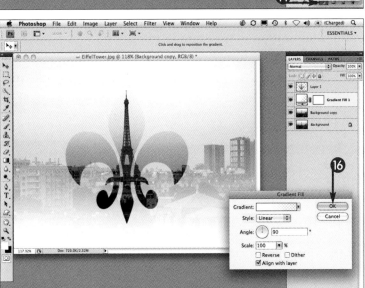

The base image is covered with a white-to-transparent gradient fill.

⑯ Click OK in the Gradient Fill dialog box or click to change the attributes.

The shape highlights the subject of the photo.

TIPS

More Options!

You can access more custom shapes than the default set by clicking the Custom Shape button (▦) in the Options bar and clicking the Shape ▼ to open the selection menu. When you click the drop-down arrow on that menu, you can select one of the shape groups at the bottom of the menu or select All to see all the installed shapes at once. Then double-click a shape thumbnail to select it.

Try This!

Create a gradient fill with a color from your image. Click the Foreground Color box to open the color picker. Move the cursor outside of the Color Picker dialog box and click a color from your image. Click OK to close the dialog box.

ACCENTUATE A SKY
with a gradient fill layer

You may have a scenic photo in which the sky is a bit dull. The lighting may have called for a different exposure setting, or you may need a neutral density filter or polarizing filter on the camera. Still, you may want to use the photo in an album or a graphic design project. You can add a little blue to darken the sky, add some black to make a gray sky more foreboding, or add an orange color to give the sky a golden glow. You can greatly improve an otherwise boring tourist photo using a gradient fill layer.

You can visually adjust the amount of color you add, and because you are using a fill layer, you can go back and increase or decrease the amount of color after you apply the gradient fill layer. You can even change the color that you applied to get a different effect or to create a more dramatic look. This technique is most effective on a photo with a large sky area and an open horizon.

① Open an image with a dull sky.

② Click the Default Colors icon to set the foreground to black.

Note: Optionally, click to select a color to use a gradient for a creative effect.

③ Click the New Fill or Adjustment Layer button.

④ Click Gradient.

The Gradient Fill dialog box appears, and a foreground-to-transparent gradient is applied to the image.

⑤ Make sure that the angle is set to 90 degrees.

6 Click Reverse
(☐ changes to ☑).

The gradient reverses to black at the top, changing to transparent at the bottom of the image.

7 Position the cursor over the image.

8 Drag upward in the image until the gradient covers only the sky and the clouds look menacing.

9 Click OK.

10 Click here and click Overlay.

11 Double-click the layer thumbnail for the gradient fill.

The Gradient Fill dialog box reappears.

12 Position the cursor over the image.

13 Drag downward in the image to increase the darkened sky or drag upward to lessen the effect.

Each time that you drag in the image with the Gradient Fill layer selected, the look of the sky changes.

TIPS

Did You Know?

Multiple layers increase the file size of your image. Because Photoshop requires more memory to work on larger files, you should merge layers that will not be changed later. Pressing ⌘+E (Ctrl+E) merges the highlighted layer with the layer below. Pressing ⌘+Shift+E (Ctrl+Shift+E) merges all the visible layers.

Try This!

You can apply a gradient fill layer on a photo showing a large body of water such as a lake or the ocean. Experiment with different foreground colors for the gradient fill for both dramatic and creative effects.

Make a selection with the
QUICK SELECTION TOOL

The Quick Selection tool in Photoshop CS4 enables you to easily select broad areas of an image by simply painting over them. You can use the Quick Selection tool to remove a background and isolate the main subject.

You can brush over different parts of a photo, varying the brush size as you work, or just click areas for a more limited selection. Once you have made your first selection, the tool automatically changes to the Add to Selection tool, so you can easily add areas without pressing any additional keys. You can subtract from the selection by pressing and holding

Option (Alt) as you paint, or using the Subtract from Selection tool in the Options bar.

This task shows the basic steps for selecting a subject and putting it on a separate layer. You can also select the background on a duplicated layer and press Delete (Backspace) to remove the background from the image, leaving just the subject on the layer. With any active selection you can click Layer in the menu and click Inverse to invert the selection.

For most selections, you will need to use the tools in the following two tasks to refine the selection.

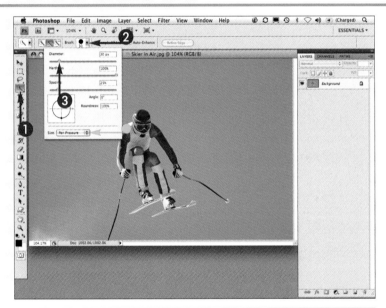

① Click the Quick Selection tool.

② Click here to open the brush picker.

③ Click and drag the Diameter slider to change the brush tip size.

● If you have a pen tablet attached, you can click here to set the brush size with pen pressure.

④ Click and drag inside the part of the image you want to select.

⑤ Click and drag in another area to be selected.

● The tool changes to the Add to Selection option.

⑥ Press ⌘+spacebar (Ctrl+spacebar) and click to zoom in.

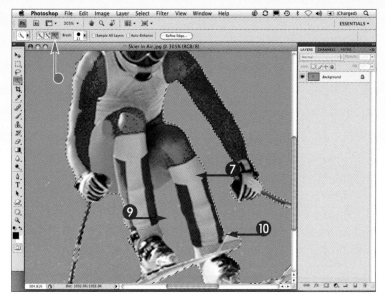

7 Continue clicking and dragging in the image to select more areas.

8 Press Option (Alt).

● The tool changes to the Subtract from Selection tool.

9 Click in areas that you want to remove from the selection.

10 Press and hold the spacebar and click in the image to move to a different area.

11 Click any other areas to remove them from the selection.

12 Press Option+spacebar (Alt+spacebar) and click to zoom out.

13 Press ⌘+J (Ctrl+J) to put the selection on its own layer.

● The selected area appears on a new layer above the Background layer.

Enhance It!

You can click the Auto-Enhance option in the Options bar to reduce the roughness of the selection boundary and extend the selection toward the edges it detects. Depending on the speed of your computer, adding the Auto-Enhance option may slow the selection process.

Keyboard Shortcuts!

To quickly change the brush size as you work, you can use the keyboard. Press the left bracket key to decrease the brush size or the right bracket key to increase the brush size.

More Options!

To quickly Zoom in and out of the photo to make it easier to select the subject, press ⌘ (Ctrl)+spacebar to zoom in and Option (Alt)+spacebar to zoom out as you select different areas.

USE REFINE EDGE
to make all selections better

The Refine Edge floating panel is accessible in the Options bar whenever any selection tool is selected. Using Refine Edge, you can clean up selections, soften or feather the edge outlines, remove edge artifacts or jaggies, and expand or contract selected areas. The panel offers various previewing options, showing the selection on different colored backgrounds or as a red masked area to help you see the edges of the areas you are selecting and the changes you are making. You can use the Refine

Edge panel with any active selection, regardless of the tool used to create the selection. Whenever there is a selection in the image, the Refine Edge button appears in the Options bar.

This task starts with a selection of the background and then inverts the selection to show the subject matter in the selection marquee. You can also select the subject directly, as in the previous task, depending on the detail in your image and what is most easily selected.

① Repeat steps 1 to 3 in the previous task.

② Click and drag in the background in the photo to select it.

③ Press ⌘+Shift+I (Ctrl+Shift+I) to invert the selection.

Note: *Optionally, click Select and click Inverse.*

● The foreground subject is selected.

④ Click the Refine Edge button in the Options bar.

The subject appears against a solid background.

⑤ Click Preview (☐ changes to ☑) to see the changes as you make them.

⑥ Click and drag the Radius slider to soften the edge outline.

⑦ Click and drag the Contrast slider to remove edge artifacts and to sharpen edges.

⑧ Click another preview button, such as the Quick Mask mode, to view the selection.

Note: *Each of the different preview buttons changes the preview mode so you can view the selection either against a white or black background or so you can see the mask or the quick mask of the selected area.*

19

⑨ Click and drag the Smooth slider to smooth the selection outline.

⑩ Click and drag the Feather slider to create a softer-edged transition.

⑪ Click and drag the Contract/Expand slider to adjust the selection edges.

⑫ Click a different preview button, such as the black background preview mode.

⑬ Repeat steps 6 to 12 to make the best selection possible.

⑭ Click OK to save the selection adjustments.

Your refined selection appears on the image and you can press ⌘+J (Ctrl+J) to put the selection on its own layer.

TIPS

Try This!
You can use a keyboard shortcut to quickly change the preview mode when using the Refine Edge panel. Press F to cycle through each preview mode. Press X to temporarily view the original image.

Did You Know?
Moving the Radius slider improves the edge of the selection and helps in areas with more detail. Increasing the Contrast amount sharpens the edges of the selection. The Smooth slider removes jagged edges of a selection, and the Feather slider adds a uniform blur to the selection edge. The Contract/Expand slider contracts or increases the edges of the selection.

PAINT A QUICK MASK
to make a detailed selection

You can select a rectangular or oval area with the Marquee tools, select freeform or geometric areas with the Lasso tools, or make other selections with the Quick Selection tool. When your image requires a more detailed or precise selection, you can use the Brush tool in Quick Mask mode to make a detailed selection or to adjust any previously selected area.

The Quick Mask mode is an editing mode in which protected areas are covered with a translucent colored mask. You paint directly on the areas you want to select, adjusting the brush size as you work

to make the selection more precise. The quick mask covers the area with a translucent red so you can see what you are selecting. You can also specify a different masking color if the area you are selecting has a lot of red in it.

Using this masking technique, you are actually masking the areas you paint, so you must invert the selection before making any adjustments. The areas you painted over are then selected, and the remainder of the image is now masked.

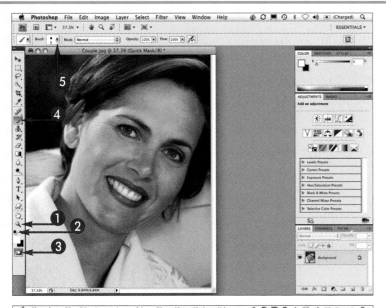

1 Click the Zoom tool and click and drag to enlarge the area you want to select.

2 Click the Default Colors icon to set the foreground color to black and the background to white.

3 Click the Quick Mask Mode button.

4 Click the Brush tool.

5 Click here to open the brush picker.

6 Select a hard-edged brush.

7 Click and drag the Master Diameter slider to adjust the size.

8 Paint over the areas you want to select.

● The painted areas are covered with a red translucent mask.

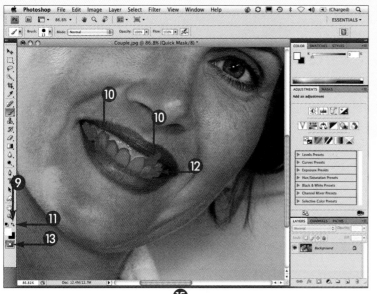

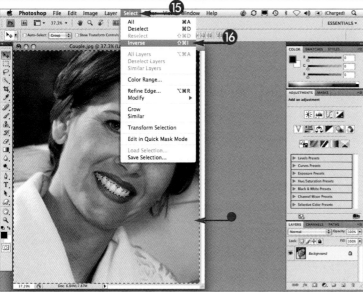

9 Click the Switch Colors icon to reverse the foreground and background colors and make white the foreground color.

10 Paint over any areas that you do not want selected.

11 Click the Switch Colors icon to make black the foreground color.

12 Continue painting until the whole area is covered in red.

13 Click the Quick Mask Mode button to turn off the Quick Mask mode.

14 Press Option+spacebar (Alt+spacebar) to zoom back out.

● Dashed lines indicate the areas that were not masked.

15 Click Select.

16 Click Inverse.

The selection now includes only the area you painted in the Quick Mask mode.

 # 20

DIFFICULTY LEVEL

TIPS

Caution!

Remember that you are creating a mask, which actually selects the inverse of the area you are painting over. You must invert the selection by clicking Select and selecting Inverse before you make adjustments to the selected area.

Important!

You may need to feather a selection before you make adjustments. After you invert the selection, click Select and click Refine Edge to adjust the selection using the Refine Edge panel as in the previous task.

More Options!

If the image you are painting on is very red, change the masking color. Double-click the Quick Mask Mode button (▣) and click the color box in the Quick Mask Options dialog box to pick a new color. You can also reduce the default mask opacity of 50% if necessary to see the selected area below the mask more clearly.

ADD LAYERS AS SMART OBJECTS
for flexible changes

A *smart object layer* is a type of layer that functions as a pointer to the original image file. This type of layer gives you creative flexibility for editing because the original pixel data of the image is preserved. You can edit a smart object layer and then change the adjustment you applied without altering the image quality.

For example, when you transform or scale a regular image layer to reduce the size, some pixels are removed. If you then transform the layer back again, you lose image quality because your previous changes permanently altered the actual pixels.

However, if you open the same photograph as a smart object layer, or convert the layer to a smart object layer, you can scale the layer without any image data loss.

You can open a document as a smart object, convert one or more layers in Photoshop to smart object layers, or move a smart object layer into another document, maintaining its quality as a smart object. You can also place an Illustrator or other vector file into a document as a smart object and maintain the vector's sharp edges or forms even when resizing.

OPEN AN IMAGE AS A SMART OBJECT

1. Click File.

2. Click Open As Smart Object.

   The Open dialog box appears.

3. Navigate to and click a file to open.

4. Click Open.

   The file opens as a smart object.

CONVERT AN OPEN IMAGE LAYER TO A SMART OBJECT LAYER

1. With an image already open, click Layer.

2. Click Smart Objects.

3. Click Convert to Smart Object.

• The layer is changed to a smart object layer and appears in the Layers panel with the Smart Object button. The layer is also renamed to *Layer 0*.

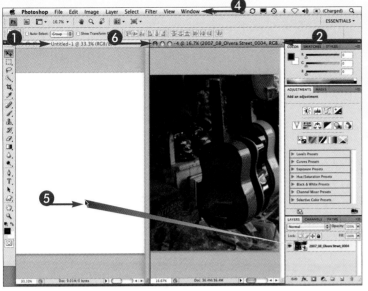

21

DIFFICULTY LEVEL

1. Open a new blank document.

2. Open a Camera Raw image as a smart object as in the first section of this task.

3. Camera Raw opens. Click OK without making any changes to the RAW file.

4. Click Window and then Float All in Windows. Then click Window and Tile so that you can view both images on-screen.

5. Click and drag the smart object layer to the blank document.

6. Click here to close the original smart object file.

   The smart object layer appears in the other document.

● You can double-click the smart object layer to reopen Camera Raw and continue to edit the RAW file.

TIPS

More Options!

You can edit the contents of any smart object layer, not just RAW files. Click Layer, Smart Objects, and Edit Contents. Click OK in the warning dialog box that appears. Edit the original file and press ⌘+S (Ctrl+S). The smart object image is updated.

Try This!

You can create duplicates of a smart object layer in a document and link them. When you replace the contents of one smart object layer, all the duplicates are automatically updated at the same time.

Did You Know?

You can place a Camera Raw image from the Bridge as a smart object layer into a Photoshop file. The smart object layer remains completely editable as a camera RAW file without any data loss.

APPLY FILTERS AS SMART FILTERS
for dynamic adjustments

Filters in Photoshop are used to add blur, reduce noise, sharpen, or style an image. When you apply a regular filter you permanently alter the pixels. By applying a smart filter instead, you can edit and change the settings of the filter at any time, even after the document has been saved and reopened. Any filter applied to a smart object layer becomes a *smart filter*.

You can apply a smart filter to the entire smart object layer or to a selection on a smart object layer. You can remove or hide smart filters at any time. You can add multiple smart filters one on top of another and then change the order of the smart filters to change the resulting effect. You can also add a mask to a smart filter. You can then paint on the mask with black to hide or white to reveal different areas of the filter and create detailed edits on specific areas, all without altering the image data.

All the Photoshop filters, with the exception of Liquify and Vanishing point, and the Shadow/Highlight and Variations adjustments and can be applied as smart filters.

① Open or convert an image as a smart object as shown in the previous task.

② Click Filter.

③ Click a filter such as Gaussian Blur.

④ Click and drag the sliders and adjust any options in the dialog box that appears.

⑤ Click OK.

● The smart filter appears below the smart object layer in the Layers panel.

● A layer mask is automatically applied to the smart filter.

⑥ Click the Brush tool.

⑦ Click here to open the brush picker.

#22

DIFFICULTY LEVEL

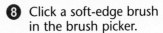
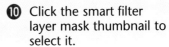
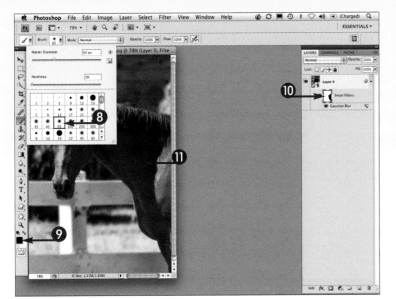

8 Click a soft-edge brush in the brush picker.

9 Press D to restore the default black and white foreground and background.

10 Click the smart filter layer mask thumbnail to select it.

11 Click in the image to paint with black to remove the filter from specific areas.

● The painted areas appear black in the layer mask, and the filters are removed from those areas in the photo.

12 Double-click the filter name to reopen the Smart Filter dialog box and adjust the settings.

TIPS

Try This!

Click the triangle by the smart object layer to reveal the smart filters or any layer effects applied to the layer. Double-click the Edit Blending Options button (⧉) next to the smart filter. A blending mode dialog box appears. Click Mode to select a different blending mode. Click Opacity to drag the slider to a different percentage.

More Options!

To change the effect, click and drag one smart filter above or below another one in the Layers panel. To delete an individual smart filter, click its name and drag it to the Layers panel trash (🗑). To delete all the smart filters on a layer at once, click and drag the text *Smart Filters* on the smart object layer to the trash.

Did You Know?

You can move a smart filter or a group of smart filters to another smart object layer in the layers panel by pressing Option (Alt) and dragging the smart filter. However, you cannot drag a smart filter onto a regular layer.

Chapter 3

Straightening, Cropping, and Resizing

A well-balanced image, free from odd-looking distortions, can mean the difference between a snapshot and a good photograph. The overall layout of the image, how it is cropped, and where the main subject is placed in relation to the background are essential visual elements in any image. Your digital photo may have buildings that appear top-heavy or out of perspective. A crooked horizon or unbalanced subject matter can make even a great image look like the work of a beginner. Your digital photos almost always need to be resized to fit your projects. Even the best photographers have images that require some cropping or resizing. You can follow similar guidelines in both design projects and photographs.

With Photoshop CS4, you can use a variety of straightening and cropping tools to improve

the composition of an image. You can also straighten and crop several crookedly scanned photos in one step. You can even make multiple photos from one original image or create a panorama from several separate images. Using Photoshop and Camera Raw, you can fix various types of camera lens distortions and correct the perspective on buildings; the software does most of the work for you.

Photoshop CS4 makes all such previously time-consuming or difficult tasks quick and easy. Tools and resampling algorithms help you straighten, crop, adjust, and resize images, saving hours of tedious work to make all your images look better.

Top 100

CROP YOUR IMAGES
to improve composition with photographers' rules

Designers and photographers use various techniques to balance an image and catch the viewer's attention. They may change the placement of the horizon to the upper or lower third of the image. They may divide the entire image into thirds horizontally and vertically and place the main subject at the intersection of the thirds. They may just offset the main subject to guide the viewer into the image. Perfectly composing a photograph in the camera's viewfinder is not always possible; however, you can recompose and improve that photo by cropping it in Photoshop.

You can use Photoshop's rulers and drag guides to divide the image into thirds as guidelines or just to mark the center of focus as a visual reference. With your image on a separate layer, you can use the Move tool to recompose your image, placing the main subject where it is most effective.

Then you can use the Crop tool to crop the image and readjust the overall layout. You can also crop visually, specify dimensions in the Options bar, use one of the preset sizes, or create a crop size and save it as a preset.

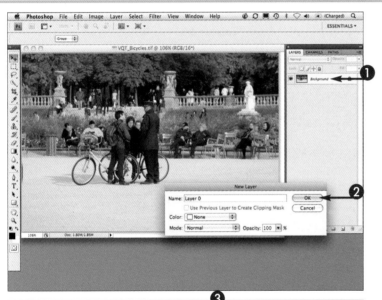

1 With the image you want to crop opened, double-click the Background layer's name.

The New Layer dialog box appears with Layer 0 for the layer's name.

2 Click OK.

The locked Background layer changes to a regular layer.

3 Click View.

4 Click New Guide.

The New Guide dialog box appears with Vertical selected.

5 Type **33%** in the Position box.

6 Click OK.

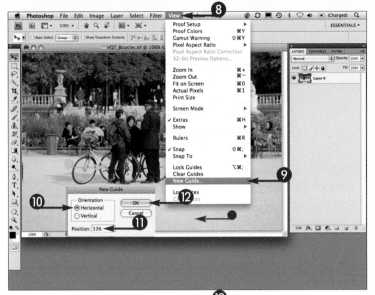

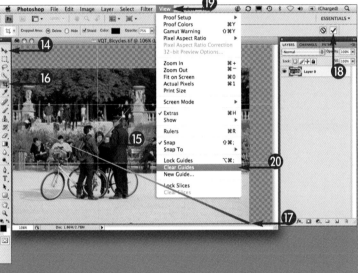

- A vertical blue guide appears on the first third of the image.

7 Repeat steps 3 to 6, typing **66%** in step 5.

- A second vertical blue guide appears on the second third of the image.

8 Click View.

9 Click New Guide.

10 In the New Guide dialog box, click Horizontal (○ changes to ◉).

11 Type **33%** in the Position box.

12 Click OK.

13 Repeat steps 8 to 12, typing **66%** in step 11.

A rule-of-thirds grid in blue is visible over the image.

14 Click the Move tool.

15 Click and drag in the image to place the main focus of the image near the intersection of two guides.

16 Click the Crop tool.

17 Click and drag across the image to select your cropped photo.

18 Click the commit button in the Options bar to accept the crop.

Note: Once the image is cropped, the guides are no longer placed at one-third intervals on the page.

19 Click View.

20 Click Clear Guides to remove the guides.

TIPS

Try This!
You can use the Crop tool () to rotate the area and get a different composition. Drag out a crop marquee with the Crop tool, and then position the cursor just outside the area. It changes to a double-headed arrow (↰). Move the cursor to rotate the cropped area. Click the commit button (✔) to commit the crop.

Customize It!
Create your own Crop tool preset. Click the Crop tool and type your values in the Options bar. Click the Tool Preset picker, the leftmost thumbnail in the Options bar. Click the New Tool Preset button (▣) on the right in the drop-down menu. Name your tool in the dialog box and click OK. Your custom cropping tool is added to the menu.

Create a
LEVEL HORIZON

You may have a photograph that is perfect for your design, but the photo was shot at a crooked angle. You can easily fix that photograph in Photoshop without doing any math to adjust the angle of the horizon line.

Photoshop includes a Ruler tool, found in the toolbox under the Eyedropper tool. This tool is intended to help you position elements precisely in a design layout and can calculate distances between two points in the unit of measure that you have set in

Preferences. When you click and drag the Ruler tool across your image, a nonprinting line is drawn, and the Options bar displays all the numeric information relating to the line and angle.

You can also use this tool to have Photoshop calculate how many degrees your image should be rotated to level the horizon and then have Photoshop straighten the photo for you. You can then use the Crop tool to cut off the angled edges of the image, giving your photograph a straight horizon line.

1 In an image with a crooked horizon line, click and hold the Eyedropper tool to reveal the Ruler tool.

2 Click the Ruler tool.

3 Click and drag from one side of the image to the other, along what should be the horizon line.

Note: You can click and drag along a building or any line that should be horizontal.

● The Ruler tool draws a line across the image.

4 Click Image.

5 Click Image Rotation.

6 Click Arbitrary.

The Rotate Canvas dialog box opens with the exact angle needed to straighten the horizon.

7 Click OK.

The image is rotated, and the horizon is more level.

⑧ Click the Crop tool.

⑨ Click and drag in the image to select the area that you want to crop.

⑩ Drag the corner anchors to the edges.

⑪ Drag the center anchors up or down to fit the image.

⑫ Click the commit button in the Options bar to commit the crop.

DIFFICULTY LEVEL

The image is cropped, and the horizon is now straight.

TIPS

Did You Know?
You can easily check the dimensions of an open photo without opening the Image Size dialog box. Select the Crop tool (🔳) and click Front Image in the Options bar. The current width, height, and resolution are shown in the data fields.

Attention!
The Crop tool retains the dimensions of the previous crop. Be sure to click Clear in the Options bar to reset the tool and remove any old settings before you click and drag the Crop marquee in a new image.

Try This!
Although you have less control over the area to be cropped, you can crop a photo using the Rectangular Marquee tool (🔲) or crop any selected area. Click and drag a selection in the image with the Marquee tool. Click Image and select Crop. The images crops to the selection's bounding rectangle.

Expand the canvas with a
REVERSE CROP

When you think of cropping, you generally think of reducing the physical size of an image by cutting away areas around the borders. In Photoshop, you can also use the Crop tool to expand your canvas, give your photo or image a wider border, or quickly create a new colored background for a photo.

Expanding the canvas with the Crop tool is quick and you can see exactly how your image appears on the enlarged canvas. In addition, using the reverse-crop method, you can create a border that is uneven,

larger on one side than the other for a page layout or a note card, or larger on the bottom than on the top as in a gallery print.

You can use this technique to enlarge your canvas visually or use precise dimensions for your final image. By specifying the width and height for your finished design in the boxes in the Options bar, you can click and drag out the crop marquee in the image and maintain the exact dimensions you typed.

① In an opened image, click the Default Colors icon in the toolbox to set the foreground to black and the background to white.

② Click the Zoom tool.

③ Click the Zoom Out box in the Options bar.

④ Click in the image several times to zoom out.

The image view becomes smaller on a gray background area.

⑤ Click the Crop tool.

⑥ Type the width and height for your finished canvas in the Options bar.

⑦ Click and drag across the entire image.

● The crop marquee appears on the image in proportion to the dimensions you set.

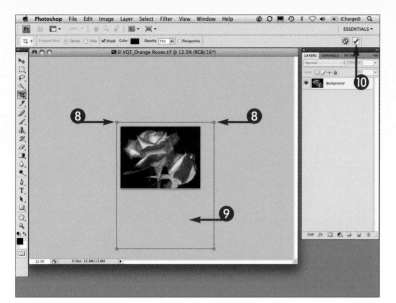

8 Click and drag the corner anchor points of the crop marquee to extend the crop area.

9 Click and drag the expanded area around your photo to fit your design.

10 Click the commit button in the Options bar to commit the crop.

● The canvas is enlarged and filled with the background color.

TIPS

Try This!
Click the Background Color box in the toolbox to open the color picker. Click another color to select it as the foreground color. Then follow the steps above to enlarge the canvas using the reverse-crop method. The extended canvas area fills with your selected color instead of white.

More Options!
If you are working on a series of images with specific sizes, you can create a custom Crop tool preset using the Tool Preset picker. You can then use your custom crop tool to quickly reverse-crop a group of photos. All your images will have the same-sized canvas, making your design and layout tasks much easier.

Change It!
Click the Crop tool (🔲) and type the width and height for your finished design in the boxes in the Options bar. When you click and drag out the crop marquee in the image, it maintains the exact dimensions you typed.

CROP AND STRAIGHTEN
in Camera Raw

Many digital cameras can save image files in the camera manufacturer's proprietary RAW format. Image files in the RAW format are like digital negatives and contain the actual picture data from the digital camera's image sensor without any in-camera processing applied. When you edit images in the RAW format, you maintain more control because you interpret the image data rather than let the camera make the adjustments and conversions automatically.

Using Photoshop CS4 and the Camera Raw converter that is installed with Photoshop CS4, you can not only open photos saved in various RAW formats but

also make color and sharpness enhancements to a variety of formats including RAW, JPEG, and TIFF. In addition, you can crop and straighten those images in Camera Raw before editing them in Photoshop.

After you crop and straighten the image files in Camera Raw, you can save them in the RAW file format and easily reprocess the images at any time. You can also continue to edit and refine them in Photoshop and save them in another file format.

Using Camera Raw to crop and straighten gives you more options for editing and saving images.

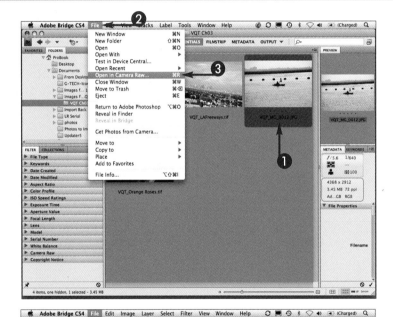

① Launch Bridge and click a JPEG, TIFF, or RAW format image.

② Click File.

③ Click Open in Camera Raw.

Note: If the file is already in a RAW format, you can open it with Photoshop CS4, which automatically opens it in Camera Raw.

The photo opens in Camera Raw.

④ Click the Straighten tool.

⑤ Click and drag on a horizontal or vertical line in the preview image.

● The preview image is rotated with the new angle, and a maximum bounding box appears.

● The Crop tool is automatically selected.

⑥ Click and drag the corner anchors to adjust the composition of the photo if necessary.

⑦ Click and drag inside the bounding box to move the entire selection in the image.

The bounding box moves to the area of the photograph that you want.

⑧ Press and hold Option (Alt).

● The Open Image button changes to Open Copy.

⑨ Click Open Copy to open the image in Photoshop without altering your original.

Note: *Pressing and holding the Option (Alt) key also changes the Cancel button to Reset so that you can start over.*

The cropped and straightened image opens in Photoshop.

TIPS

Did You Know?
You can select and crop multiple images at once to the same size in Camera Raw. All the selected images are displayed on the left of the dialog box and the first one is shown in the main window. Click the Select All button and then the Synchronize button; both buttons are on the left pane of the dialog box. Select the Crop check box. Click OK to close the dialog box. Select the Crop tool () and crop the image in the main window. All selected images are cropped in the same way.

More Options!
You can crop to specific proportions in Camera Raw. Click and hold the Crop tool. Click a preset from the pop-up menu or click Custom. In the Custom Crop dialog box, type the exact ratio or dimensions and click OK. The Camera Raw Crop tool is set for your specific size.

STRAIGHTEN CROOKED SCANS
quickly

When you are not bogged down with repetitive tasks, you can be more productive and creative. Photoshop has many features to help both your productivity and your creativity, such as automated image processing.

Scanning images one at a time is one of those projects that can be very time-consuming. You have to scan one image, crop it, and save it — and then lift the scanner top, reposition another image on the scanner bed, and start over.

Using a flatbed scanner with a large scanning area, you can scan multiple images at one time and let

Photoshop separate these into multiple files. Photoshop's Automate command for cropping and straightening photos even saves time when scanning just one photo. You can place a photo on the scanner bed without lining it up perfectly because Photoshop's Crop and Straighten Photos command can crop and straighten that one scan.

The Crop and Straighten Photos command works best when the images have clearly defined edges and there is at least 1/8-inch between each image. The command may work more quickly if all the images have similar tones.

① In Photoshop, open a file with multiple scans.

② Click File.

③ Click Automate.

④ Click Crop and Straighten Photos.

● Photoshop automatically crops and separates the images onto separate windows as tabs.

⑤ Click Window.

⑥ Click Arrange.

⑦ Click Float All in Windows.

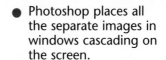

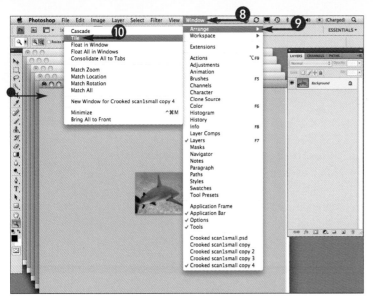

- Photoshop places all the separate images in windows cascading on the screen.

8 Click Window.

9 Click Arrange.

10 Click Tile.

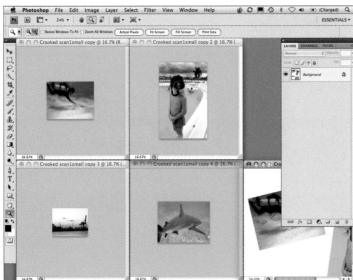

Photoshop arranges the original scan and all the separate images on the screen.

Important!

Photoshop does not replace the original scan with the separated photos, and it does not automatically save the separate images. Instead, Photoshop renames each separated file using the same name as the original scan and labels it "copy," "copy 2," and so on. Be sure to click File and click Save As to rename and save each file.

More Options!

You can scan multiple images at once and decide to keep only one of them. Make a selection border around that one image, including some background. Press and hold Option (Alt) as you select File, Automate, and then select Crop and Straighten Photos. Photoshop crops and straightens that one photo and puts it in a separate file.

CREATE MULTIPLE IMAGES
from one original

Although tools such as the Crop and Straighten Photos command are meant as productivity aids to crop and straighten multiple images at one time, you can use the same tool in various creative ways.

You can create multiple images from one file by using the command to divide one photograph into multiple sections. You can make individual photographs from each section of the original or apply a diptych or triptych look to an image, making two or three panels for the image, which you can print and frame separately.

Select a plain, rectangular frame shape as a custom shape to designate the areas that you want to crop into new images. Photoshop turns those separate shapes into separate images that you can save as new files. The trick to this technique is to leave a small margin around each of the shape selections and to create a separate layer for each shape when you use the Custom Shape tool. If you do not want the shape as part of your final print, you can delete it because the shape is on a separate layer.

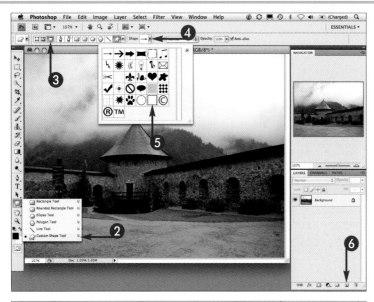

❶ Open a wide photograph.

❷ Click and hold the Rectangle tool and select the Custom Shape tool.

❸ Click the Fill Pixels button in the Options bar.

❹ Click the Custom Shape picker in the Options bar.

❺ Select the Square Thin Frame shape.

❻ Click the New Layer button in the Layers panel.

● A new empty layer is placed above the background.

❼ Click and drag a frame shape in the image.

❽ Repeat steps 6 and 7 twice to have two more layers and two more frame shapes.

Note: Keep at least a 1/8-inch space between each shape.

❾ Click here.

❿ Click Merge Down.

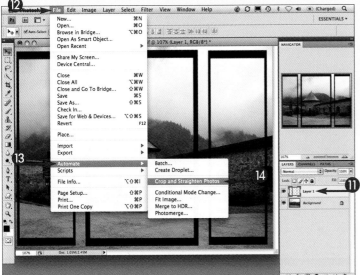

DIFFICULTY LEVEL

⑪ Repeat steps 9 and 10 until there is only one frame layer above the Background layer.

Note: Optionally, Shift+click all three frame layers and click Layer and then Merge Layers.

⑫ Click File.

⑬ Click Automate.

⑭ Click Crop and Straighten Photos.

Photoshop separates the segments and creates three new files with the name of the original plus "copy," "copy 2," and "copy 3."

⑮ Repeat steps 5 to 10 of Task #27 to separate and tile the windows.

⑯ Click the close button of the original file.

⑰ Click and drag each file to align the three new separate files to view the triptych.

TIPS

Important!

Be sure to create a new layer for each frame that you draw. You can then resize and rotate the shapes by clicking Edit and selecting Free Transform to change the frame shapes using the transformation anchors. Merge all the custom shape layers into one layer before applying the Crop and Straighten Photos command.

More Options!

You can drag the shape layer to the trash (🗑) or you can modify the shapes to add a framed look. Select the shapes by ⌘+clicking (Ctrl+clicking) the shape layer. Click Edit and click Fill. Select a color for the frames. Then click Layer, click Layer Style, and apply a bevel and drop shadow to the shape layer.

CHANGE YOUR PERSPECTIVE
with the Crop tool

When you photograph an object from an angle rather than from a straight-on view, the object appears out of perspective, displaying *keystone distortion*. For example, the top edges of a tall building photographed from ground level appear closer to each other at the top than they do at the bottom. If you photograph a window and cannot get directly in front of it to take the shot, the window appears more like a trapezoid. Depending on the photograph, you can correct this type of distortion with a number of Photoshop's tools.

The Crop tool in Photoshop CS4 has a special option that enables you to transform the perspective in an image and quickly adjust the keystone distortion. Your image must have an object that was rectangular in the original scene for the Crop tool's perspective function to work properly. You first adjust the cropping marquee to match the rectangular object's edges and then extend the marquee to fit your image. When you click the commit button, Photoshop crops the image as large as possible while maintaining the angles of the rectangular object.

① Open a photo containing a distorted rectangular object.

② Click the Crop tool.

Note: If there are any dimensions showing in the fields in the Crop tool Options bar when you first select the Crop tool, click the Clear button in the Options bar to remove them.

③ Click and drag a cropping marquee in the image.

The selected area is light, and the area that you want to crop away is dimmed.

④ Click to select Perspective (☐ changes to ☑).

⑤ Click and drag each corner anchor of the cropping marquee and align it with a corner of an object, such as a window, that is rectangular but that appears at a perspective angle in the photo.

Note: To zoom in with the crop marquee showing, press ⌘+ spacebar (Ctrl+spacebar) and click in the image. Press Option+ spacebar (Alt+spacebar) and click in the image to zoom out.

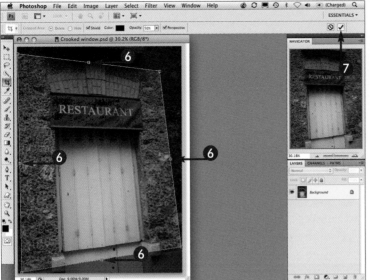

6 Click and drag each of the center anchor points to fit the edges of the entire image.

7 Click the commit button in the Options bar to commit the crop.

DIFFICULTY LEVEL

Photoshop realigns the image and changes the perspective.

TIPS

Attention!

If Photoshop shows an error, you may not have placed the corner handles correctly. Click the cancel button (⊘) in the Options bar and adjust the cropping marquee. Also, the Crop tool (🔲) may not fix the perspective distortion if it is applied to an image that has already been cropped for size.

Keyboard Shortcuts!

Press C to access the Crop tool. Press Return (Enter) to commit the perspective crop or Esc to cancel it. Or Control+click (right-click) in the image and select Crop or Cancel from the menu.

Change It!

Click the word *Opacity* in the Options bar and drag to change the darkness of the shield on cropped areas, or click in the Color box and select a different color for the shield. You can also turn the shield off by clicking the check box to deselect it.

STRAIGHTEN BUILDINGS
with one filter

Depending on the focal length of a camera lens or the f-stop used, a photograph may show common lens flaws such as barrel and pincushion distortion. *Barrel distortion* causes straight lines to bow out toward the edges of the image. *Pincushion distortion* displays the opposite effect, where straight lines bend inward. If the camera tilts up or down or at any angle, the perspective also appears distorted. The Lens Correction filter in Photoshop CS4 can help you fix these and other lens defects easily.

When you photograph tall buildings, the buildings may appear to be larger at the top than at the bottom. The Lens Correction filter enables you to easily line up the perspective of the buildings with a vertical plane. You can use the filter's image grid to make your adjustments more accurately, or you can turn the grid off if you choose. The filter even has an option to let you select how to correct the missing areas along the edges that occurred when the perspective was repaired.

① Open an image as a smart object or open a file and convert it to a smart object layer.

Note: *See Task #21 for information about smart objects.*

② Click Filter.

③ Click Distort.

④ Click Lens Correction.

The Lens Correction dialog box appears with a large preview of the image and a grid overlay.

⑤ Drag the Vertical Perspective slider to align the tallest building with the grid.

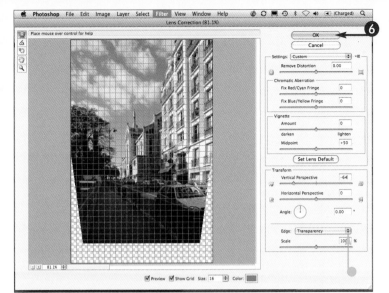

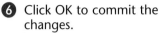

The image appears with a changed perspective plane.

● You can view the edge against a dark background by clicking here and selecting Background Color, or view the image with the edge extended by selecting Edge Extension.

6 Click OK to commit the changes.

The adjusted image reopens in Photoshop.

7 Click the Crop tool.

8 Click and drag in the image.

9 Click the anchors of the crop area to adjust your image.

10 Click the commit button in the Options bar.

The image is cropped, and the buildings appear straight.

TIPS

Try This!
You can edit the adjustment by double-clicking the Lens Correction smart filter in the Layers panel to reopen the Lens Correction dialog box before cropping the final image. You can reset the adjustments in the dialog box by pressing Option (Alt). The Cancel button changes to Reset. Click Reset to remove the changes and start over.

More Options!
You can save the Lens Correction settings and reapply them to other images. Set the options in the Lens Correction dialog box. Click the Manage Settings menu button (⊞) next to the Custom Settings and choose Save Settings. The saved settings appear in the Settings drop-down menu.

Did You Know?
In addition to barrel and pincushion distortion, the Lens Correction filter can fix both *chromatic aberration*, a colored fringe along the edges of objects, and *vignetting*, the appearance of darker corners or edges in the image.

CREATE A PANORAMA
from multiple photos

You can combine multiple photographs into one continuous image to create a panorama. For example, you can take two or more overlapping photographs of a scenic horizon, or even a number of scans of parts of a large document, and then assemble them in Photoshop with the Photomerge command. You can combine photos that are tiled horizontally as well as vertically.

The Photomerge command in Photoshop CS4 can automatically position and blend each layer using individual layer masks. You can also choose to blend the images manually using Interactive Layout.

To make any Photomerge project as successful as possible, photos or scans intended for merging should have an overlap of 25 to 40 percent. You should also maintain the same exposure for each photograph or keep the same scanning settings for each scan. If you are shooting the photos, use a tripod to keep the camera level so the photos line up correctly. By shooting in the Portrait mode or vertically, and shooting more images, you have a larger area to crop from for your final image, giving you a taller and more realistic result.

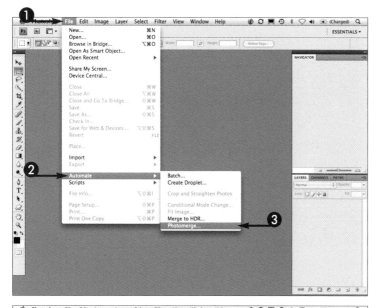

1. In Photoshop, click File.
2. Click Automate.
3. Click Photomerge.

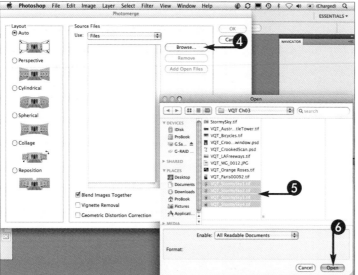

The Photomerge dialog box appears.

4. Click Browse.

The Open dialog box appears.

5. Navigate to and ⌘+click (Ctrl+click) the images to select them.

6. Click Open.

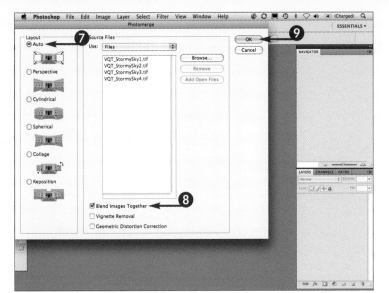

The selected files are listed in the dialog box.

7 Click Auto to select the automatic layout.

8 Make sure that Blend Images Together is selected.

9 Click OK.

Photoshop aligns the images based on content and blends them into a single image.

Note: The new image is a multilayered file.

10 Click the Crop tool.

11 Click and drag across the blended image to make your final panorama.

12 Adjust the corner anchors to fit your image.

13 Click the commit button in the Options bar.

The panorama is cropped to the selected edges.

TIPS

More Options!

The Perspective option (see step 7) uses one image as a reference and adjusts the perspective of the other images to match by overlapping the content of the reference image. The Cylindrical option reduces the bowed shape that can occur in some merged photos, and Spherical has the opposite effect. Collage and Reposition help Photoshop align uneven images.

Change It!

In the Photomerge dialog box, you can add more files to be included in the merge by clicking the Browse button again and navigating to the new source files to be added. You can always remove a file from the Source Files list by selecting the file and clicking Remove.

RESIZE YOUR IMAGE
with minimal visible loss

You often need a different size image than the original. You can resize images using the Image Size dialog box.

By deselecting the Resample Image check box in the dialog box, you can adjust the width, height, or resolution without affecting image quality or pixel dimensions. However, to change the overall size of an image, you must check the Resample Image box; Photoshop resamples by adding or removing pixels to adjust for the new size.

Photoshop's *interpolation methods* — the way it assigns values to added pixels and smoothes

transitions between juxtaposing pixels — work well to preserve the quality and detail as long as the size changes are not extreme. Third-party plug-ins (see Chapter 10) are better for enlarging greater than 150 to 200 percent.

The generally recommended resampling method for reducing image size is Bicubic Sharper, although Bicubic Smoother is intended for enlarging. However, many photographers find that depending on the image, the Bicubic Sharper resampling method, along with a resolution of 360 ppi, actually works best both for enlarging and reducing photos.

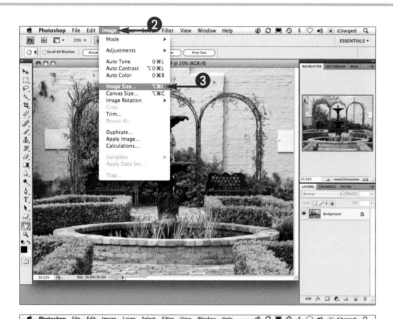

① Open a photo that you want to enlarge.

● The current size of the image as shown on-screen appears here.

② Click Image.

③ Click Image Size.

The Image Size dialog box appears, showing the current size of the opened image.

④ Make sure that the Resample Image check box is selected.

⑤ Double-click in the Width box to highlight the contents.

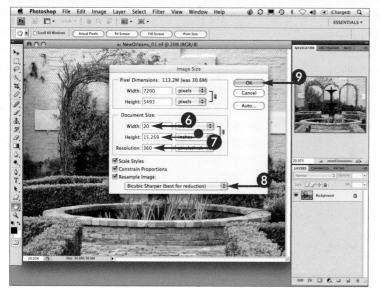

6 Type the width that you want for the final printed image.

● The height automatically adjusts proportionally.

7 Type **360** in the Resolution box.

8 Click here and select Bicubic Sharper (best for reduction).

9 Click OK.

A progress bar may appear depending on the speed of the computer's processor and the size of the image while Photoshop processes the enlargement.

The enlarged photo appears.

10 Click here to check the file size in the window frame.

TIPS

Test It!

Make two copies of an image. Enlarge the first using Bicubic Smoother and the second using Bicubic Sharper. Crop the same 4-x-6-inch section on both enlargements and paste these into two new documents. Because resampling may reduce detail and sharpness, apply the Smart Sharpen filter with the same settings to each new document and print them for comparison.

Did You Know?

A resolution of 150 to 360 ppi is generally recommended for inkjet printing. Images for on-screen viewing only need a resolution of 72 ppi. Images intended for a printing press require a resolution of twice the *line screen* of the press, referring to the number of lines of dots that appear per linear inch (lpi) on the printed piece. If the line screen is 133 lpi, the resolution should be 266 ppi. Rounding up to 300 ppi is generally recommended.

Chapter 4

Retouching Portraits

You can use Photoshop to give your subjects a digital makeover and make them look more beautiful, younger, and healthier. However, it is so easy to alter images in Photoshop that new users often overdo it and make people look like plastic versions of themselves. You are trying to enhance a person's best features and minimize other areas, not turn him or her into someone else. If your subject looks at his photo and thinks that he looks good, you have done your job well.

You can use the tools in Photoshop CS4 to remove blemishes and red eye, enhance the eyes, whiten teeth, soften the face, and more. You can also change a model's hair color or eye color to fit a client's request. You can add a catch light to the eyes even if it was not captured by the camera to enhance a portrait.

You can even reduce wrinkles and smooth the skin without plastic surgery.

Applying the enhancements on separate layers enables you to preserve the original image as well as blend or reduce the changes, making them appear more natural. You should always work on a duplicate of the original file even when you make minor enhancements. To finalize the image, select Flatten Image from the Layer menu before saving it with a new name. Like a magician, you should not reveal your tricks or show the original unretouched photo to the subject!

Because these enhancements should be subtle, a pen tablet is particularly useful when retouching portraits.

Top 100

REMOVE BLEMISHES
and improve the skin

You can greatly improve a portrait by removing skin imperfections. Blemishes may be natural, but they are rarely a desirable feature in a photograph. With Photoshop, you can easily remove or reduce the number of blemishes. You can even leave some while making them less obvious.

As with many other projects in Photoshop, you can use a variety of tools to reduce or remove blemishes. Depending on the areas that need to be retouched, the Clone Stamp tool, the Patch tool, and the Healing Brush can all be used; however, the Spot Healing

Brush is the most effective tool for removing small imperfections. The Spot Healing Brush automatically samples the areas around the spot to be removed and blends the pixels so you do not need to specify the source sample. The key to using the Spot Healing Brush is to work in stages on separate layers and to adjust the brush as you work such that the brush size is just slightly larger than the blemish.

You can then change the opacity of each layer and make the changes less obvious. If you do not like the changes, you can simply discard the layers.

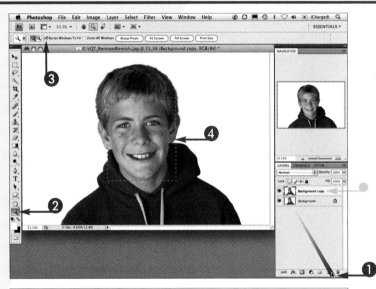

1 With the image open, drag the Background layer over the New Layer button to duplicate it.

● A Background copy layer is added, but the screen does not change.

2 Click the Zoom tool.

3 Click Resize Windows To Fit (☐ changes to ☑).

4 Click and drag over the blemish areas to zoom in.

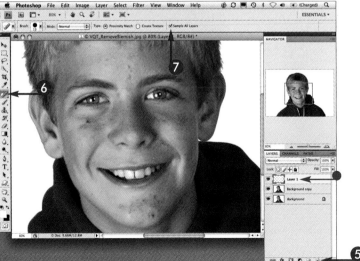

The image is enlarged and fills the screen.

5 Click the New Layer button to add a new empty layer.

● A new layer is added in the Layers panel, but the screen does not change.

6 Click the Spot Healing Brush.

7 Click Sample All Layers (☐ changes to ☑).

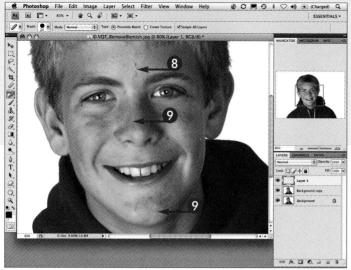

8 Move the cursor over a blemish in the photo and press the left bracket key to reduce the brush size or the right bracket key to increase the brush size.

Note: The brush size should be just larger than the blemish that you want to remove.

9 Click each of the worst blemishes of a similar size first.

Photoshop removes the blemishes and blends the surrounding skin area.

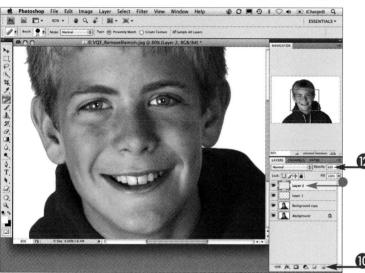

10 Click the New Layer button to add another empty layer.

11 Repeat steps 8 to 10, clicking the other blemishes.

● Layer 2 should be highlighted in the Layers panel.

12 Click here and drag the Opacity slider for Layer 2 to the left until the skin looks natural.

TIPS

More Options!

Once you have finished removing the blemishes, you can combine all the blemish repair layers with the Background copy layer, leaving just the original Background layer and the Background copy layer. You can then quickly compare the before and after images by turning on and off the visibility button () for the Background copy layer.

Did You Know?

If you use a pen tablet rather than a mouse, you can set the size in the brush picker to respond to Pen Pressure. Then set the initial brush size to be just larger than the largest blemish. To vary the size as you brush, press harder to remove large blemishes and press lightly to remove smaller blemishes.

REMOVE BLEMISHES
and improve the skin

The Spot Healing Brush generally removes blemishes and imperfections and makes the skin appear cleaner. However, the blemishes often discolor the surrounding skin tone, and removing the blemishes can leave spots or streaks of mismatched colors on your subject. You can easily improve the overall skin tone and smooth any blotches the Healing Brush may have left using the skin-smoothing technique, as taught by Jane Conner-ziser.

Known as one of the best photo retouchers in the professional photography industry, Jane teaches classes in portrait photography, facial retouching, and fine-art portrait painting at her Digital Art School in Florida, as well as across the United States and internationally. You can learn more about Jane's many classes and seminars at www.janesdigitalart.com.

This technique adds a special dodge and burn layer to your image. You can control the amount of tonal adjustment and improve the skin without making the photo appear retouched and without altering your original file.

⑬ Press Option (Alt) and click the New Layer button.

The New Layer dialog box appears.

⑭ Type a name such as Skin Tone in the Name field.

⑮ Click here and select Overlay for the mode.

⑯ Click Fill with Overlay-neutral color (50% Gray).

⑰ Click OK.

● A gray layer in Overlay mode appears in the Layers panel.

⑱ Click the Brush tool.

⑲ Click here and select a small soft-edged brush.

⑳ Click here and reduce the brush opacity to about 3%.

㉑ Click the Default Colors icon to reset the default colors to black and white.

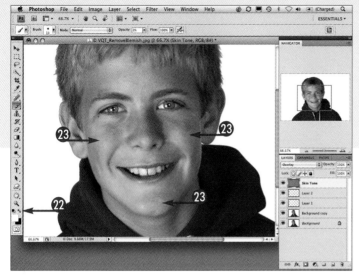

㉒ Click the Switch Colors icon to reverse the colors, making white the foreground color.

㉓ Paint over any dark spots in the image to smooth the skin.

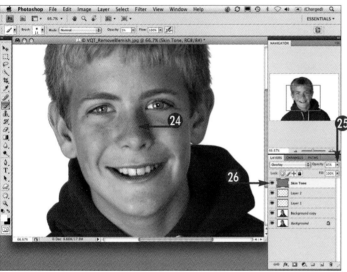

The skin tone appears smoother.

Note: The skin tone changes are very subtle and should be more visible on your monitor and on a printed photo than in the photo on these pages.

㉔ Continue painting over any dark areas, adjusting the size of the brush tool as necessary.

㉕ Click here and drag the Opacity slider to the left to reduce the effect for a more natural look.

㉖ Click the visibility button for the gray layer multiple times, turning it off and on to compare the image before and after the adjustment.

The skin tone is smoothed and appears natural rather than over-corrected.

TIPS

More Options!

You can press X to reverse the background and foreground colors and paint with black to darken any areas that appear too light. However, if your image starts to appear unnatural, open the History panel and click back several steps to undo the changes. Then continue painting until the skin tone appears natural.

Attention!

You may not see much of a change as you paint with the Brush opacity set to 3%; however, when you turn off the visibility button ( ) for the layer, you will definitely see the changes. You can increase or decrease the brush opacity one or two percent, brush over an area, and then check the changes by toggling on and off the visibility button.

REDUCE WRINKLES
with a soft touch

You can remove wrinkles with Photoshop in a variety of ways, including cloning them away with the Clone Stamp tool or patching them using the Patch tool. However, if you remove all the wrinkles and give a person perfectly smooth skin, the effect is not believable. Using the Healing Brush tool and a separate layer, you can maintain more control over the corrections and give your subject a rejuvenated yet natural appearance.

You can modify the Healing Brush to a medium softness and change its shape and angle so that your brush strokes are not as visible when you literally paint away the wrinkles. You can create a special wrinkle-removing brush by changing attributes in the brush picker in the Options bar. The effect appears even more realistic if you use a pressure-sensitive pen tablet and set the Healing Brush to respond to pressure.

After you brush away the years, you can change the opacity of the altered layer to reintroduce just enough wrinkles to appear natural.

① Click and drag the Background layer thumbnail over the New Layer button to duplicate the layer.

② Click the Zoom tool and zoom in to enlarge the areas with wrinkles.

③ Click the New Layer button to add a new empty layer.

④ Click and hold the Spot Healing Brush tool and select the Healing Brush tool.

⑤ Click here to open the brush picker.

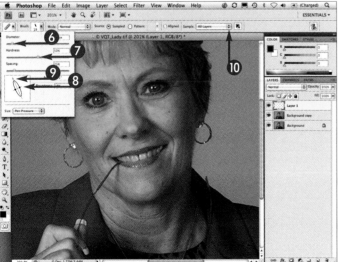

⑥ Set the Diameter slider to a brush size wide enough to cover the deepest wrinkles.

⑦ Drag the Hardness slider to the midpoint to build a brush with just slightly soft edges.

⑧ Click one dot on the circle in the thumbnail and drag toward the center to change the roundness of the brush.

⑨ Drag the arrowhead to change the angle of the stroke in the direction of the deepest wrinkles.

⑩ Click here and select All Layers.

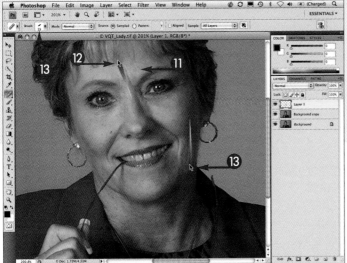

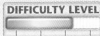
⑪ Option+click (Alt+click) an area of clear skin near one wrinkle to sample.

⑫ Click and drag directly on the first wrinkles to paint them away.

⑬ Click here and repeat steps 8 to 12, changing the brush angle and roundness for the other wrinkles.

⑭ With the top layer selected, click here and drag the slider until the wrinkles appear diminished and still natural.

The wrinkles on the face are less pronounced, and the person appears slightly rested and younger.

TIPS

Try This!

To make painting more natural try using a pen tablet. By setting the rocker switch on the pen to the Option (Alt) key, you can press the switch to sample areas with the Healing Brush tool. Also, use many small strokes rather than one larger one when you paint over wrinkles with the Healing Brush and sample nearby areas of clear skin often. The skin tones will match more closely, and the results appear more natural.

Try This!

You need to zoom in and out often when removing wrinkles. Instead of changing tools when the Healing Brush is selected, press ⌘+spacebar (Ctrl+spacebar) and click to zoom in. Press Option+spacebar (Alt+spacebar) to zoom out.

REMOVE RED EYE
to quickly improve any photo

You can remove the red eye effect from your photos quickly using either the Red Eye tool in Photoshop or the Red Eye Removal tool in Camera Raw.

Red eye is caused by the reflection of a camera flash in a person's retina. When you shoot in a darkened room, the subject's irises are wide open and their pupils enlarged, increasing the chances for red-eye photos. Using a camera with the flash mounted directly above the lens also causes more red eyes than using a bounce flash or a flash unit that is positioned away from the camera lens.

The default settings for pupil size and darken amount for both tools are the same and can be adjusted to fit your image. You can quickly apply the Red Eye tool in Photoshop to one eye. If necessary, undo the correction, adjust the darken amount in the Option bar, and apply the tool again. In Camera Raw, you can more easily control the effect as you apply the Red Eye removal tool by adjusting the correction on each eye individually.

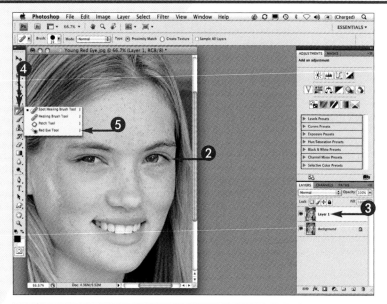

REMOVE RED EYE IN PHOTOSHOP

❶ In Photoshop, open a photo that has a red eye effect.

❷ Press ⌘+spacebar (Ctrl+spacebar) and click and drag over the eyes to zoom in.

❸ Press ⌘+J (Ctrl+J) to duplicate the background layer as a safety step.

❹ Click and hold the Spot Healing Brush tool to see the other tools.

❺ Click the Red Eye tool.

❻ Click and drag over one eye.

The red is replaced by a dark gray.

❼ Repeat step 6 for the other eye.

REMOVE RED EYE IN CAMERA RAW

① In Photoshop, click File.

② Click Open.

③ Navigate to the red eye photo in the Open dialog box.

④ Click here and select Camera Raw.

⑤ Click Open.

DIFFICULTY LEVEL

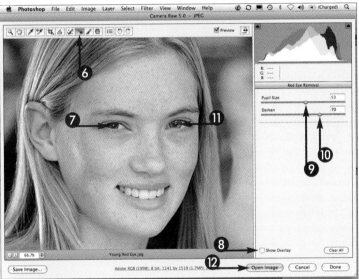

The photo opens in Camera Raw.

⑥ Click the Red Eye Removal tool.

⑦ Click and drag an area across one eye, including some of the surrounding face in the selection rectangle.

The red is replaced by a neutral gray.

⑧ Click Show Overlay to deselect it (☑ changes to ☐).

⑨ Click and drag the Pupil Size slider to adjust the size of the gray area covering the pupil.

⑩ Click and drag the Darken slider to adjust the strength of the gray area.

⑪ Repeat steps 7 to 10 for the other eye.

⑫ Click Open Image to open the image in Photoshop.

TIPS

Try This!

In Photoshop, press J to select the Spot Healing Brush tool ().
Then press Shift as you press J again three times to select the Red Eye tool (⬚).

More Options!

You can remove the red-eye effect from all photographs, whether they are scanned from film or prints or start out as digital files.

Did You Know?

You can often avoid red eye by using the red-eye reduction feature included with some cameras. This feature minimizes the red-eye effect by firing several flashes an instant before the photo is taken, forcing the pupils to close slightly just as the final flash and shutter are released.

CHANGE EYE COLOR
digitally

The eye color often appears grayer or darker in photos than the actual color of the eyes when you look at the person directly. You can improve many photos by adding a little color to the iris of the eyes. You can simply add a little more color or you can change the color to a different hue.

When you colorize the eyes, you are looking for a natural eye color. You can also select any color as the foreground color and paint in the irises. If you have another photo of the same person where the eye color appears more natural, you can sample the eye

color from the first photo and paint it into the one with the grayed eyes. Colorizing the eyes naturally depends on the specific brush options you set in the Options bar.

You can also use the same technique to apply one person's eye color to another subject's eyes. Agencies often request a specific eye color for a model to better blend into the color scheme of an advertising piece. You can save time by using Photoshop to change the eye color in the original photo and avoid finding and photographing a different model.

① Click and drag the Background layer over the New Layer button to duplicate the layer as a safety step.

② Click the Zoom tool and zoom in to enlarge the eyes.

③ Click the Eyedropper tool.

④ Click here and select 3 by 3 Average.

⑤ Click in the iris to set a reference color as the foreground color.

⑥ Click the Brush tool.

The Options bar changes.

⑦ Click here to open the brush picker.

⑧ Drag the Master Diameter slider to set a brush size just smaller than one-half the iris.

⑨ Click and drag the Hardness slider to 50% so there is only a slightly soft brush edge for better blending.

⑩ Click the Airbrush button to enable it.

⑪ Click the Foreground Color box in the toolbox.

The Color Picker dialog box appears.

⑫ Click and drag the Hue slider to another color.

⑬ Click OK to close the color picker.

⑭ Click the New Layer button to add a new empty layer.

⑮ Click here and select Color for the layer blend mode.

⑯ Click and drag over both irises to paint in the new color.

⑰ Click the Eraser tool and erase if you paint over other areas.

⑱ Click here and drag the Opacity slider to the left until the eye color appears natural.

The irises of the eyes are now a different color.

More Options!

If you have another photo with an appropriate eye color, you can use the Color Replacement tool instead of the standard Brush tool. The tools are in the same group in the tool box. Option+click (Alt+click) in the first photo using the Color Replacement tool (✏) to sample the color of the eyes that you want to use. Then apply the color on the empty layer of the image you are correcting, using a soft-edged brush.

Did You Know?

Dogs' and cats' eyes often show a greenish or white eye when they are photographed with a flash. The Red Eye removal tool (👁) does not remove that effect. You can, however, paint in the eye color using the techniques described in this task.

Add a gradient layer to
LIGHTEN THE IRISES

The eyes are generally considered the most important feature in a portrait. You can add interest to the eyes and draw the viewer in by giving the eyes a digital brightening effect. You can improve the eyes in a variety of ways in Photoshop. Some methods work better on one image than another, so learning and trying various techniques lets you improve your images according to your subject and the project's requirements.

You must apply the gradient on a separate layer, not only to protect the original image and make it easy

to undo the effect, but also so you can adjust the strength of the eye brightening to fit your photo and make it look natural. You adjust the layer opacity as you view the effect on-screen before flattening the layers and saving the file. This technique is very quick and often gives just enough sparkle to an otherwise dark eye.

Like all portrait retouching, the effect should be subtle and yet still brighten the subject's eyes.

① Click the New layer button in the Layers panel to add a new layer.

② Click the Default Colors icon to reset the default colors to black and white.

③ Press X to reverse the default colors, making the foreground color white.

④ Click the Zoom tool and zoom in to enlarge the eyes.

⑤ Click the Gradient tool.

The Options bar changes.

⑥ Click the Radial gradient.

⑦ Click here and select the Foreground (white) to transparent gradient.

● Reverse should be unchecked and Dither and Transparency should be checked.

⑧ Click in the center of one pupil and drag to the edge of the iris.

⑨ Repeat step 8 for the second eye.

10 Click here to change the layer blend mode.

11 Click Overlay.

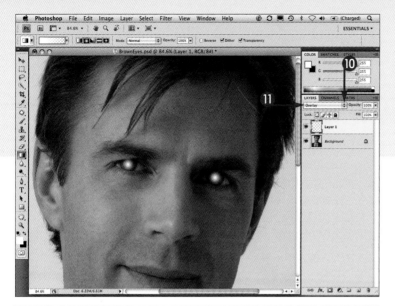

The bright white spots blend into and lighten the irises.

12 Click the word *Opacity* and drag to the left to reduce the layer opacity until the eye color appears lighter but still natural.

The irises of the eyes are now brighter.

13 Click the layer visibility button to turn it off and compare the before and after views.

Did You Know?

The default gradient always uses the current foreground and background colors in the toolbar. Set the foreground color before you select the gradient tool and then press G to quickly select the Gradient tool. You can also access the other tools on the toolbox by pressing a specific letter, such as V for the move tool or Z for the Zoom tool. When multiple tools are grouped together, like the Spot Healing Brush, the Healing Brush, the Patch tool, and the Red Eye tool, you can press the one-letter keyboard shortcut to access the first tool and then repeatedly Shift+click the letter to cycle through all the grouped tools.

BRIGHTEN THE EYES
by lightening the whites

You can quickly enhance any portrait by lightening the whites of the eyes. The eyes are the most important feature of the face and the key to a person's individuality. Whether the whites of the eyes are bloodshot or just appear dull, lightening them can enhance the whole face. Brightening and desaturating the white area draws the viewer into the subject's personality.

Lightening the whites of the eyes is a multistep and multilayer process. You first select the whites and remove the redness using a Hue/Saturation adjustment layer. Then you brighten the eyes with a Curves adjustment layer and change the blending mode of the layers.

The whites of people's eyes are not completely white, so this adjustment requires not only making a precise selection, but also viewing the entire photo as you apply the changes. Because the adjustments are on separate layers, you can easily go back and modify the adjustments to enhance the overall image and keep the subject looking natural.

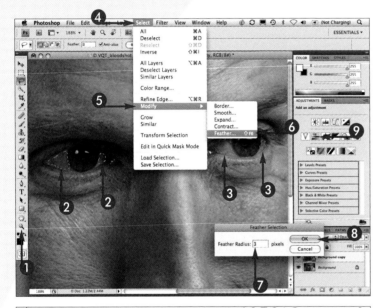

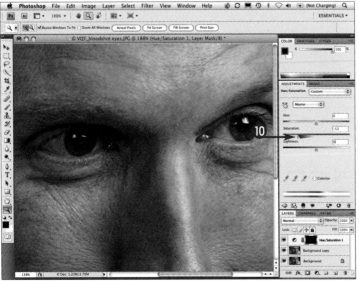

1 With the Background layer duplicated, click the Zoom tool and zoom in on the eye area.

2 Click the Lasso tool and draw a selection around the white area of one eye.

3 Press Shift and select the other white areas of the eyes.

Note: You can also click the Add to Selection button ( ) and continue selecting other areas.

4 Click Select.

5 Click Modify.

6 Click Feather.

7 Type **3** for the Feather Radius.

Note: The feather radius depends on your photo's size.

8 Click OK.

9 Click the Hue/Saturation button.

The panel changes to the Hue/Saturation panel, and a Hue/Saturation layer appears in the Layers panel.

10 Drag the Saturation slider to the left just enough to remove the redness.

The whites appear gray.

11 Press ⌘+0 (Ctrl+0) to zoom out and view the whole face.

⑫ Click and drag the Lightness slider to the right slowly just enough to lighten the whites.

⑬ With the Hue/Saturation layer still selected, click and drag the Opacity slider to the left if necessary to reduce the effect until the eyes look brighter but still natural.

The subject's eyes appear bright without appearing artificially lightened.

TIPS

More Options!
In most panels, dialog boxes, and Options bars, clicking and dragging on the word associated with a slider activates the scrubby sliders. The cursor changes to a pointing finger. Click and drag across the word, changing the amount in the data field.

Did You Know?
Pressing Shift as you select with a selection tool enables you to add to a selected area or add a separate selection. Pressing Option (Alt) as you drag over a selected area enables you to remove areas from that selection.

Try This!
With the selection tool still active, you can quickly access the Feather dialog box, or other options, once you make a selection by Control+clicking (right-clicking) in the selection area. A contextual menu appears, listing options such as Feather and Select Inverse.

ADD DEPTH TO EYES
to emphasize them

Removing red eye and lightening the whites of the eyes improves any portrait photograph. You can also make your subject more interesting by adding other adjustments that emphasize the eyes. You can add more contrast to the iris by lightening some areas and darkening others. You can add depth to the eyes by darkening the eyelashes and the natural outline of the eyes. This digital technique is similar to dodging and burning in the darkroom.

Instead of using Photoshop's Dodge and Burn tools on the image, however, you can use the Brush tool

on separate empty layers and vary the opacity of each layer to control the adjustments. Painting with white lightens areas. Painting with black darkens areas, lengthens the eyelashes, and adds definition to the eyes. Using the Opacity setting in the Layers panel, you can fine-tune the adjustments before you finalize the image.

Making the eyes sparkle by using a variation of digital dodging and burning in Photoshop helps draw the viewers' attention to the eyes and engages them in the photo.

① Click and drag the Background layer over the New Layer button to duplicate it.

② Click the New Layer button.

● A new empty layer is added to the Layers panel.

③ Double-click in the Opacity data field and type **10** to view a more realistic adjustment as you work.

Note: You can increase or decrease the Opacity before saving the file.

④ Click the Zoom tool and click and drag across both eyes to zoom in.

⑤ Click the Default Colors icon to reset the foreground and background colors to the defaults.

⑥ Click the Switch Colors icon to reverse the foreground and background colors and set the foreground to white.

⑦ Click the Brush tool.

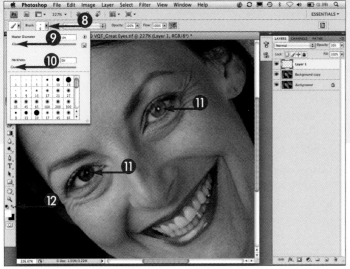

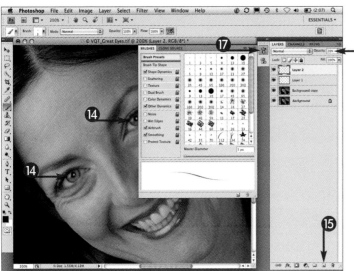

8 Click here to open the brush picker.

9 Click and drag the Master Diameter slider to select a small brush that fits inside the iris.

10 Click and drag the Hardness slider to 0% to build a very soft brush.

11 Paint in the center of each iris.

12 Click the Switch Colors icon to reverse the foreground and background colors and set the foreground to black.

13 Press the left bracket key to reduce the brush size.

14 Paint with black around the edges of the irises and in the pupils.

15 Click the New Layer button to add a second empty layer.

16 Double-click in the Opacity data field and type **20** to view a more realistic adjustment on this layer as you work.

17 Click the Brushes button if it is on-screen, or press F5 to open the Brushes panel.

#39

DIFFICULTY LEVEL

Did You Know?

You can save and reuse an eyelash brush. With the settings that you create for Brush Tip Shape (see step 19), click the panel menu button (▦) on the right in the Brushes panel. Click New Brush Preset. Type a name in the dialog box and click OK.

Try This!

Press D to set the foreground and background colors to the default black and white. Press X to quickly switch the foreground and background colors as you digitally dodge and burn.

Try This!

To lighten dark brown eyes, try setting the foreground color to a dark red or burgundy color instead of white. Paint in the irises on a separate layer and adjust the opacity. Adding red to dark brown eyes softens the look.

ADD DEPTH TO EYES
to emphasize them

Retouching portraits is always tricky. You want to improve the image and still preserve the person's character. Because the eyes can define personality, enhancing the eyes almost always helps the overall portrait and helps the viewer focus on the subject.

When you work on any portrait and especially when you work on the eyes, you need to make small changes. Large changes are too often obvious, and your subjects want to see themselves and be seen at their best, not different. Make small changes and repeat these on several layers. You can easily adjust the opacity of each layer independently, creating more variations in brush strokes and colors. With adjustments on multiple layers, it is also easier to change or delete enhancements that do not seem natural.

Using a pressure-sensitive pen tablet also gives more variety to brush strokes. Use light brush strokes instead of heavy ones. Many of the brush options can be set to respond to pressure or tilt, allowing you to alter brush styles with fewer trips to the Brushes panel.

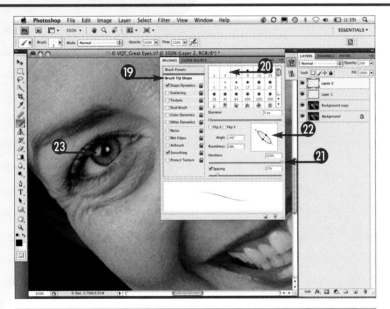

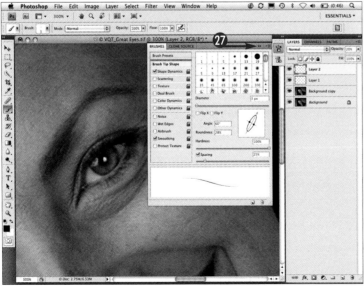

⑱ Press ⌘+spacebar (Ctrl+spacebar) and then click in the image to zoom in to see the eyelashes.

⑲ Click Brush Tip Shape.

⑳ Select a very small brush to match the size of the eyelashes.

㉑ Click and drag the Hardness slider to 100% to build a completely hard-edged brush.

㉒ Drag the brush angle and the dots on the roundness icon to conform the brush shape to the eyelashes of one eye.

㉓ Paint over the eyelashes one at a time to darken them.

㉔ Repeat steps 22 and 23 to adjust the brush for different angled eyelashes.

㉕ Press the spacebar and click and drag in the image to move to the other eye.

㉖ Repeat steps 22 to 24, adjusting the brush to fit the shape of the lashes of the other eye.

㉗ Click here to close the Brushes panel.

㉘ Press Option+spacebar (Alt+spacebar) and click in the image to zoom out to see the whole face.

㉙ Click Layer 1 to highlight it.

㉚ Click in the Opacity data field.

㉛ Press the keyboard up or down arrows to increase or decrease the layer opacity until the irises look natural.

㉜ Click Layer 2 to highlight it.

㉝ Click in the Opacity data field.

㉞ Press the keyboard up or down arrows to increase or decrease the opacity until the eyelashes look darker but still natural.

The eyes now appear stronger and still natural and help focus the viewer's eyes.

㉟ Click here and select Flatten Image to finalize the photo.

TIPS

More Options!

You can add eyeliner to the eyes in a photograph. First add another layer. Lower the opacity to about 18%. Paint with black at the edge of the eyelashes on each eye. Click in the Opacity data field and use the keyboard up and down arrows to increase or reduce the opacity of the layer until the eyeliner looks natural.

Did You Know?

You can use the same technique shown in this task to enhance light eyebrows. Add a layer and reduce the opacity to 8%. Open the Brushes panel and click Brush Tip Shape. Set the hardness to 0% and change the size, angle, and roundness to match the shape of the eyebrows. Paint a few smooth strokes over both eyebrows using black. Change the layer's opacity as needed.

ADD A CATCH LIGHT
to make the eyes come alive

When the light source — whether it comes from a camera flash, side lighting, or a natural light source — reflects in the subject's eyes, it forms a catch light. A *catch light*, also called a *specular highlight*, in a subject's eyes adds life and sparkle to the subject and brightens the overall photograph. More importantly, it draws attention to the subject's eyes and engages the viewer.

If the subject in a photograph does not have any specular highlights in the eyes or if the subject's eyes

appear somewhat dull, you can use Photoshop to add catch lights. The trick is to make them look real.

Jane Conner-ziser, one of the most experienced and well-respected portrait retouching masters, teaches this technique in her classes and instructional videos. Jane creates catch lights with diffused edges and emphasizes the use of two separate layers, one for the glow and the other for the sparkle of catch lights. By placing them on separate layers, you can adjust the catch lights to achieve a natural, realistic look.

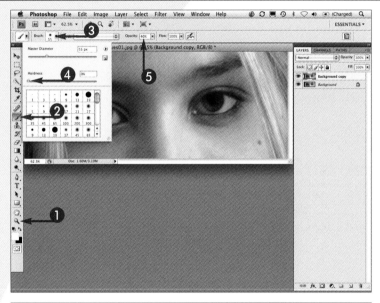

1. With the Background layer duplicated, click the Zoom tool and zoom in on the eye area.

2. Click the Brush tool.

3. Click here and select a brush slightly larger than the final catch light should be.

4. Click and drag the Brush Hardness slider to 0%.

5. Click Opacity in the Options bar and drag the slider to 40%.

6. Press D to reset the foreground and background colors.

7. Press X to reverse the colors, making white the foreground color.

8. Click the New Layer button to add a new empty layer.

9. Click once in each eye to create the catch lights.

10. Click here and drag the Hardness slider completely to the right (100%) to build a hard brush with no edge softness.

11. Click here and drag the slider to the right to return the brush opacity to 100%.

12. Click the Layer Mask button to add a layer mask.

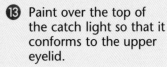

The foreground color changes to black.

⑬ Paint over the top of the catch light so that it conforms to the upper eyelid.

⑭ Click here and drag the layer opacity to about 70% to slightly better blend the effect.

⑮ Click the New Layer button to make a new empty layer.

40

DIFFICULTY LEVEL

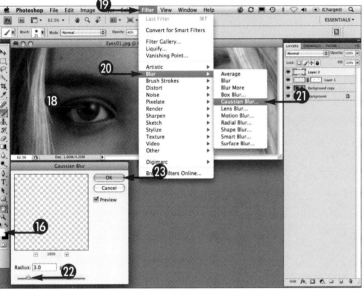

⑯ Press X to reverse the default colors, making the foreground color white.

⑰ Press the left bracket key multiple times to reduce the brush size to about half the previous size.

⑱ Click once in the center of each catch light.

⑲ Click Filter.

⑳ Click Blur.

㉑ Click Gaussian Blur.

The Gaussian Blur dialog box appears.

㉒ Click and drag the Radius slider between 1.5 and 3 pixels to soften the edges.

㉓ Click OK.

A soft-edged catch light with a sparkle in the center appears in each eye.

 TIPS

More Options!
You can refine the catch lights more by viewing the whole face at once. Press Option+spacebar (Alt+spacebar) and click to zoom out. Click and drag the Layer Opacity slider for each of the catch light layers until you see a bright sparkle with a natural diffused edge.

Important!
The catch lights must correspond to the natural direction of the light to appear natural. If the light is coming from the right, the catch lights should be on the right side of the pupils, just slightly above the center.

Did You Know?
Studio portrait lighting is often arranged to intentionally create catch lights to help draw attention to the eyes. Different types of photographic lighting produce different styles of catch lights.

SHARPEN JUST THE EYES
to add focus

The final step to enhancing the eyes in a photograph is to sharpen the eye area. You want to add focus and draw the viewer into the photo, but you may not want to sharpen the rest of the face or the skin. You can selectively sharpen the eyes by using a Sharpen filter and then applying the filter with the History panel and History Brush.

You can use not only the Unsharp Mask filter for sharpening, but also the Smart Sharpen filter. This

filter is not only easier to use, but it also has added features including a much larger preview.

After you sharpen the entire portrait, you can hide the effect using the History panel to go back to a version of the photo before the sharpening was applied. Then using the History Brush, you can paint the sharpening effect on the eye area where you want the focus.

❶ Click and drag the Background layer over the New Layer button to duplicate it.

❷ Double-click the Zoom tool to view the image at 100%.

❸ Press the spacebar, click in the image, and move it to see the eyes.

❹ Click Filter.

❺ Click Sharpen.

❻ Click Smart Sharpen.

The Smart Sharpen dialog box appears.

❼ Click in the Preview window and drag to see the eyes area.

❽ Click here and select Lens Blur.

❾ Click and drag the Radius slider to 1.5 to increase the area to be sharpened.

❿ Click and drag the Amount slider to sharpen the eye, generally between 80 and 115 percent.

⓫ Click More Accurate (☐ changes to ☑).

⓬ Click OK to apply the sharpening.

The sharpening is applied to the Background copy layer.

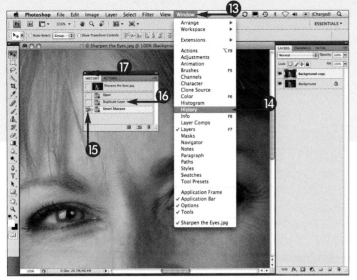

⑬ Click Window.

⑭ Click History to open the History panel.

Note: When the History panel opens, you can click and drag it on the screen so you can see the eyes.

⑮ Click the box to the left of the Smart Sharpen step to set the source for the History Brush.

⑯ Click the previous state named Duplicate Layer in the History panel.

⑰ Click here to close the History panel.

⑱ Click the History Brush tool.

⑲ Click here to open the brush picker.

⑳ Select a totally soft-edge brush (0%) that is large enough to cover the edge of the eyes.

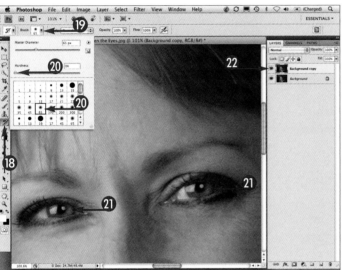

㉑ Paint over the eyes, eyelashes, and eyebrows with the History Brush to apply the sharpening.

㉒ Click the visibility button for the Background copy on and off to compare before and after sharpening.

The sharpening is applied only to the eye areas.

TIPS

Attention!
The Smart Sharpen filter applies only to one layer. If you have made other adjustment layers, you must merge them before applying the sharpening. Press ⌘+Option+Shift+E (Ctrl+Alt+Shift+E). The adjustment layers and the Background layers merge in the new layer. All the adjustment layers, Background copy, and original Background layers remain unchanged.

Did You Know?
Always view the image at 100% magnification when you use a sharpening filter to get the most accurate view on-screen of your changes. Still, the amount of detail visible in a print may be slightly different from what you see on the screen. The amount of detail can vary depending on the type of printer and paper used.

WHITEN TEETH
to improve a smile

You can greatly improve every portrait in which the subject is smiling by applying a little digital tooth whitening. Yellow teeth always dull a smile as well as the overall look of the photo.

You first select the teeth and soften the selection, to avoid a visible line between the areas that are lightened and the rest of the image. Although there are many ways to make a selection in Photoshop, using the Quick Mask mode or the Quick Selection tool as described in Chapter 2 works well when making a detailed selection such as selecting a person's teeth.

After the teeth are selected, whitening is a two-step process. You have to remove the yellow and then brighten the teeth by adjusting the saturation. As in the previous tasks, duplicate the Background layer as a safety step and zoom in to make the detailed selection. Then zoom out to see the whole image before adjusting the color. Digital tooth whitening should be a subtle adjustment to keep the smile and the person looking natural.

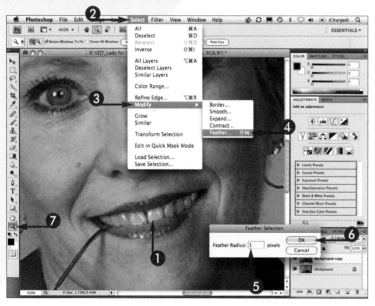

① Zoom in and make a selection of the teeth using the Quick Mask mode or the Quick Selection tool.

Note: *To use the Quick Mask mode, see Task #20. To use the Quick Selection tool, see Task #18.*

② Click Select.

③ Click Modify.

④ Click Feather.

The Feather Selection dialog box appears.

⑤ Type **1** in the Feather Radius field to slightly soften the edge of the selection.

⑥ Click OK.

⑦ Click the Zoom tool and zoom out to see the whole image.

⑧ Press ⌘+H (Ctrl+H) to hide the selection marquee.

The selection marquee is no longer visible, but the teeth are still selected.

⑨ Click the Hue/Saturation button to create a new adjustment layer.

The Hue/Saturation pane appears in the Adjustments panel and a Hue/Saturation layer is created in the Layers panel.

⑩ Click here and select Yellows.

⑪ Click and drag the Saturation slider slowly to the left to remove the yellow.

⑫ Click here and select Master.

⑬ Click and drag the Lightness slider slowly to the right to brighten the teeth.

⑭ Press ⌘+D (Ctrl+D) to deselect the teeth.

⑮ Press ⌘+Shift+E (Ctrl+Shift+E) to merge all the visible layers into one layer.

 TIPS

Try This!

When zooming in on an image, press and hold the spacebar; the pointer temporarily changes to the Hand tool. You can click and drag around your image with the Hand tool and easily move to the area that needs to be adjusted. When you release the spacebar, you change back to the tool that was previously selected.

Did You Know?

Feathering softens the edge of a selection and smoothes the transition between two distinct areas. You can also click Select and click Refine Edge to feather the selection edge. The default settings of the Refine Edge dialog box include a one-pixel feather. Click OK in the dialog box and continue lightening the teeth as shown here.

Add a soft-focus effect to
MAKE A PORTRAIT GLOW

You can apply Photoshop's filters to mimic the photographic filters used in traditional film photography. However, by using a combination of Photoshop filters, layers, and blending modes, you can add special effects and create unique images with a painterly quality that go beyond the possibilities of film photography. You can add a soft-focus effect to a portrait that not only minimizes skin imperfections but also adds a romantic glow to the subject's skin and still keeps the subject's main features in focus.

You first apply the filter and then modify the effect using the blending modes and the opacity settings. When the overall effect is pleasing, you can apply a mask to refocus the eyes and other areas.

By converting the layer you are working on to apply Smart Filters, you can control the effects and continue to adjust the effects with layer modes and opacity changes and edit the photo without affecting any pixels. Converting a duplicated layer is great for experimenting with different creative techniques. If you do not like the changes, simply delete the layer.

① Click and drag the Background layer over the New Layer button to duplicate it.

② Click Filter.

③ Click Convert for Smart Filters.

④ Click OK in the message box.

● The Background copy layer is changed into a smart object layer.

⑤ Click Filter.

⑥ Click Blur.

⑦ Click Gaussian Blur.

The Gaussian Blur dialog box appears.

⑧ Click and drag the Radius slider to blur the image.

Note: Use a blur of about 4 to 8 pixels for low-resolution and 10 to 14 pixels for high-resolution images.

⑨ Click OK to apply the blur.

 # 43

DIFFICULTY LEVEL

⑩ Click here and select the Screen blend mode.

The image is lightened.

⑪ Click the Layer mask button to add a layer mask.

The foreground color is set to black.

⑫ Press B to select the Brush tool.

⑬ Click here to open the brush picker.

⑭ Click a soft-edged brush just large enough to outline the eye area.

⑮ Click the Airbrush button.

⑯ Click here and drag the slider to the left until 40% appears in the Opacity field.

⑰ Paint over the eyes and other important features to bring them out.

⑱ Click here and drag the Opacity slider to the left to get the amount of glow that you want.

The soft focus is applied to the overall portrait while keeping the main features of the subject in sharp focus.

TIPS

Did You Know?

Dragging the Background layer over the New Layer button (⬚) automatically names the duplicated layer "Background copy." You can also duplicate the Background layer by pressing ⌘+J (Ctrl+J). The duplicated Background layer is then named "Layer 1."

Try This!

To experiment with the amount of Gaussian Blur, or any other smart filter, double-click the filter name in the Layers panel to reopen the dialog box. Change the slider amounts and watch the changes on your image.

More Options!

You can select and modify brushes from either the brush picker in the Options bar or from the floating Brushes panel. When you edit or save a brush in one place, the brush is automatically updated in the other.

Chapter 5

Changing and Enhancing Colors and Tone

Color is the heart of Photoshop. Whether you work on a design or a photograph, you often adjust the hue, saturation, and brightness of an image. Using Photoshop, you can fine-tune shadows and highlights or completely alter the overall tone of a photograph. You can transform a color photograph into a grayscale image, colorize an old grayscale image, or make a color image look like an antique colorized photograph. You can also tone a photo as photographers used to do in the darkroom. And you can create these effects in many different ways.

Because some pixel information is discarded whenever you make color and tonal adjustments, you should apply corrections on a duplicate layer, on separate layers, or on a smart objects layer. Photoshop CS4's adjustment layers and the new Adjustments panel also help you make some changes

without permanently altering pixel values. In addition, opening or converting an image or a layer to a new smart object enables you to apply most filters as smart filters, making them continuously editable and nondestructive. You can reedit adjustment layers and smart filters before you flatten the image.

Camera Raw, included with Photoshop CS4, not only adds powerful controls for editing images, but can also open a variety of file formats, including RAWs, JPEGs, and TIFFs, so you can start with nondestructive edits in Camera Raw for most photos.

Whenever you make color or tonal adjustments, start by calibrating and profiling your monitor as discussed in Task #9. Otherwise, you may be changing colors that are not really in the image, and what you see on your monitor can look very different when it is printed.

Top 100

IMPROVE AN UNDEREXPOSED PHOTO
in two steps

You may find a photograph that is perfect for your project or has the subject just the way you want, but it is underexposed. Fixing an underexposed photograph with traditional photography tools was difficult. Fixing such a photo with Photoshop is much easier, and there are many ways you can accomplish the correction. You can use a variety of Photoshop filters and adjustments to correct the exposure. However, you can sometimes make a quick correction using a duplicated layer and altering the layer blend mode. This two-step technique is worth a try before you work with any of the other methods.

Depending on the photo, the exposure may appear corrected the first time that you apply the technique. For other images, you may need to repeat the steps once or even twice. You can even apply a half step by duplicating the layer with the changed blend mode and reducing the effect by changing the Opacity slider of the layer. You can also adjust the Fill slider to lower the effect of the layer without altering any layer styles on that layer.

① With an underexposed photo open in Photoshop, click and drag the Background layer over the New Layer button to duplicate it.

② Click here and select Screen.

The photo appears lighter.

Note: The photo may look fine this way, or you may need to add another layer and change it as in steps 3 and 4.

③ Click and drag the Background copy layer over the New Layer button to duplicate the copy.

④ Click here and drag the Opacity slider to the left to change the opacity of the top layer and the amount of lightening.

The underexposed image exposure is improved.

IMPROVE AN OVEREXPOSED PHOTO
in three steps

DIFFICULTY LEVEL

An overexposed photograph is impossible to salvage with traditional darkroom techniques. Too much light means that there is nothing in the film to print. Digital photography and Photoshop can improve photos in almost magical ways. Although it may be easier to lighten a dark photo, you can easily reduce some of the highlights in an overly bright photograph and often improve the image. You can use the Shadows/Highlights command in the basic mode to effectively reduce the highlights.

With most dialog boxes in Photoshop, when you move the slider to the right you increase the amount. When you use the Shadows/Highlights adjustment to reduce the highlights, it works in the opposite fashion.

By applying the Shadows/Highlights command on a smart object layer you can continue to adjust the exposure nondestructively. This three-step technique for improving an overexposed photo is worth testing before spending time with other methods or discarding the photo.

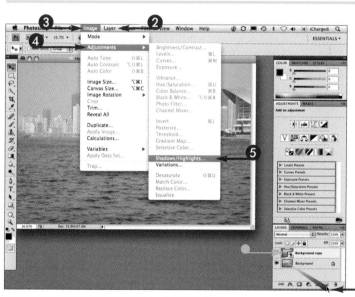

① Click and drag the Background layer over the New Layer button to duplicate it.

② Click Layer, click Smart Objects, and click Convert to Smart Object from the menu.

● The Background copy layer is converted to a smart object.

③ Click Image.

④ Click Adjustments.

⑤ Click Shadows/Highlights.

⑥ Click and drag the Shadows slider to the left to 0%.

⑦ Click and drag the Highlights slider to the right until the image looks the way you want.

● You can click Show More Options (□ changes to ☑) to refine the adjustment using the other sliders.

⑧ Click OK.

The image exposure is improved.

REMOVE A COLORCAST
to improve the overall color

Whether you have a scanned image or one from a digital camera, your image may show a colorcast due to improper lighting, white balance settings, or other factors. A *colorcast* often appears as a reddish, bluish, or greenish tint over the whole image. Photoshop has many tools that you can use to remove colorcasts, including the White Balance setting in Camera Raw; sometimes you may need to try different ones, depending on the photograph. Using the Match Color command as shown here to remove a colorcast is simple and often works well.

Intended for matching the colors between two images, the Match Color command uses advanced algorithms to adjust the brightness, color saturation, and color balance in an image. Because you can adjust the controls in different combinations, using this command on just one image gives you better control over the color and luminance of the image than many other tools.

When using the Match Color command on a duplicated layer, you can use the layer's Opacity slider to blend the results with the Background layer to achieve the best color for your image, as well as compare the before and after images.

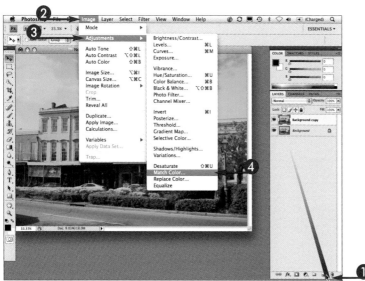

① Click and drag the Background layer over the New Layer button to duplicate it.

② Click Image.

③ Click Adjustments.

④ Click Match Color.

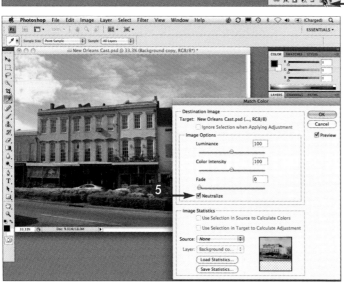

⑤ Click Neutralize to remove the colorcast (☐ changes to ☑).

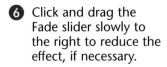

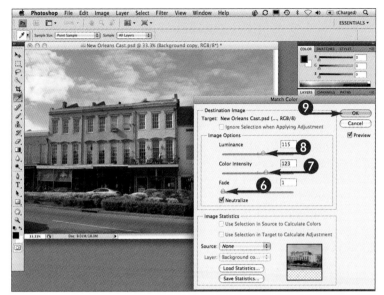

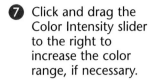

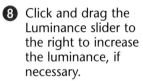

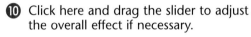

6 Click and drag the Fade slider slowly to the right to reduce the effect, if necessary.

7 Click and drag the Color Intensity slider to the right to increase the color range, if necessary.

8 Click and drag the Luminance slider to the right to increase the luminance, if necessary.

9 Click OK to apply the change.

10 Click here and drag the slider to adjust the overall effect if necessary.

The colorcast is removed and the colors appear more natural.

TIPS

Did You Know?

You can view the floating Histogram panel and see the color changes as they are made. Click Window and click Histogram to display the Histogram panel. Click and drag the Histogram panel so that you can keep it open and still see the image and your other panels.

More Options!

If there is an area in the image that is normally neutral gray, you can also correct a colorcast using the Levels command. Click the Levels button ([icon]) in the Adjustments panel to create a new adjustment layer. Click the Gray Point eyedropper, the middle eyedropper in the Levels pane. Click in the part of the image that should be neutral gray to neutralize the colorcast. If necessary, click another area until the colors appear natural.

COLORIZE
a black-and-white photograph

Hand-coloring a photograph can be a difficult process using traditional paints and traditional film photos. With Photoshop, hand-coloring an old black-and-white image is much easier. You can use any black-and-white photo, called a *grayscale image,* and paint areas using any colors that you choose.

You can start with larger areas and then focus in on specific parts to colorize individually and on additional layers. By making selections of detailed areas and then applying the colors, you can be as precise as necessary to achieve the effect. Zoom in

to select and paint detailed areas and then zoom out to see the overall effect. Continue making different selections and choosing other colors until the whole image is colorized. After the entire image is painted, you can lower the opacity of each colored layer as a final touch.

You can vary the size of the Brush tool as you paint using the left and right bracket keys. If you are using a pressure-sensitive stylus and tablet, open the Brushes panel, click Shape Dynamics, and set the Control to Pen Pressure.

① Click Image.

② Click Mode.

③ Click RGB Color.

The color mode changes, but the image on the screen does not.

④ Click the New Layer button in the Layers panel.

⑤ Click here and select Soft Light.

⑥ Click the Quick Selection tool.

⑦ Click Sample All Layers in the Options bar (☐ changes to ☑).

⑧ Click in an area to make a selection.

Note: You can use any of the other selection tools to complete the selection.

⑨ Click in the foreground color in the toolbar.

The Color Picker dialog box appears.

⑩ Click and drag the Color slider to select a color range.

⑪ Click in the Color Preview box to select a color.

⑫ Click OK to close the dialog box.

13 Press B to select the Brush tool.

14 Click here to open the brush picker.

15 Click a soft-edged brush.

16 Paint over the selected areas to apply the color.

17 Click here and drag the Opacity slider for the layer to adjust the color.

18 Repeat steps 4 to 17 until the entire image is painted.

The black and white photo now appears in color.

TIPS

Try This!

Instead of clicking the foreground color, simply click in the Set Foreground Color box in the Color panel to open the color picker without changing tools. You can also move the cursor over the Color panel and click in the color ramp to select a color — all without changing tools. Click and drag the RGB sliders to adjust the colors.

More Options!

You can select realistic colors for skin tones or hair by sampling the colors from another color image. Keep the other image open on the screen while you are colorizing the grayscale photo. With the color picker open, move the cursor outside the dialog box to sample real colors from the color image. Then paint in the grayscale image with those colors.

Change a color photo into a
CUSTOM GRAYSCALE PHOTO

You can convert a color image to black and white using many different tools and techniques in Photoshop, and because there are no fixed rules on which colors in an image should match specific levels of gray, you can create a variety of different grayscale images from just one color photograph.

The Black and White adjustment in Photoshop CS4 offers a powerful conversion method with complete visual control. You interactively determine which shade of gray is applied to any particular color range in the image by moving the sliders in the

Adjustments panel. And because you are editing using a nondestructive adjustment layer, the original image data is preserved.

Although you can access the Black and White adjustment layer from the menu, using the Adjustments panel in Photoshop CS4 is faster. In addition, the Black and White pane of the Adjustments panel includes a number of presets that you can use or modify, or you can create and save your own preset.

① Click here and select Essentials to make sure the Adjustments panel is open.

② Open an image to convert to grayscale.

③ Click the Black and White adjustment layer button.

The image converts to a default grayscale image.

④ Click Auto to see the changes.

The grays in the image change.

Note: The Auto function in the Black & White Adjustments pane maps the colors to grays differently from the Default setting.

⑤ Click and drag any of the sliders to vary the grays according to the colors in the image.

The gray tones change.

6 Click here and select one of the presets, such as Infrared.

48

The grayscale image changes accordingly.

7 Click and hold the View Previous State button to temporarily view the previous black and white conversion.

8 Click and drag any of the sliders to customize the preset settings.

TIPS

Important!

Converting a color image to grayscale is not the same as changing the mode to grayscale, which in effect throws away image data. When you convert a color image to grayscale, you map individual colors to different shades of gray, preserving the same complete tonal range that exists in the color image. The image remains in RGB mode.

Change It!

Checking the Tint check box in the Black and White pane enables you to color-tone the grayscale image. Drag the Hue slider to the color that you want and then move the Saturation slider to increase the amount of tint.

More Options!

You can also convert a color image when you open the image in the Camera Raw dialog box. Click the HSL/Grayscale tab and click the Convert to Grayscale check box. Adjust the color sliders to alter the grayscale values corresponding to the colors in the underlying image.

ADD A CREATIVE TOUCH
with a little color

You can hand-color an old grayscale photograph with Photoshop to create an antique look. You can also start with a color image, convert it to grayscale as in Task #48, and then colorize it to get a very different look; this type of colorization is much easier to accomplish. You can colorize the entire photo or just one area for effect. You can brush the color into specific areas and even create a more or less muted colorized effect by changing the opacity of the brush as you paint. Start with a low opacity setting and bring the original color back gradually.

If you have already saved a grayscale version of the photo without the original layers, you can still use the method shown here. First open both the original color image and the converted grayscale photo. Using the Move tool, hold the Shift key as you click and drag the grayscale version onto the original color photo. Then follow steps 4 to 13 of this task using the Eraser tool instead of the Brush tool to paint a very creative image.

① Open a color photo.

② Follow steps 3 to 5 of Task #48 to apply a black and white adjustment layer.

The photo appears in grayscale.

The color photo is the Background layer. The Black and White adjustment layer with a white mask appears as the second layer.

③ Click the mask thumbnail in the Layers panel to select it.

④ Click the Default Colors icon to reset the foreground and background colors to black and white.

⑤ Click the Switch Colors icon if necessary to reverse the colors, making the foreground color black.

⑥ Click the Brush tool.

⑦ Click here to open the brush picker.

⑧ Select a brush size.

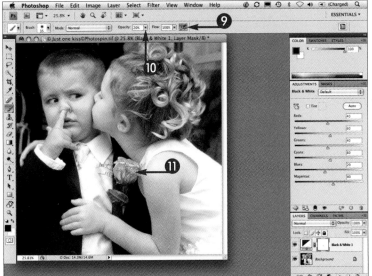

⑨ Click the Airbrush button.

⑩ Double-click here and type **20** to lower the opacity.

⑪ Paint over the area to be colorized.

 # 49

DIFFICULTY LEVEL

⑫ Double-click here again and type **40** to increase the opacity.

⑬ Press the left bracket key several times to reduce the brush size.

⑭ Paint over parts of the colored area to increase the color.

The image is selectively colorized and the viewer's attention is drawn to the perfect spot.

TIPS

Keyboard Shortcut!

You can change the size of the Brush tool by pressing the right bracket key to increase the size and the left bracket key to reduce the size. You can also change the opacity of the Eraser tool () by clicking once in the Opacity data field and pressing the up arrow on the keyboard for an increase or the down arrow for a decrease.

Did You Know?

You can vary the hardness or softness of the Eraser or Brush tools using the keyboard instead of the brush picker. Click the Eraser or Brush tool to select it. Hold the Shift key down as you repeatedly press the right bracket key to increase the hardness or the left bracket key to increase the softness.

DODGE AND BURN
with a special layer

Dodging and *burning* are photographic terms describing the traditional darkroom method for brightening and darkening tones in an image. You can effectively dodge and burn a digital image in Photoshop.

Although Photoshop CS4 includes digital dodge and burn tools, these tools directly affect the pixels on the layer, making your edits permanent and destructive. Using a separate layer and the Brush tool to dodge and burn not only adjusts the image nondestructively, it also gives you greater control over the adjustment.

You can digitally dodge and burn on a separate layer with two different methods. One uses a separate empty layer in the Soft Light blend mode. The other uses a separate layer filled with neutral gray in the Overlay blend mode. With either type of layer, you dodge by painting with white and burn by painting with black on the layer. By setting the brush opacity to about 30% to start, you can increase the effect as you work by brushing over an area multiple times.

Both methods give you complete control over dodging and burning digitally.

USE A LAYER IN THE SOFT LIGHT BLEND MODE

1 Click the Default Colors icon to reset the foreground and background colors to black and white.

2 Click the New Layer button to create a new empty layer.

3 Click here and select Soft Light for the layer blend mode.

4 Click the Brush tool.

5 Click here and select a soft-edged brush.

6 Double-click here and type **30** to set the brush opacity to 30%.

7 Click and drag to paint with black in the light areas of the image to darken, or digitally burn them.

8 Click the Switch Colors icon to reverse the foreground and background colors, making the foreground color white.

Note: You can also press X to reverse the foreground and background colors.

9 Click and drag to paint with white in the dark areas of the image to lighten, or digitally dodge them.

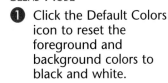

USE A LAYER IN THE OVERLAY BLEND MODE

1 Click the Default Colors icon to reset the foreground and background colors to black and white.

2 Press Option (Alt) and click the New Layer button to create a new empty layer.

The New Layer dialog box appears.

3 Click here and select Overlay.

4 Click Fill with Overlay-neutral color (50% gray) (☐ changes to ☑).

5 Click OK.

● A new layer appears filled with gray in the Layers panel but the image in the main window is unchanged.

6 Repeat steps 4 to 9 in the Soft Light Blend mode method described in the first part of this task.

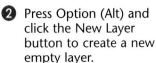

DIFFICULTY LEVEL

TIPS

More Options!

You can even create separate layers for dodging and burning using either method. Name one layer Burn and the other Dodge. You can then adjust the layer opacity of the dodge or burn layer individually to give you even more control and use the Layer panel's Opacity slider to adjust the effect.

Try This!

If the darkening or lightening is not as strong as you want, you can just release the mouse button and click and paint over the same area again. Because you are using the brush at a low opacity to start, you can paint over an area multiple times to increase the effect.

Did You Know?

When you use a layer filled with 50% gray in the Overlay blend mode, the layer displays a gray thumbnail in the Layers panel, but appears as a transparent layer over the image in the main window.

Increase saturation subtly using a
VIBRANCE ADJUSTMENT LAYER

Vibrance is similar to saturation in that they both increase or decrease the intensity of the colors. Unlike saturation, vibrance affects only the less saturated areas and minimizes any effect on the more saturated areas in the image, thus increasing the intensity of the colors while maintaining a more natural appearance. The Vibrance adjustment also improves skin tones better than the Saturation adjustment, which saturates all the colors in the image.

You can increase the intensity of the colors in an image without altering the original pixels by using a Vibrance adjustment layer. You can apply the

adjustment by clicking Layer, selecting New Adjustment Layer, and selecting Vibrance. However, you can also use the Adjustments panel, which enables you to quickly apply a variety of image modifications as nondestructive adjustment layers. The panel includes one-click buttons as well as a number of presets for the various options.

You can adjust both the vibrance and the saturation using the sliders in the Adjustment panel's Vibrance pane to increase the intensity of the colors in your image.

① Open an image.

② Click Window.

③ Click Adjustments to open the Adjustments panel.

> *Note: Optionally, click Essentials to have the Adjustments panel included in the right panel.*

④ Click the Vibrance button.

The Vibrance adjustments pane appears.

⑤ Click and drag the Vibrance slider to the right to increase the intensity of the colors.

⑥ Click and drag the Saturation slider slightly to the right to increase all the colors if necessary.

The colors in the image intensify.

7 Click and hold the View Previous State button to view the image before the adjustment.

The adjustment is temporarily hidden.

8 Release the mouse to view the adjustment again.

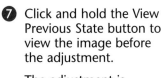

9 Click and drag to adjust the sliders to increase or decrease the vibrance and saturation.

10 Click the Return to Adjustment List arrow to view all the options in the Adjustments pane, and apply more adjustments if desired.

TIPS

More Options!

You can remove the Vibrance or any adjustment layer and return to the list of Adjustments by clicking the trash can (🗑) in the Adjustments pane.

You can return to the list of adjustments by clicking the arrow (◀) any time without removing the adjustment you just applied.

Try This!

Click the visibility button (👁) in the Adjustments pane to temporarily turn off the effect of the adjustment layer. Click the Previous State button (🔄) in the Adjustments pane or press the backslash key to temporarily view the previous adjustment state. Click the Reset button (🔄) to reset the adjustment to the default settings.

Did You Know?

When you apply adjustments as adjustment layers, a mask is automatically created. You can then paint on the mask with black to hide the adjustment on certain areas, allowing the original image to appear.

Chapter 5: Changing and Enhancing Colors and Tone 115

USE CAMERA RAW
to visually adjust any photo

Most digital cameras can create JPEGs and sometimes TIFF files. Advanced digital cameras can also write a manufacturer's proprietary camera RAW format, such as NEF or CR2. The RAW file format is the most direct representation of what the camera sensor captured because the data is not processed or compressed in the camera. Such proprietary RAW files require specific software to convert the file in the computer. Photoshop CS4 includes Camera Raw to convert RAW images. However, Camera Raw is a powerful image editor on its own.

Camera Raw automatically launches whenever you open a proprietary manufacturer's RAW file. However, you can set the Camera Raw preferences to open both JPEGs and TIFFs automatically as well to take advantage of the many editing tools.

You can then open any photo using Camera Raw and make specific adjustments, including cropping, straightening, spot removal, and fixing red eye. You can work with one or multiple images at one time before opening each photo individually in Photoshop to make more specific adjustments.

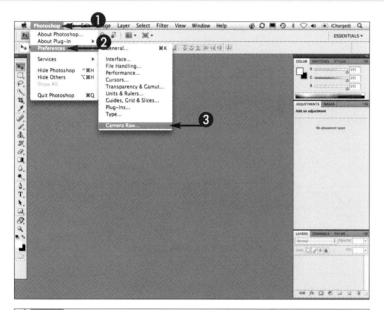

SET THE CAMERA RAW PREFERENCES TO OPEN JPEGS AND TIFFS

① Click Photoshop (click Edit).

② Click Preferences.

③ Click Camera Raw.

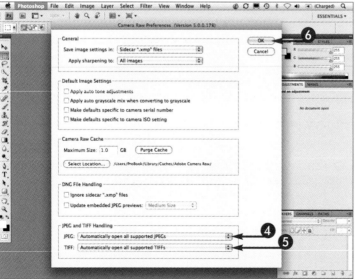

The Camera Raw Preferences dialog box appears.

④ Click here and select Automatically open all supported JPEGs.

⑤ Click here and select Automatically open all supported TIFFs.

⑥ Click OK to save the Camera Raw preferences.

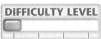

① In Photoshop, click File and select Open.

The Open dialog box appears.

② Click a JPEG or TIFF to open it in Camera Raw.

③ Click Open.

The file automatically opens in Camera Raw.

④ Click the Crop tool.

⑤ Click and drag in the image to crop it.

⑥ Click Open Image.

The cropped version of the image opens in Photoshop.

TIP

Did You Know?

A camera RAW file is a file format that contains the unprocessed and uncompressed picture data exactly as captured by the digital camera's image sensor, along with the information about how the image was captured, called the image's *metadata*.

A camera's JPEG file is a photo file that has been processed and compressed by the digital camera's internal processor.

Photoshop Camera Raw is software that interprets the camera RAW file to build and process the color image you see on your monitor.

When you adjust a RAW file in Photoshop Camera Raw, the adjustments are saved as metadata and all the original image data is preserved. When you edit a JPEG file in Camera Raw, you are adjusting pixels that have already been altered by the camera.

RECOVER HIGHLIGHTS
with Camera Raw

The Recovery slider is one of the many valuable tools in Camera Raw. The Recovery slider can often reduce or remove the clipped highlights. Clipped or blown highlights print as completely white areas because the image has no pixel information in these areas. Clipped highlights can ruin an otherwise good photograph and are often difficult to control with other tools.

With an image open in Camera Raw, you can see the blown-out highlights by clicking the Highlight Clipping warning triangle in the histogram. The highlights

without any colored pixels appear in red. Conversely, clicking the Shadow Clipping warning triangle in the histogram makes the overly dark shadow areas or completely black areas with no tonal range appear in blue.

The Recovery slider works in combination with the Exposure slider. Using both sliders, you can improve the exposure and prevent most of the highlights from being completely blown out. The Exposure and the Recovery sliders are located on the Basic tab.

① Open Bridge.

② Click a photo to select it.

③ Click File.

④ Click Open in Camera Raw.

Note: You can also open most camera manufacturers' RAW files by double-clicking the file in any folder or in Bridge.

The photo opens in Camera Raw.

⑤ Click here to view the overexposed highlights.

⑥ Click here to view the underexposed shadows.

- White highlights appear in red, and black shadows appear in blue.

7 Click and drag the Recovery slider slowly to the right to lessen the red colored areas.

The red colored highlights are reduced.

8 Click and drag the Exposure slider slowly to the left to reduce the red colored highlights more.

9 Repeat steps 7 and 8 as needed to adjust the photo.

10 Click Open Image to open the image in Photoshop.

Note: Optionally, click Save Image to save the image with the new adjustments.

The blown-out highlights are reduced and the photo displays a better exposure.

TIPS

Did You Know?

The latest version of Camera Raw includes an Adjustment Brush tool ( ) so you can selectively paint Exposure, Clarity, Brightness, and other adjustments onto specific areas of a photo. You can then refine the amount of the adjustments by moving the appropriate sliders. You can also use the Graduated Filter tool ( ) in Camera Raw to apply a gradual blend of selected adjustments over specific areas of the photo.

Try This!

You can quickly access the Camera Raw preferences from within Camera Raw by clicking the Open preferences dialog button ( ) in the Camera Raw toolbar.

More Options!

The Fill Light slider in Camera Raw performs changes similar to the Shadows/Highlights adjustment in Photoshop CS4. The Fill Light slider brightens only the shadows without changing other values. The Blacks slider changes the black points in the photo, darkening it.

IMPROVE A SKY
with the Camera Raw graduated filter

When you first open an image in Camera Raw, the interface displays the tools in a top toolbar and numerous color and tone adjustments on the Basic tab. These sliders help you adjust the tone, white balance, and saturation of the overall image. On other tabs, you can adjust different tones and colors individually, make lens corrections, alter colors in the image, sharpen and reduce noise, and even save some of your settings as presets so that you can reapply them to similar images.

The Graduated Filter tool enables you to apply tonal changes similar to a photographic graduated filter. For example, you can easily dramatize an open sky in a landscape photo by changing the exposure, saturation, clarity, or color of just the sky and completely change the mood of the image.

With Camera Raw, you control the colors in the image by what you see on the screen, so it is essential to work with a properly calibrated and profiled monitor as discussed in Task #9.

① Open an image with a large sky area in Camera Raw.

② Click the Graduated Filter tool.

The Graduated Filter tool options appear under the Histogram.

③ Click Show Overlay (☐ changes to ☑).

④ Press and hold Shift and click and drag from the top of the image to where the sky meets the foreground.

The Graduated Filter overlay appears with two adjustment pins on the image.

⑤ Click and drag the Exposure slider to the left to darken the sky.

⑥ Click and drag the other sliders on the Graduated Filter panel to increase the intensity of the sky.

Note: Optionally, click the Color box and select a graduated filter color to apply to the sky.

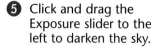

The sky in the photo changes as you move the sliders.

⑦ You can click Open Image to open the photo in Photoshop or Shift+click Open Image to open the photo as a smart object in Photoshop.

● You can click Save Image to convert and save the image with the Graduated Filter adjustment.

● You can click Done to apply the changes and close the dialog box without opening the image in Photoshop.

More Options!

Once you have applied the Graduated Filter settings, you can continue to adjust the image in Camera Raw. Click the Zoom tool (🔍) to return to the Basic panel. The adjustments you applied with the graduated filter remain on the image. You can then use any of the other tools in the toolbar or the sliders and tabs in the right panel to edit the photo.

Try This!

You can apply multiple Graduated Filter adjustments to an image by applying one and then selecting New (○ changes to ◉) to start another one. You can always go back and edit any adjustment. Make sure that Show Overlay is selected and click the Graduated Filter pin on the image. Edit is automatically selected (○ changes to ◉) so you can move the adjustment sliders to change the applied graduated filter.

CREATE A SPLIT TONE
for a special effect in Camera Raw

Creating split-tone effects in the traditional darkroom was difficult and labor-intensive. With Camera Raw included with Photoshop CS4, you can easily create a split-tone look, in which a different color is applied to the shadows and highlights. You can also visually add or remove tones while previewing the image.

This feature of Camera Raw lets you associate hue and saturation with the lightest colors separately from the hue and saturation values associated with the darkest colors in the image. You can then adjust the Balance slider to emphasize the tone of the highlights or the tone of the shadow areas.

Because you create the split tone in Camera Raw, the alteration to the image is completely nondestructive. The original image always remains intact. You can reopen Camera Raw to change the color or saturation amounts any time to adjust the effect.

You can apply a split tone to either a grayscale or a color image; however, the toning is often most effective on a grayscale photo with high contrasts.

1 In Photoshop, click File and select Open.

The Open dialog box appears.

2 Navigate to the file and click to select it.

3 Click here and select Camera Raw, if it is not already selected.

4 Click Open.

The Camera Raw dialog box appears.

5 Click the Split Toning tab.

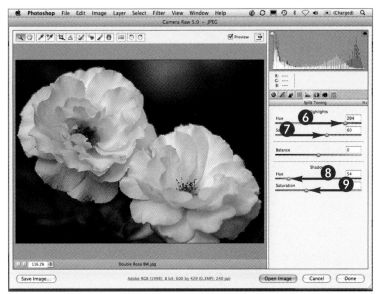

6 Click and drag the Highlights Hue slider to select the color for the highlights.

7 Click and drag the Highlights Saturation slider to increase the saturation in the highlight areas.

8 Click and drag the Shadows Hue slider to select the color for the shadows.

9 Click and drag the Shadows Saturation slider to increase the saturation in the shadow areas.

10 Click and drag the Balance slider to the right to shift the toning more into the highlights or to the left to emphasize the tones in the shadows.

11 Repeat steps 6 to 10 to adjust the split tone effect.

12 Click Open Image to open the toned image and continue editing it in Photoshop.

Note: Optionally, click Save Image to save it with the adjustments and a different name.

The grayscale image appears as a traditional split-tone image with different colored shadows and highlights.

TIPS

Did You Know?

You can automatically open any image from Camera Raw as a smart object in Photoshop. Press Shift and the Open Image button changes to Open Object. Once in Photoshop, you can double-click the smart object layer to reopen the image in Camera Raw and edit the settings.

More Options!

If you add a split tone to a color image, you can still convert it to grayscale after applying split toning. Using the HSB/Grayscale tab ( ) in Camera Raw, you can also change the effects of the split toning.

Try This!

Leave the Saturation slider set to 0 and press the Option (Alt) key as you drag the Hue sliders. The preview shows a 100% saturation of that hue. After you select the hue, move the Saturation sliders to the amount that you want.

Making Magic with Digital Special Effects

Since Photoshop's inception, photographers and graphic designers alike have been using the application for digital imaging and photo manipulation. Photoshop can transform an average shot into a good photograph, a good photograph into a great one, and a great image into creative fine art. Photoshop CS4 adds even more power and control to digital image editing. Just as with the previous versions, there are many different ways to create a design or enhance a photograph. You can use the old tools in new ways and in combination with the new techniques to create, improve, or completely alter any image.

You can simulate the effect of using traditional photographic filters to enhance the colors or change the areas in focus in an image. You can draw attention to one part of the image using a vignette or simulate traditional photographic effects with a digital filter. Using the Merge to HDR feature, you can combine multiple exposures to realize a photo with a wider range of tones than the camera can capture in one shot. You can also use the flexibility of smart objects and Camera Raw to vary the luminosity of a photo. You can even use parts of a photo and multiple layers to create an original design. The Vanishing Point filter enables you to add or remove items in an image while maintaining the basic perspective.

Photoshop CS4 not only offers more methods for altering images, but also gives you more opportunities to be creative.

Top 100

APPLY A PHOTO FILTER  #56
for dynamic adjustments

Different lighting conditions produce different color temperatures on the image. Photographers sometimes use colored lens filters to correct for the lighting differences, change the color balance in their photos, or even create a more dramatic image. You can alter the white balance setting on digital images in both Camera Raw and Photoshop, as shown in Chapter 5. You can also use the Photo Filter adjustment in Photoshop to apply a traditional lens filter effect to an image whether it is digital or scanned from film. Because Photoshop considers the Photo Filter an adjustment rather than a filter, you find the Photo

Filter adjustment under both the Image ⇨ Adjustments and Layer ⇨ New Adjustment Layer menus. However, using the Adjustments panel is the quickest and easiest way to access this adjustment.

Using a Photo Filter adjustment can visually change the time of day in the photo, turning midday into sunset. You can also revive an image, turning a bland photo into a dramatic one, by applying a blue or violet filter across the entire image, or warm a cool photo by applying a warming filter.

DIFFICULTY LEVEL

① Click here and select Essentials to set up the workspace.

② Click the Photo Filter adjustment layer.

Note: Using a Photo Filter adjustment layer does not alter the original image until you flatten the layers.

The Photo Filter options appear in the Adjustments panel.

● Make sure that Preserve Luminosity is selected.

③ Click here and select a colored filter.

④ Click and drag the Density slider to the right to increase the effect if necessary.

The Photo Filter adjustment is applied to the entire image.

Note: You can duplicate the layer to increase the effect or change the layer blend mode to Hue to soften the effect.

Add a quick dark vignette effect to
FOCUS ON THE SUBJECT

57

A dark vignette around the edges of a photograph is often due to the light falloff in the camera lens. However, darkening the edges of an image can also help focus the viewer's eye on the subject in the center of an image. For other images, a darkened edge can simulate the look of an old photograph. Used on a portrait, it can create a dramatic look by appearing to focus a soft light on the subject. With a landscape, you can simulate a burned-in edge, essentially enhancing the center of the image.

You can create a vignette effect in many ways with Photoshop. Most methods involve separate layers and multiple steps. This quick vignette technique uses the Lens Correction filter, almost opposite from the way it was intended, and makes adding a darkened- or lightened-edge vignette very fast. When you apply the filter as a smart filter, the effect is also completely editable even after it has been applied.

DIFFICULTY LEVEL

① Open an image as a smart object or convert it using one of the methods described in Task #21.

② Click Filter.

③ Click Distort.

④ Click Lens Correction.

The Lens Correction dialog box appears.

⑤ Click Show Grid to remove the grid lines (☑ changes to ☐).

⑥ Click and drag the Amount slider to the left for a dark-edge vignette effect.

Note: You can move the Amount slider to the right to create a light-edge vignette.

⑦ Click and drag the Midpoint slider to control how far the darkened areas extend into the photograph.

⑧ Click OK.

The smart filter is applied to the image.

Add action with a
SIMULATED MOTION BLUR

You can add a sense of movement to action shots by using a filter to simulate the motion of the subjects. Photoshop includes a number of blur filters, including one for motion blur. Unlike the Gaussian Blur filter, which blurs pixels in clusters, the Motion Blur filter blurs pixels in both directions along straight lines. You can choose the angle of movement and the distance in pixels that are affected by the blur in the filter dialog box to simulate both the direction and speed of motion of the subject of the photo.

The Motion Blur filter blurs the entire image, removing all details. Both the subject matter and the

background are blurred, making the photo look as though the camera and not the subject was moving when the shot was taken. By adding a layer mask filled with black to hide the motion blur, you can then selectively paint in white over certain areas to create the illusion of movement while keeping the main subject and the background in focus. Apply the filter as a smart filter on a previously converted smart object layer, and you can edit the amount of blur after applying it for even more visual control.

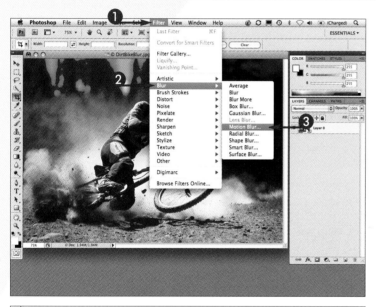

1 With the image as a smart object layer (see Task #21), click Filter.

2 Click Blur.

3 Click Motion Blur.

The Motion Blur dialog box appears.

4 Click and drag the straight line in the circle to rotate the angle of the motion.

5 Click and drag the distance slider to adjust the amount of blur.

6 Click OK.

58

DIFFICULTY LEVEL

- The filter is applied to the smart object layer.

⑦ Press D to reset black as the foreground color.

⑧ Click the Layer Mask icon for the smart filter.

The mask appears with a line around it, and the foreground color changes to white.

⑨ Press Option+Delete (Alt+Backspace) to fill the smart filter layer mask with black.

The motion blur effect is hidden, and the mask is filled with black.

⑩ Click the Brush tool.

⑪ Click here and click a soft-edge brush from the brush picker.

⑫ Click the Switch Colors icon to reverse the foreground and background colors so that white is the foreground color.

⑬ Paint in the image over the areas where you want the motion blur to appear.

The motion blur is applied to specific areas and the subject appears to be moving through the background.

TIPS

Did You Know?

You can also use the Wind filter for a linear motion effect. Instead of selecting the Motion Blur filter, click Filter, Stylize, and then Wind. Click From the Right or From the Left to select the direction of the movement. Click OK to close the dialog box. Then follow steps 7 to 12 in this task to selectively paint in the appropriate motion.

More Options!

After applying the Motion Blur smart filter, you can instead leave the blur over the entire image and paint back the subject and foreground to bring them back into focus. Click the mask to select it as in step 8 and press X if necessary to reverse the foreground and background colors so that black is the foreground color. Paint with black over the areas that you want in focus.

Chapter 6: Making Magic with Digital Special Effects

BLEND SEPARATE PHOTOS
for the best group shot

Photoshop CS4 includes an Auto-Align Layers command to help you combine separate photos for panoramas or for composites. Auto-Align Layers analyzes edges and common elements in each image and brings them into alignment with each other. This tool works very well when combining multiple photos of a group so that everyone looks their best in the final photo.

You can drag all the separate images onto one of the images, making multiple layers. When you run the Auto-Align Layers command, Photoshop matches each layer with the others so that the similar shapes and forms match as much as possible. You can then add a layer mask to the layers to merge the images, erasing the unwanted parts of each layer. For group shots, you erase the closed eyes or grimaces to reveal the best expressions of everyone in the group.

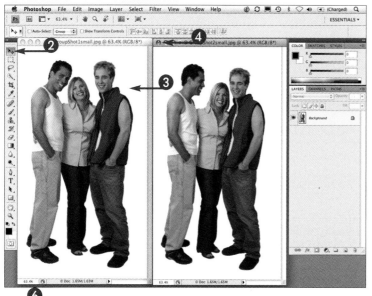

① Open the photos to combine.

② Click the Move tool.

③ Click and drag one photo on top of the other.

④ Click here to close the photo that you just dragged.

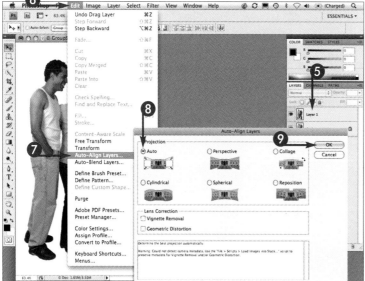

⑤ Press Shift and click each layer to select it.

⑥ Click Edit.

⑦ Click Auto-Align Layers.

The Auto-Align Layers dialog box appears.

⑧ Click a projection style, depending on the elements in the photos (○ changes to ◉).

Note: *In this example, you are trying to align people in a group shot; Auto Projection will work best.*

⑨ Click OK.

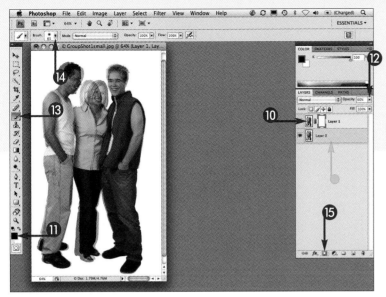

● Photoshop aligns the photos by the content and renames the layers Layer 0 and Layer 1.

⑩ Click the top layer to select it.

⑪ Press D to set the foreground color to black.

⑫ Click here and drag the top layer's opacity to 60% to see the shapes below.

⑬ Click the Brush tool.

⑭ Click here and select a soft-edged brush.

⑮ Click the Layer Mask button to add a layer mask to the top layer.

⑯ Paint with black on the top layer to show the best group shots.

Note: The top layer's mask should still be selected.

● The mask displays the painted areas in black.

⑰ Click here and drag the top layer's opacity back to 100%.

The final image blends the preferred subjects from both images.

● You can click the Crop tool and crop the image to final size.

TIPS

Caution!
Make sure that the top layer's mask is still selected and that the foreground color is set to black when you paint on the photo to reveal the parts of the image on the layer below.

Did You Know?
Photoshop automatically selects one alignment projection option (see step 8) based on the contents of the images you are combining. You can try it and then press ⌘+Z (Ctrl+Z) to undo the auto-alignment and try a different option.

More Options!
The Auto-Blend Layers command blends separate layers and tries to reduce or eliminate the perspective differences as well as the differences in colors or luminance without leaving a seam. This command works well for scenic photos.

Chapter 6: Making Magic with Digital Special Effects

MERGE MULTIPLE RAW PHOTOS
to 32-bit HDR

Dynamic range in a photo refers to the ratio between the dark and bright areas. The human eye can adapt to different brightness levels, but the camera cannot. Using Photoshop CS4, you can merge multiple photos of the same scene but with different exposures into a *high dynamic range* (HDR) image. The merged image can display luminosity levels even beyond what the human eye can see, and far more shades of the colors in the visible world than any camera can capture in a single photo. Although HDR images are often used for motion pictures and special lighting effects in some high-end photography, Photoshop

CS4's Merge to HDR command enables the still photographer to create detailed yet realistic images with a wide dynamic range.

The Merge to HDR command works best on a series of photos taken with a tripod so that only the lighting of the image differs and nothing is moving. The aperture and ISO of the images should be the same in each photo. The shutter speed should vary from one to two f-stops in each direction. You can merge to HDR with at least three photos; however, you can include more photos with varying shutter speeds so your photos have a large variation in the image tones.

OPEN MERGE TO HDR FROM BRIDGE

❶ In Bridge, ⌘+click (Ctrl+click) to select the images to merge.

   Note: Photos taken specifically to use with the Merge to HDR command would normally appear in sequential order.

❷ Click Tools.

❸ Click Photoshop.

❹ Click Merge to HDR.

   Note: Continue the steps starting with step 9 below.

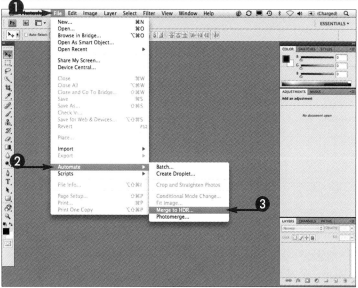

OPEN MERGE TO HDR FROM PHOTOSHOP

❶ In Photoshop, click File.

❷ Click Automate.

❸ Click Merge to HDR.

132

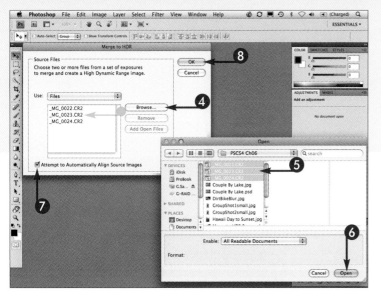

The Merge to HDR dialog box appears.

④ Click Browse.

The Open dialog box appears.

⑤ Navigate to and ⌘+click (Ctrl+click) to select the images to use.

⑥ Click Open.

● The files appear in the list box.

⑦ Click Attempt to Automatically Align Source Images (☐ changes to ☑).

⑧ Click OK.

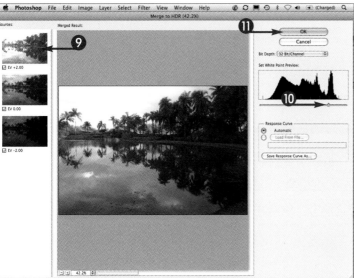

Photoshop opens, analyzes, aligns, and combines the images into one multilayered file.

The larger Merge to HDR dialog box appears.

⑨ If necessary, click to deselect a source image.

⑩ If necessary, click and drag the White Point Preview slider just enough to see all the details in the image.

Note: The White Point Preview adjustment is applied when you open the image in Photoshop. The slider does not delete any of the merged image data, which remains in the merged file. You can adjust the white point again later by clicking View and then 32-bit Preview Options.

⑪ Click OK.

Photoshop merges the files into a document named Untitled_HDR.

More Options!

Refine the merged image even more by converting it to a 16-bit or an 8-bit image. Click Image, click Mode, and click either 8 or 16 bits/Channel. An HDR Conversion dialog box appears. Click and drag the Gamma slider to the left to increase the contrast or to the right to decrease the contrast. Then click and drag the Exposure slider to the desired brightness. Click OK to finish the conversion.

Did You Know?

The *bit depth* describes how much color information exists per pixel in an image. A greater number of bits per pixel translates into greater color accuracy, with more shades of each color or more shades of grays in the image.

Apply a split-neutral density filter using
SMART OBJECTS

You may have photographed a scene with a vibrant sky, but the resulting photo did not reflect the drama that you saw. The light in the sky or a reflection of water may have created a dynamic range larger than what the camera could capture. Photographers sometimes use a split-neutral density filter on the lens to capture such a large dynamic range. Using a tripod, you can also take multiple exposures of the same scene and combine the images using Photoshop's Merge to HDR command. However, you can effectively simulate a neutral-density filter or a

multi-exposure photograph using a combination of Camera Raw and smart object layers.

Using two copies of a smart object layer, you can use Camera Raw to adjust a photograph — first to emphasize the foreground and next to edit a copy and emphasize the background or sky. You can then use a layer mask to combine the best exposures of both images. You can also edit each layer again before flattening and saving the final image file with a new name.

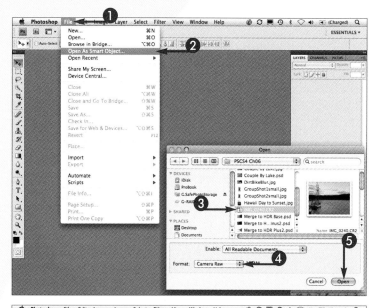

1. Click File.
2. Click Open As Smart Object.

   The Open dialog box appears.
3. Click a file to select it.
4. Click here and select Camera Raw.
5. Click Open.

Camera Raw opens.

6. Move the sliders to simulate the best exposure for the foreground.
7. Click OK.

● The file is opened in Photoshop as a smart object.

⑧ Click Layer.

⑨ Click Smart Objects.

⑩ Click New Smart Object via Copy.

● The smart object layer is duplicated but not linked to the original.

⑪ Double-click the Smart Object icon on the new smart object layer.

The image opens in Camera Raw again.

⑫ Repeat steps 6 and 7, but this time select the best exposure for the sky.

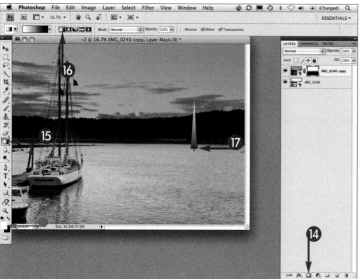

⑬ Press D to set the foreground and background colors.

⑭ Click the Layer Mask button to add a layer mask to the top layer.

● White becomes the foreground color.

⑮ Click the Gradient tool.

⑯ Click the Linear gradient.

⑰ Press Shift and click and drag from just above the horizon to just below the horizon.

The gradient on the mask allows the properly exposed sky from the top smart objects layer to be seen on the smart objects photo layer with the well-exposed foreground.

#61

DIFFICULTY LEVEL

TIPS

Caution!

You must duplicate the smart object layer using the menu path Layer, Smart Objects, New Smart Object via Copy to edit each one independently. If you duplicate the smart object by dragging it over the New Layer button in the Layers panel, the smart object layers are linked to each other, and editing one edits the other at the same time.

More Options!

If the file is in the RAW format, you can start from Bridge. Double-click the RAW file to open Camera Raw. Make your adjustments for the foreground. Shift+click Open Object. The file then opens as a smart object, and you can continue with the rest of the steps in the task starting at step 8.

ADJUST DEPTH OF FIELD
with a Lens Blur filter

You can draw the attention of the viewer into the main subject of an image by controlling the depth of field, or defining the part of the image that is in focus and blurring other areas. Photographers control the depth of field by changing the aperture setting on the camera. A small opening results in a greater depth of field with more of the image in focus. A larger aperture creates an image with less depth of field and only the center of the image in focus. You can use Photoshop's blur filters to selectively adjust the depth of field in your digital images.

Use the Lens Blur filter and a white-to-black gradient on an Alpha channel, a special type of channel for saving a selection, to create a smooth transition from the focused areas to the out-of-focus areas in the photo. Click one area in the image to set the main focal point. Areas with the same level of gray in the Alpha channel as the selected area are now in focus. All other areas are blurred, depending on the level of gray in the Alpha channel.

① With a photo open, click the Channels tab in the Layers panel.

② Click the New Channel button to add a new black Alpha channel.

Note: Optionally, you can press F once to view the photo against a gray background.

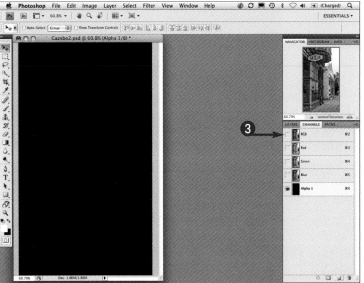

The image is covered with black, and the channel is named Alpha 1.

③ Click the Visibility box for the RGB channel to see the image.

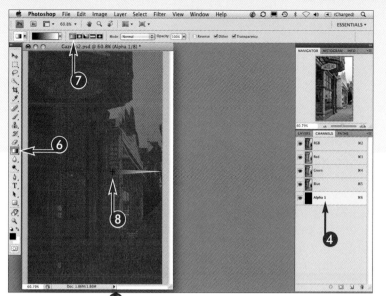

All the channels are visible, and a red mask covers the image.

62

DIFFICULTY LEVEL

④ Click the Alpha 1 channel to highlight it.

⑤ Press D to select the foreground and background colors.

⑥ Click the Gradient tool.

⑦ Click the Linear gradient.

⑧ Press and hold the Shift key as you click and drag in the image from the background toward the foreground.

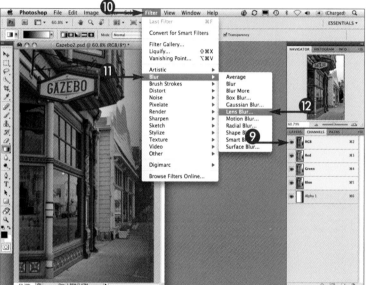

The red mask area appears as a red gradient.

⑨ Click the RGB channel to highlight it.

⑩ Click Filter.

⑪ Click Blur.

⑫ Click Lens Blur.

More Options!

You can keep a selected area in focus when you apply the Lens Blur. Make a selection. Click Select and then Save Selection. Type a name in the data field in the Save Selection dialog box and click OK. Next, click the Channels tab and deselect the visibility button of the new channel. Click the RGB channel to select it and click the Layers tab. Now when you apply the Lens Blur filter, everything in the selection remains in focus.

Try This!

You can create a channel with two selections, one for the main subject and the second for an area slightly farther in the background. Fill the first selection with white and the second with a light gray. Apply the Lens Blur filter with this channel as the source. Your image now has areas with three distinct levels of focus.

ADJUST DEPTH OF FIELD
with a Lens Blur filter

Photoshop includes other blur filters. All the blur filters can soften or blur either a selected area or the entire image. These filters smooth the transitions between areas of contrast from hard edges or shaded areas by averaging the pixels that are juxtaposed to any lines or edges in an image. The Lens Blur filter works best for creating or simulating depth of field in a photo because it uses a depth map to determine the position of the pixels to blur. You can set the specific area to start blurring the focus in the image

by specifying the source for the depth map. Using the Lens Blur filter with a separate Alpha channel or a layer mask as the source enables you to specify exactly what is in sharp focus and how much depth of field to apply. The Lens Blur filter also enables you to determine the shape of the iris to control how the blur appears. By changing the shape, curvature, or rotation of the iris in the Lens Blur dialog box, you control the look of the Lens Blur filter.

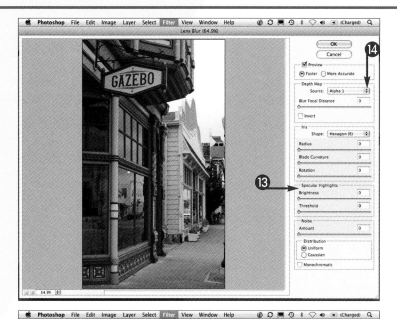

The Lens Blur dialog box appears.

⑬ Click and drag all the sliders to the left to remove any blur effect.

⑭ Click here and select Alpha 1.

⑮ Click the main subject in the image to assign the point of focus.

⑯ Click Invert to set the blur to the background (☐ changes to ☑).

⑰ Click and drag the Radius slider to the right to blur the background.

● If necessary, click and drag the Blur Focal Distance slider to adjust the point of focus.

Note: The Blur Focal Distance number corresponds to the level of gray at the targeted point in the Alpha channel.

⑱ Click OK.

The Lens Blur filter is applied to the image in the areas covered by the red gradient.

#62 CONTINUED

⑲ Click the visibility button on the Alpha 1 channel to deselect it and hide the red mask.

⑳ Click the Layers tab.

The main subject in the image is sharp while the rest of the image gradually blurs out of focus as it gets farther away from the focal point.

TIPS

Attention!

Film grain and noise are removed when the Lens Blur filter is applied. You can replace some of the noise and make the image look more realistic. First, zoom in to see the image at 100%. Click and drag the Amount slider in the Noise section of the Lens Blur dialog box until the image appears less changed and then click OK.

Did You Know?

Applying a Lens Blur filter rather than a Gaussian Blur filter preserves more of the geometric shapes in the original image. Highlights in the image also reflect the Shape setting that is chosen in the Iris section of the Lens Blur dialog box. You can smooth the edges of the iris and rotate it by changing the Blade Curvature and Rotation settings.

Use the Auto Blend tool to create
GREATER DEPTH OF FIELD

The depth of field you can capture depends on the type of camera, the aperture, and the focusing distance. Larger apertures — or smaller f-stop numbers — and closer focal distance produce images with a shallower depth of field, or less of the image in focus. Using smaller apertures — larger f-stop numbers — produces photos with greater depth of field or more of the overall image in focus.

Sometimes you cannot use as small an aperture as you would need to create a photo with a very large depth of field because of the distance involved, or because of the lighting conditions. You can combine multiple shots and blend them together using the capabilities in Photoshop CS4 to create a larger depth of field.

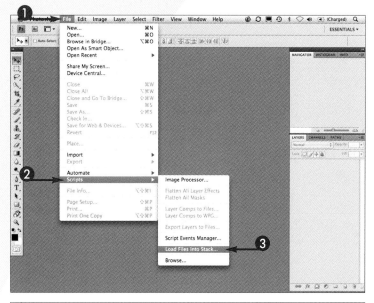

① Click File.

② Click Scripts.

③ Click Load Files into Stack.

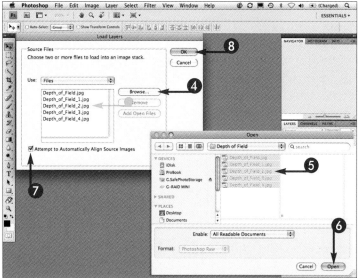

The Load Layers dialog box appears.

④ Click Browse.

The Open dialog box appears.

⑤ ⌘+click (Ctrl+click) multiple photos to select them.

⑥ Click Open.

● The files appear in the Load Layers dialog box.

⑦ Click Attempt to Automatically Align Source Images (☐ changes to ☑).

⑧ Click OK.

● The images all open as individual layers of one file named *Untitled1*.

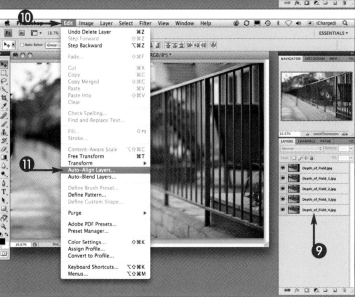

9 Click the first layer and Shift+click the last layer to select all the layers at once.

10 Click Edit.

11 Click Auto-Align Layers.

TIPS

Did You Know?

Depth of field occurs as a gradual transition, with everything in front of and behind the focusing distance of the camera lens losing sharpness.

Try This!

You can also start by selecting the files and opening them all as separate files. Then click File, Scripts, and Load Files into Stack. In the Load Layers dialog box, click Add Open Files to select all the currently open files and click OK, and then continue with step 9 above.

Did You Know?

The Auto-Align Layers command aligns the layers based on similar content, such as corners and edges, in each of the different layers.

Use the Auto Blend tool to create
GREATER DEPTH OF FIELD

To create the best blend for extending the depth of field of the final image, you should use a tripod and use the manual focus of the camera. With the full image in the viewfinder or on the camera's LCD, manually focus on the area closest to the camera and take the first shot. Then change only the focus point to see the next area over in sharp focus. Continue taking photos until all the areas are in focus in at least one shot.

The Auto-Blend Layers command only works with RGB or Grayscale images and does not work with smart object layers or Background layers. And although the Auto-Blend dialog box does have an option for blending multiple images into a panorama, the Photomerge command generally produces better photo blends for panoramas.

You can use as many photos as required to capture each area of the scene in sharp focus.

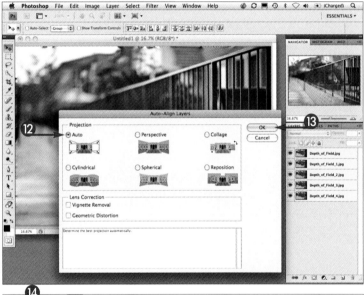

The Auto-Align Layers dialog box appears.

⑫ Click an alignment option (○ changes to ⦿).

Note: The Auto projection option, in which Photoshop analyzes the images for content and positions them in the layout, generally works well when blending images with overlapping areas to increase depth of field. You can experiment with other projection layouts.

⑬ Click OK.

A progress bar appears as the layers are automatically aligned.

Note: You may not see a noticeable change on screen.

⑭ With all the layers still selected, click Edit.

⑮ Click Auto-Blend Layers.

The Auto-Blend Layers dialog box appears.

⑯ Click Stack Images (○ changes to ⊙).

⑰ Click Seamless Tones and Colors (☐ changes to ☑).

⑱ Click OK.

A progress bar appears as the layers are blended based on the content, and layer masks are created.

The layers are blended using the layer masks and the depth of field is increased, reflecting all the points in sharpest focus of each layer.

TIPS

More Options!

The Auto-Blend Layers command can also be used to create a correctly illuminated composite from multiple images of a scene with different over- or underexposed areas.

Attention!

Although you did select Attempt to Automatically Align Source Images in the Load Layers dialog box (step 7), the Auto Blend Layers command generally works best if you apply the Auto-Align Layers command before attempting to auto blend the layers.

More Options!

You can also convert video frames shot against a static background into layers and then use the Auto-Align Layers command to combine these frames and add or delete specific areas from the frames.

CREATE A SILHOUETTE
for a custom design

Many advertising layouts are designed with a silhouetted person or object against a plain, colored background. You can easily create a similar design by making a selection in a photograph and using that selection in a background document. The silhouette design can be very effective, not only as an advertising piece but also as a business card, a greeting card, a postcard, or an original logo.

Not all objects in a photograph can be used as a silhouette. The subject needs to have a detailed

enough shape when contrasted against a background to not only stand out but also be recognizable. People or objects that are angled or positioned parallel to the plane of the photograph often work best. The size of the object is not important because you can transform and resize the silhouetted item to fit your design. You can use just one silhouette or combine any number of objects from various photos and place these on any colored background. Just add some text to complete the design.

CREATE THE SILHOUETTES AND BACKGROUND

① Open the photos with the objects for the silhouettes and a new blank document with the width, height, and resolution set for the custom layout.

② Press D to set the foreground color to black.

③ Click the Quick Select tool.

● Optionally, you can click the Lasso tool to select the subject.

④ Click and drag a detailed selection around the subject.

⑤ Press ⌘+J (Ctrl+J) to put the selected area on its own layer.

⑥ Press ⌘ (Ctrl) and click the Layer 1 thumbnail to target the selection and make it active.

⑦ Press Option+Delete (Alt+Backspace) to fill the selection with black.

⑧ Repeat steps 3 to 7 for any additional photos.

⑨ Click the blank document to select it.

⑩ Click the foreground color in the toolbox.

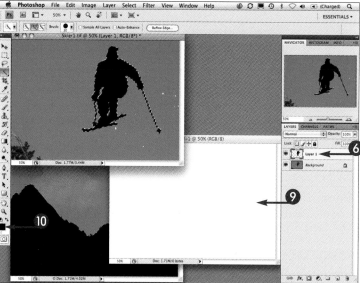

The color picker appears.

⑪ Click to select a color for the new document.

⑫ Click OK.

Note: *If a Warning triangle (Out of Gamut indicator) appears next to the selected color, it indicates that a color will not print exactly as seen on the screen. You can click the color swatch under the Out of Gamut indicator and Photoshop automatically changes the color selection to the closest In Gamut (printable) color.*

⑬ With the blank document selected, press Option+Delete (Alt+Backspace) to fill the layer with the new foreground color.

The new document fills with the foreground color.

More Options!

Pressing ⌘+Tab (Ctrl+Tab) enables you to cycle through all open documents. You can select the one that you need to work on without clicking and dragging the others out of the way in the document window.

Did You Know?

If all your documents open as tabs, you can click Window, Arrange, and then Float All in Windows and view each image in a separate window. You can also click Window, Arrange, and then Cascade to make all the open documents align and occupy the least amount of space on-screen.

More Options!

Press ⌘++ (Ctrl++) to enlarge the preview. Press ⌘+– (Ctrl+–) to reduce the preview. Press ⌘+spacebar (Ctrl+spacebar) and click to zoom in even with another tool selected. Press Option+spacebar (Alt+spacebar) and click to zoom out.

CREATE A SILHOUETTE
for a custom design

The silhouette technique can be used in a variety of ways. It can be the main part of the design or a secondary element in the overall piece. A wedding thank-you note, for example, may have a small silhouette of the couple kissing on the inside or back of the card.

You can make variations to the silhouette and the background depending on the purpose of the piece. Highlighting specific areas such as a bracelet or a belt adds dimension and focus to the silhouette. Select these areas as the first step. Jump the

selections to a separate layer and fill them with white to contrast against the black silhouette, and then continue creating the silhouetted form. Place the highlights layer above the silhouette layer and merge these two layers. For a more subtle overall effect, you can apply a gradient to the background layer instead of using a solid color. Place the most important part of the silhouette over the lightest part of the gradient. As the gradient gets lighter, the silhouette stands out more due to the increased contrast.

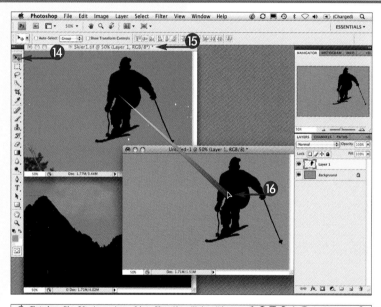

⓮ Click the Move tool.

⓯ Click one of the photos to activate it.

⓰ Click the black silhouette and drag it onto the new document.

⓱ Repeat steps 14 to 16 for any additional silhouettes.

● The silhouettes appear on separate layers in the new document.

⓲ Click Auto-Select (☐ changes to ☑).

⓳ Click Show Transform Controls (☐ changes to ☑).

⓴ Click the Close button to close each of the original photos used for silhouettes.

Note: Do not save the changes to the images when the dialog box appears.

㉑ With the new design document selected, press ⌘++ (Ctrl++) to enlarge this document.

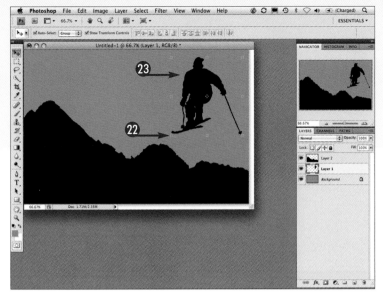

22 Click the first silhouette. Then press Shift and drag the corner of the transformation anchors to resize the silhouette.

23 Click and drag the silhouette into position.

24 Press Return (Enter) to apply the transformation.

25 Repeat steps 22 to 24 for any additional silhouettes.

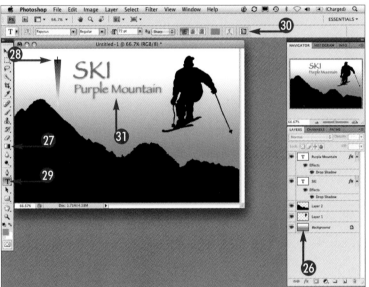

APPLY A GRADIENT

26 Click the Background layer to select it.

27 Click the Gradient tool.

28 Shift+click and drag in the image to create a gradient from the foreground color to white.

ADD TEXT TO YOUR DESIGN

29 Click the Type tool.

30 Select a color, font, and size in the Type tool's Options bar.

31 Click in the image and type some text.

32 Press Return (Enter) to apply the text.

64 CONTINUED

TIPS

Keyboard Shortcuts!
Pressing ⌘+T (Ctrl+T) opens the Transformation controls. You can press Return (Enter) instead of clicking the commit button (✔) on the Options bar to apply the transformation. You can press Esc instead of clicking the cancel button (⊘) to cancel the transformation.

Did You Know?
Selecting the Auto-Select check box on the Options bar enables you to click an item in a multilayered document; the layer that contains the item is automatically selected in the Layers panel.

Try This!
Selecting the Show Transform Controls check box on the Options bar makes the transformation anchors appear. You can then click and drag the corner anchors to resize items quickly.

BECOME A DIGITAL ARCHITECT
with the Vanishing Point filter

The Vanishing Point filter helps Photoshop recognize the third dimension of objects so that you can manipulate items in perspective. Using the Grid tool, you create a grid over a rectangular area. You must align the anchor points of the grid precisely with the corners of a rectangular area in the photo. With the first grid area set, you can extend the grid by pulling on the anchor points to cover a larger area with a blue grid in the same perspective. You can then pull a secondary plane around 90 degree corners to add more perspective planes to the image.

With Photoshop CS4, you can also rotate the secondary plane by any amount to fit a perpendicular or even an angled plane in the photo.

After all the grids or perspective planes are defined, you can change the look of the image by erasing items, copying objects from one area of the image to another, or adding items from other images, all while keeping the perspective in the original photo.

1. Open a main image.

2. Click the New Layer button to add a new layer.

3. Open a second image to be used on the main image.

4. Press ⌘+A (Ctrl+A) to select the entire second image.

   Note: You can select just an area.

5. Press ⌘+C (Ctrl+C) to copy the image.

6. Click here to close the second image.

7. Click Filter.

8. Click Vanishing Point.

#65

DIFFICULTY LEVEL

The Vanishing Point dialog box appears.

● The Create Plane tool is automatically selected.

9 Click four corners of an area that shows the perspective of the photo to create a blue grid.

10 Click the Edit Plane tool.

11 Click and drag the center points of the grid to extend the plane.

12 Press ⌘ (Ctrl) and click and drag a center point to create a perpendicular plane.

TIPS

Caution!
When you plan to copy an item or a layer from one photo to paste into another in perspective, be sure to copy the item first to save it to the Clipboard *before* you choose the Vanishing Point filter.

Did You Know?
When you are in the Vanishing Point dialog box, you can use the Zoom tool (🔍) to enlarge the area where you plan to apply the anchor points of the plane. You can also zoom temporarily in as you are placing or adjusting the anchor points by pressing and holding X.

Important!
You can use the Vanishing Point filter to increase the size of the building beyond the boundaries of the existing photo. Increase the canvas size by clicking Image and Canvas Size and then add width or height to one side of the existing image.

BECOME A DIGITAL ARCHITECT
with the Vanishing Point filter

You can expand a building to make it look taller than it is by creating and then extending the perspective plane above the top of the existing building and then using the Vanishing Point stamp tool to clone in more building. You can also increase the length of a structure by extending the grid past the edge of the existing building. You can add or erase the windows of a structure, add or remove a roof, or even add signs on any building and easily place the signs in perspective.

Using the Vanishing Point grids takes a little practice. The first grid is the most important and must be accurate. A blue grid shows a correct perspective plane. A red or yellow grid must be adjusted using the anchor points until the grid turns blue. However, even with a blue grid, you may need to readjust the anchor points to fit the perspective of the building or the subject after you extend the grid. By carefully adjusting the anchor points, you can match the perspective and change the architecture of any structure.

- The grid extends at a 90 degree angle.

⑬ Press Option+click (Alt+click) and drag a center point to rotate the plane into position.

- The perspective plane swings around and aligns at a different angle.

⑭ Press ⌘+V (Ctrl+V).

- The pasted image appears in a corner of the Vanishing Point dialog box.

⑮ Click and drag the second image over the perspective plane.

- The second image snaps into perspective on the plane.

⑯ Click the Transform tool.

⑰ Press Shift+click and drag the corners of the second image to adjust it into position.

⑱ Click OK.

The sign is applied and follows the perspective of the building.

- You can click here and select a different blending mode, such as Darker Color, to make the colors of the second image blend into the first.

TIPS

More Options!
You can also use the Vanishing Point filter to add designs to boxes or book covers and make the designs fit the perspective of the box or book.

Did You Know?
You can paint with a color in Vanishing Point and the brush size and shape scale and change orientation to fit the plane's perspective.

Try This!
You can create grids in Vanishing Point and save them on a separate layer in the Photoshop document. Click the New layer button (⬜) in the Layers panel. Click Filter and click Vanishing Point. Create the grids using the Vanishing Point tools. Click the Settings and Commands for Vanishing Point button (▦) in the Vanishing Point dialog box. Click Render Grids to Photoshop. Click OK, and the grids appear on the top layer of the file.

ERASE ITEMS IN PERSPECTIVE
with the Vanishing Point filter

You can use the Clone Stamp tool, the Patch tool, or the Healing Brushes to erase unwanted items in a photo. If the areas are natural as in a sky or grass, cloning and patching is fairly easy. If the area being patched or cloned includes architectural elements and perspective, removing them becomes more difficult. You can use the Vanishing Point filter in Photoshop CS4 to help you remove items in an image while maintaining perspective.

You can edit the image in Photoshop before and after using the Vanishing Point filter. By creating a

separate layer in Photoshop before applying the Vanishing Point filter, you can more easily adjust those areas once you are back in the main Photoshop window.

After you have finished editing the file, save it as a PSD, TIFF, or JPEG so the perspective planes you drew in Vanishing Point will be saved with the file. You can then reopen the file, reopen the Vanishing Point filter, and continue to erase or edit in perspective at a later date.

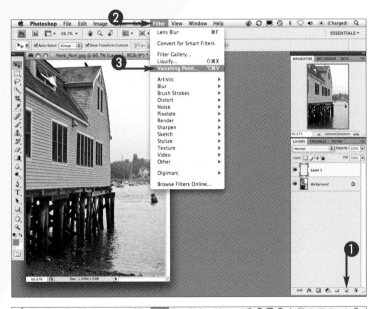

① Click the New Layer button in the Layers panel to add an empty layer above the Background layer.

② Click Filter.

③ Click Vanishing Point.

The Vanishing Point dialog box appears.

④ Click the Create Plane tool.

⑤ Click four corners of an area that shows the perspective of the photo to create a blue grid.

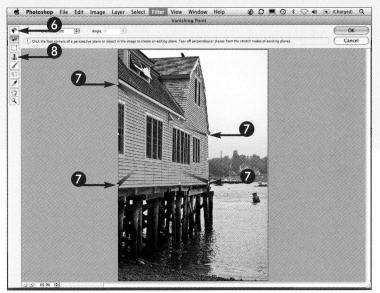

6 Click the Edit Plane tool.

7 Click and drag the points of the grid to extend the plane.

8 Click the Stamp tool.

#66

9 Option+click (Alt+click) in an area in the perspective plane to establish the sampling point.

10 Click and drag carefully using short strokes in the area of the photo to be erased.

11 Repeat steps 9 and 10, resampling several times to keep the look natural.

12 Click OK.

The edits are applied to the top layer.

● You can click Layer and select Flatten Image, and then click File and select Save As to save the new version of the photo.

TIPS

Caution!
If your grid is yellow or red, use the Edit Plane tool to adjust the anchor points until the grid turns blue. You can also press Option (Alt), which changes the Cancel button to Reset. Click Reset to start over.

Important
When erasing with the Vanishing Point Stamp tool (), Option+click (Alt+click) a straight line in the area to be sampled. Then click along the same line in the area to be removed to help align the parts you will be cloning.

Did You Know?
You can use the Stamp tool options and choose a Heal mode. Click the Heal ● and select On to blend the cloned strokes with the texture of the sampled image. Select Luminance to blend the cloned strokes with the lighting of the surrounding pixels.

ADD A SIMULATED REFLECTION
to an object with the Clone Stamp tool

You can create a reflection or a mirror image of the subject in a photo using Photoshop with a variety of techniques and different tools. Creating a perfectly mirrored reflection of the subject is tricky and can involve many techniques and tools for selecting objects, duplicating and transforming layers, adjusting opacity, and more. However, you can quickly create a simulated mirror image of the subject in a photo using the Clone Stamp tool and the Clone Source feature of Photoshop CS4, as shown by Russell Brown, the Senior Creative Director at Adobe.

The Clone Source tabbed panel enables you to see the reflection as a guide before you paint it; however, this panel must be moved away from the main image window to function correctly as a preview of what you are painting. You create the reflection on a separate layer so you can adjust the look using the layer opacity or a blended layer mask, or both.

Depending on the subject matter, angle of the subject, and intended use of the photo, your mirrored image can be convincingly realistic.

① Click the Clone Stamp tool.

② Click the New Layer button on the Layers panel to create a new layer.

③ Click here and select All Layers.

④ Click the Clone Source panel toggle button to open the Clone Source panel.

⑤ Click to uncheck Clipped, Auto Hide, and Invert if these are selected (☑ changes to ☐).

⑥ Click and drag the Clone Source panel so it does not touch the image window.

⑦ Click Show Overlay (☐ changes to ☑).

⑧ Click the Maintain Aspect Ratio button to turn it off and unlink the Width and Height.

⑨ Click in the Height box and type **–100** to set the vertical scale.

Note: Optionally, click the H and drag to the left until –100 shows in the box.

⑩ Click the word *Opacity* and drag to the left to reduce the preview opacity to 50% or lower so you can see both the reflection and the original subject as you work.

⑪ Press Option (Alt) and click at the bottom of the subject to be mirrored to sample it.

⑫ Move the cursor away from the image window.

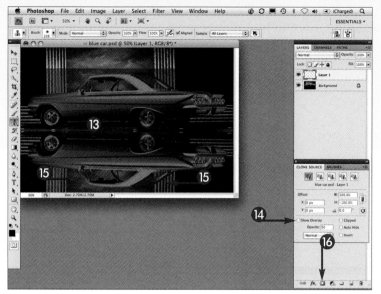

The reflection appears as an overlay on the image.

⑬ Click and drag using the Clone Stamp tool and a large brush to paint in the reflection.

Note: Start painting close to the spot you originally sampled in step 11.

⑭ Click Show Overlay to turn off the overlay (☑ changes to ☐).

⑮ Click and drag with the Clone Stamp tool to finish painting in the reflection.

⑯ Click the Layer Mask button to add a layer mask.

⑰ Press D to reset the foreground and background colors to white and black.

Note: The foreground color should be white after adding a layer mask and pressing D.

⑱ Click the Gradient tool.

⑲ Click and drag from the bottom of the original subject to the bottom of the reflection using a white to black gradient.

The reflection appears to fade away from the subject.

⑳ Click and drag the Layer Opacity slider to make the reflection appear realistic.

● You can click here to change the layer blending mode to see if other modes, such as Soft Light, make the reflection more realistic.

TIPS

Did You Know?
The Clone Stamp reflection technique works well on product shots and can also be used as a creative tool for special effects with rasterized type.

More Options!
The Clone Source feature works with the Healing Brush tool (🖌) as well as with the Clone Stamp tool.

Try This!
You can change the offset values in the Clone Source panel to change the distance of the reflection from the subject. You can also vary the angle of the reflection by clicking and dragging on the angle icon or typing a set number of degrees in the Clone Source panel.

Blend one image into another with a
DISPLACEMENT MAP

You can paste one image onto another and blend the pasted image into the Background layer by changing the blend mode. The layer blending modes control how the colors in the top image combine with the pixels in the underlying image. They do not affect the texture of either image. To make the top image blend into the texture of the base image and make the final image appear more realistic, you can use the Distort filter and a special file called a *displacement map*.

A displacement map is a grayscale version of an image saved as a Photoshop file. The Displace filter then uses the displacement map essentially as an applied texture. The black areas are the low points and the light areas are the high points of the contours of the original image.

You create a displacement map of the background image and save it as a Photoshop file. Then you apply the Displace filter to the second image to be placed of top of the background image.

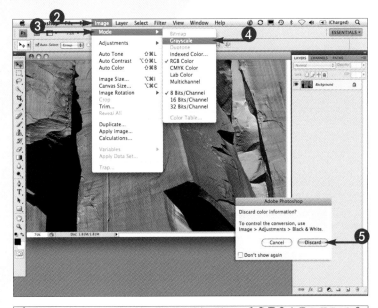

① Open the photo that will be the background image.

② Click Image.

③ Click Mode.

④ Click Grayscale to convert the image to grayscale.

⑤ Click Discard in the warning box that appears.

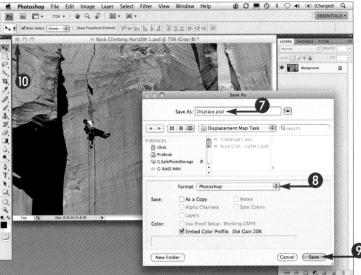

The image is converted to grayscale.

⑥ Press ⌘+Shift+S (Ctrl+Shift+S).

The Save As dialog box appears.

⑦ Type **Displace** in the name field.

⑧ Click here and select Photoshop.

⑨ Click Save.

⑩ Click here to close the grayscale Displace image.

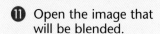

⓫ Open the image that will be blended.

⓬ Click Filter.

⓭ Click Distort.

⓮ Click Displace.

The Displace dialog box appears.

⓯ Type a lower value such as 10 to 30 in both the Horizontal and Vertical scale fields.

Note: The scale is the amount the filter will shift the selected pixels to make them wrap to the contours of the base image, based on the brightness values in the displacement map. A low to middle value generally creates a more realistic result for this task.

⓰ Click Stretch To Fit (○ changes to ◉).

⓱ Click Repeat Edge Pixels (○ changes to ◉).

⓲ Click OK.

TIPS

Did You Know?

If your grayscale image has very strong contrasts, you can reduce the amount of texture in the displacement map image by somewhat blurring the image after changing it to grayscale. Click Filter and select Blur and then Gaussian Blur. Increase the Radius slightly and click OK. Then save the image as the displacement image in the Photoshop (.psd) format.

More Options!

You can add a layer mask to hide the effect on certain areas of the image. For example, you could add a layer mask and paint with black over the rock climber to make the sign appear to be painted on the rocky surface only, and behind the rock climber.

Blend one image into another with a
DISPLACEMENT MAP

The Displace filter applies the displacement map to wrap one image precisely over the other, forcing the top layer to reflect the contours of the base layer. Other Photoshop filters such as Conté Crayon, Glass, Lighting Effects, and Texturizer also load other images or textures to produce their effects. However, not all these filters load the second image in the same way. The Displace filter specifically distorts an image based on the different values of gray in the displacement map image. The greater the contrast in the gray values, the more texture appears in the blended image.

This technique works best if both original images are the same size and resolution. You can start by clicking Image and selecting Image Size to resize the two photos to match. If the images are not the same size, the Displace filter either resizes or tiles the map, depending on the settings you select in the Displace dialog box. Stretch to Fit resizes the map, whereas the Tile option repeats the map, creating a pattern (see steps 16 and 17).

A dialog box appears.

⑲ Navigate to select the displacement image you saved earlier.

⑳ Click Open.

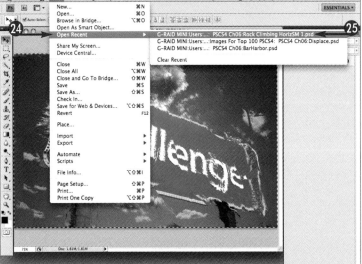

The image is distorted.

㉑ Press ⌘+A (Ctrl+A) to select the entire image.

㉒ Press ⌘+C (Ctrl+C) to copy the image.

㉓ Click File.

㉔ Click Open Recent.

㉕ Click to select the image for the background again.

- The background image opens.

26 Press ⌘+V (Ctrl+V) to paste the distorted image as a layer on top of the background image.

27 Click here and change the blending mode of the top layer to Multiply.

28 Click on the word *Opacity* and drag to the left to reduce the layer opacity to fit your image.

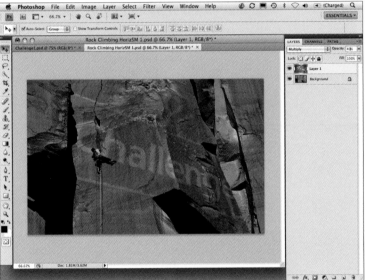

The top layer blends into the background layer, wrapping around the contours in the background image.

TIPS

Important!

Photoshop cannot recognize a displacement map image with layers. Be sure to flatten any image you plan to use as the displacement map before saving it as a Photoshop (.psd) file.

Try This!

You can convert the photo to a black and white image using the Adjustments panel. Use the sliders to control the amount of dark and light areas for the contours of the displacement map. Flatten the image before saving it as the displacement Photoshop file.

More Options!

You can apply a slight Gaussian Blur filter to the distorted layer to make it blend even more with the underlying background layer.

Designing with Text Effects

If a picture is worth a thousand words, then a picture with words has even more persuasive powers. Although Photoshop CS4 is not a page-layout application, you can add text to photographs for impact or to create an original design. You can also create special text effects to give personality to the words or even use the words alone to create the design.

With Photoshop, you can apply effects to text in more creative ways and more quickly than is possible using traditional tools. Not only can you see the end result instantly, but you also have complete creative freedom to make changes without wasting any paper or ink. By combining layer styles, patterns, colors, and fonts, you can create type with just the right look for your project. You can use text on images and make the words appear as part of

the photograph and, conversely, make the photo appear as part of the text.

When you type in Photoshop, the text is placed on a type layer as *vectors,* or mathematically defined shapes that describe the letters, numbers, and symbols of a typeface. You can warp, scale, or resize the words, edit the text, and apply many layer effects to the text while preserving the crisp edges. Some commands, such as the filter effects, painting tools, and the perspective and distort commands and tools, however, require the type to be *rasterized,* or converted to a normal layer filled with pixels. Be sure to edit the text before rasterizing because, once the type layer has been converted, the letters are essentially pixels on a layer and are no longer editable as text.

Top 100

PAINT DIFFERENT COLORS
into a text title

You can customize a title for an album page or any line of text by applying different colors to the words or to individual letters. Although you can colorize type while it is still a vector shape by selecting different colors or by adding a layer effect such as a Color Overlay or a Gradient Overlay, the text must be rasterized and turned into pixels in order to use any of Photoshop's painting tools. Once the type is turned into pixels, you can paint different colors on text using the brushes or the Gradient tool on whole words, individual letters, or even parts of letters.

When you type with the Type tool in Photoshop, the letters appear in the current foreground color. You can select a different foreground color before you type or you can change the text color after you type by highlighting the words with the Type tool and changing the color thumbnail in the Options bar. In order to add color to any kind of type, the document must be in RGB mode.

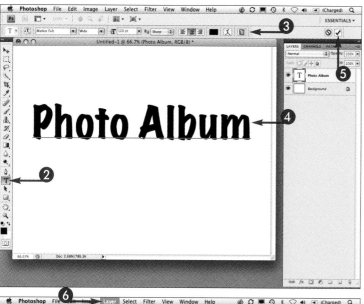

① Open any document or create a new one with the color mode set to RGB.

② Click the Type tool.

③ Select the font family, style, size, and alignment in the Options bar.

④ Click in the image and type the words for the title.

⑤ Click the commit button in the Options bar.

⑥ Click Layer.

⑦ Click Rasterize.

⑧ Click Type.

● The type layer changes to a pixel layer in the Layers panel but the image does not change.

⑨ ⌘+click (Ctrl+click) the layer thumbnail in the Layers panel to select the text.

A selection marquee individually outlines the letters.

⑩ Click the Brush tool.

⑪ Click the Foreground Color box.

The color picker appears.

⑫ Click in the color picker to select another foreground color.

⑬ Click OK to close the color picker.

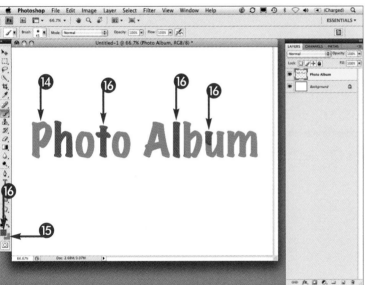

⑭ Paint over a letter or part of a letter with the brush to change the color.

⑮ Press X to reverse the foreground and background colors.

⑯ Repeat steps 11 to 14 to change each letter's color.

More Options!

You can select the Gradient tool (▣) and a colored gradient from the Gradient Editor in the Options bar. Click and drag across any individually selected letters to create a variegated color fill. You can click and drag multiple times, changing the angle or direction with each stroke. Each time you drag, the fill style changes.

Try This!

You can select colors for painting from any open image on your desktop. With the Color Picker dialog box open, move the cursor out of the dialog box and over another image. The cursor changes to an eyedropper. Click anywhere in the other photo to select that color. The color automatically appears in the color box in the color picker. Click OK to select that color as the foreground color.

ADD A DOUBLE-NEON GLOW
to text for a unique design

You can easily give any text a double-neon glow effect using a variation of a technique taught by Colin Smith of PhotoshopCAFÉ. Colin is an award-winning Photoshop and Flash designer and teaches the new media through his instructional videos called the *Photoshop Secrets* video training series. He also writes the CAFÉ cup, a free subscription newsletter, and runs the PhotoshopCAFE.com Web site, a powerful resource for Photoshop-related news.

The double-neon glow can be very effective for creating album or Web page titles. Set against a dark background, the glowing letters quickly capture your viewer's attention. You can easily change the way the letters glow on the screen by changing the background layer color or adding a gradient background. The double-glow effect surrounding the letters can be varied anytime and changed by simply double-clicking the effect button in the Layers panel to reopen the Layer Style dialog box. By keeping the text as a type layer, you can edit the text and maintain the glow, so you can use the double-glow technique for multiple applications.

1. Open a new blank document.
2. Click the Type tool.
3. Select the font family, style, and size in the Options bar.
4. Click in the image and type your text.
5. Click the commit button to commit the type.
6. Click the Layer Style button.
7. Click Outer Glow.

The Layer Style dialog box appears.

8. Click and drag to increase the spread slider to about 13%, which is just over 1/8 the text size.

   Note: You can reopen any layer style by double-clicking on its name in the layers panel later to readjust the amounts if necessary.

9. Click and drag to increase the size to about 15 pixels or 1/8 the text.

10. Click Drop Shadow (☐ changes to ☑).

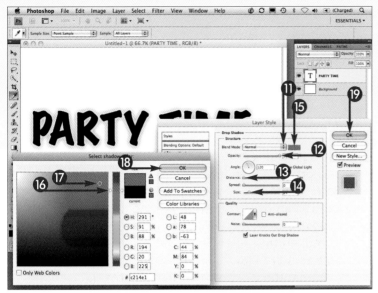

The dialog box changes.

⑪ Click here and select Normal.

⑫ Click and drag the Opacity slider to 100%.

⑬ Click and drag the distance to 0 pixels.

⑭ Increase the size slider until it looks good in the preview.

⑮ Click the color box.

The Select Shadow Color dialog box appears.

⑯ Click and drag the color slider.

⑰ Click in the color box to select a glow color.

⑱ Click OK to close the Shadow Color dialog box.

⑲ Click OK to close the Layer Style dialog box.

⑳ Press D to reset the foreground color to black.

㉑ Click the Background layer to select it.

㉒ Press Option+Delete (Alt+Backspace) to fill the background with black.

● You can double-click the name of any layer style in the Layers panel to readjust the neon glow.

The text appears with a neon glow against a dark background.

TIPS

Attention!

The double-neon glow technique works best on a dark background; however, it does not need to be black. You can also select the Gradient tool () and click and drag across the Background layer to create a gradient color fill.

Keyboard Shortcuts!

With the Type tool (T) selected, pressing Return (Enter) moves the cursor to the next line; pressing ⌘+Return (Ctrl+Enter) or Enter on the numeric keypad applies the type or any transformations. Pressing Esc cancels the type layer.

Try This!

Type some text with the Type tool. Before clicking the commit button (✓), press and hold ⌘ (Ctrl) to open the transformation anchor points. Click and drag the anchors while pressing ⌘ (Ctrl) to transform the type.

CREATE A CUSTOM WATERMARK
to protect your images

If you upload your proofs to a Web site for client approval or if you sell your digital artwork online, you want people to see the images but not to use the files without your permission. You can add a custom watermark with a transparent look to any image to protect it and still keep the image visible.

A custom watermark can be as simple as your name and the copyright symbol. After typing your name on a type layer and adding a large copyright symbol as

a shape layer, you can add any kind of bevel or embossed style to your personalized watermark. You can even copy the two layers to another photo to apply the same custom watermark. To give a transparent look to each layer, you can lower the Fill opacity, which affects only the fill pixels, leaving the beveled areas appearing like a glass overlay. You can also use the same technique to give a transparent look to any text, shape, or other layer on any image.

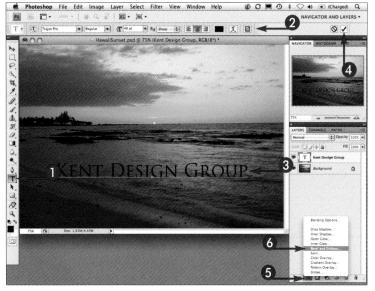

① With the image open, click the Type tool.

② Select the font family, style, and size in the Options bar.

③ Click in the image and type the text for your watermark, such as your name or company name.

④ Click the commit button.

⑤ Click the Layer Style button.

⑥ Click Bevel and Emboss.

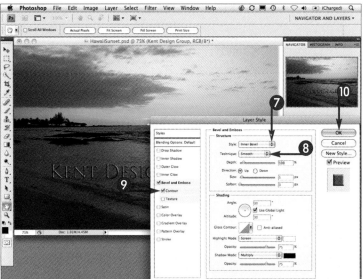

The Layer Style dialog box appears.

⑦ Click here and select Inner Bevel.

⑧ Click here and select Smooth.

⑨ Click Contour (☐ changes to ☑) and the Contour pane appears in the Layer Style dialog box.

⑩ Click OK.

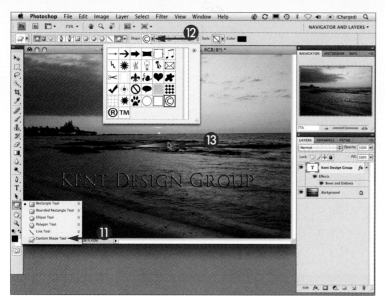

⑪ Click and hold the Rectangle tool and select the Custom Shape tool.

⑫ Click here and select the copyright symbol.

⑬ Press Shift and click and drag in the photo to create a copyright symbol.

The copyright symbol appears on the image and as a shape layer in the Layers panel.

⑭ Press Option (Alt) and click and drag the Layer Style button from the type layer to the shape layer to copy the effect.

The same emboss style is applied to the copyright symbol.

⑮ Double-click in the Fill data field and type **0**.

⑯ Click the type layer to select it and repeat step 15.

The name and copyright symbol appear embossed on the image.

Caution!

There are three options on the Options bar for the Custom Shape tool. When you select the Shape tool for the copyright symbol, make sure that the Shape Layer button (◻) is highlighted on the Options bar rather than the Paths or Fill Pixels button.

Did You Know?

The Layers panel includes two types of sliders. The Opacity slider affects the visibility of both the filled pixels and the layer style. The Fill slider affects only the transparency of the filled pixels without changing any style that is applied.

Try This!

Double-clicking the Type thumbnail in the Layers panel selects and highlights all the type on that layer. Double-clicking the blank space next to the name of a layer opens the Layer Style dialog box.

FILL A SHAPE WITH TEXT
to create unique effects

In Photoshop, you can type text in several ways. When you type, the text is placed on a type layer and the words remain editable until you rasterize, convert it to a shape layer, or flatten the layer. You can then scale, skew, or rotate it to fit a design. You can also control the flow of the characters you type within a bounding box by typing text as a paragraph, either horizontally or vertically. For text in a rectangular shape, you can use the Type tool to drag diagonally and define a bounding area and then click and type the text. Typing text as a paragraph is

useful for creating brochures, scrapbooks, or various design projects.

You can also use custom shapes as text bounding boxes for unique designs. You can drag out any shape selected from the custom shape picker using the Custom Shape tool and type into the shape as a bounding box. You can also use the Pen tool to create an original path to use as the bounding box. You can then fill the shape with paragraph text to create unique visual effects.

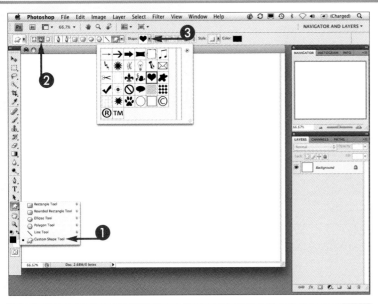

① Click and hold the Rectangle tool and select the Custom Shape tool.

② Click the Paths button in the Options bar.

③ Click here and click a shape to select it.

④ Click and drag in the image to create the shape.

Note: Press Shift to constrain the shape and press the spacebar to reposition the shape as you drag.

⑤ Click the Type tool.

⑥ Select the font family, style, size, and color.

⑦ Click a text alignment.

⑧ Click inside the shape.

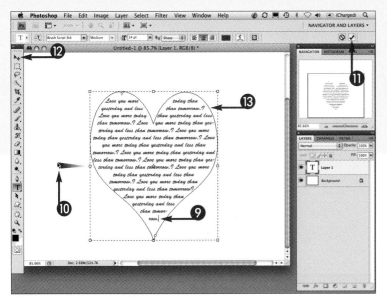

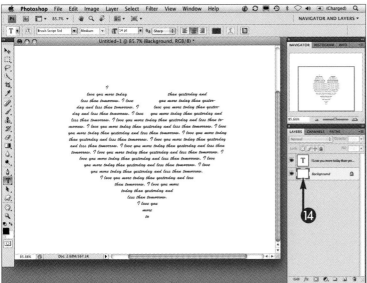

A bounding box surrounds the shape.

⑨ Type the text until the shape is full.

⑩ Click and drag the anchor points around the shape to alter the form if necessary.

⑪ Click the commit button.

⑫ Click the Move tool.

⑬ Click and drag in the shape to reposition it on the page.

⑭ Click the Background layer in the Layers panel to view the text without the outline of the shape.

TIPS

Did You Know?

Click the right-pointing arrow (▶) on the custom shape picker in the Options bar to load more shapes. Select All from the choices in the menu and click Append to add these to the current set.

More Options!

You can purchase and load professionally designed custom vector shapes from third parties, such as GraphicAuthority.com. You can also copy the purchased custom shapes file directly into the Presets folder of the Photoshop CS4 application to have the shapes automatically appear in the Custom Shapes menu after restarting Photoshop.

Try This!

You can copy text from another document and paste it into the shape. Select the text in the other document, and press ⌘+C (Ctrl+C) to copy. Click the Photoshop document. Use the Type tool (T) to click in the shape. Press ⌘+V (Ctrl+V) to paste the text.

WARP TYPE
for a fun effect

You can create many different effects with type by warping the letters into various shapes. Although you can warp text on a rasterized layer, the letters lose their sharp edges and appear fuzzy. Using Photoshop's Warp Text feature gives text a completely new look and keeps the text sharp-edged and editable.

Type the text and then use the Warp Text dialog box to transform it. You can select from a variety of warp styles and use the sliders to alter the look. You can control the direction of the warp as well as the size of the letters. Because the warp style is an attribute of the type layer, you can change the style at any time by reselecting the layer with the Type tool and opening the Warp Text dialog box. As long as the text is on an editable type layer, you can change the letters and color them individually. With the text on a separate layer, you can apply any layer styles before or after warping the text.

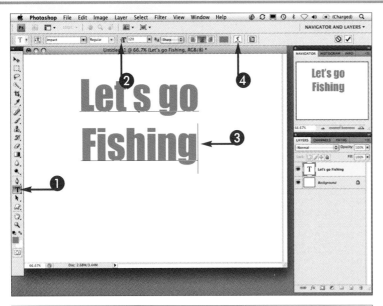

❶ In a new blank document, click the Type tool.

❷ Select the font family, style, size, justification, and color.

❸ Click in the document and type the text.

❹ Click the Warp Text button.

The Warp Text dialog box appears.

❺ Click here and select a warp style such as Fish.

The text in the image changes to match the style selected.

⑥ Click and drag the Bend slider to change the amount of warp.

⑦ Click and drag the Horizontal Distortion slider to adjust the direction of the effect.

⑧ Click and drag the Vertical Distortion slider to change the effect.

⑨ Click OK to commit the warp.

⑩ Click the commit button to apply the text.

The style of warp and the changes to the text are committed.

● You can change the text color; see the tip section for more information.

TIPS

Did You Know?

You can change the color of the text after you warp it. Select the Type tool (T) and click and drag across the text to highlight it. Click the foreground color in the toolbox, select another color from the color picker, and click OK to close the dialog box. Click the commit button (✓) in the Options bar.

More Options!

To see the color of the type as you change it, highlight the type. Then press ⌘+H (Ctrl+H), the keyboard shortcut to Hide Extras. The type remains selected but the highlighting is not visible. When you select another foreground color in the color picker, you instantly see the color on your text.

ADD PERSPECTIVE TO TYPE
and keep it sharp

When you warp a type layer, the letters always bend the shape to some degree, even if you set the Bend slider to 0. Although using the Perspective function found under the Edit menu's Transform submenu more accurately gives the illusion of text disappearing into the distance, this function is unavailable for a type layer. If you rasterize the layer and turn the letters into pixels to use the Perspective transformation, the characters blur as you change the angles. You can, however, add realistic

perspective to type and preserve the crisp edges by converting the type layer to a shape layer.

Converting type to shapes changes the type layer into a layer with a colored fill and a linked vector mask showing the outline of the letters. The outline is actually a temporary path and appears in the Paths panel as well. The text is no longer editable, but you can alter the vector mask, modify the paths, add layer styles, and use all the transformation tools to change the look.

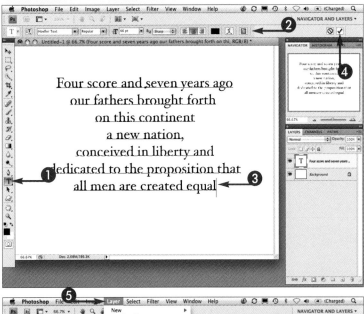

1 In a new blank document, click the Type tool.

2 Select the font family, style, size, justification, and color.

3 Click in the image and type the text.

4 Click the commit button.

5 Click Layer.

6 Click Type.

7 Click Convert to Shape.

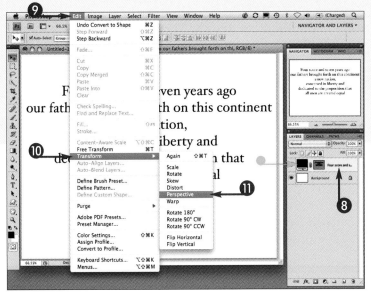

- The type layer in the Layers panel changes to a fill and vector mask.

Note: The type may appear jagged if the vector mask remains selected.

8 Click the vector mask to deselect it.

9 Click Edit.

10 Click Transform.

11 Click Perspective.

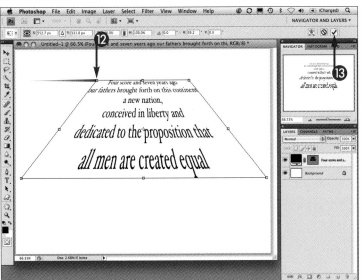

The text has a bounding box with anchor points.

12 Click one of the top corner anchors and drag toward the center top anchor.

The text appears to be lying down on a perspective plane.

13 Click the commit button.

The text retains its sharp edges even as it appears in a perspective plane.

TIPS

Change It!
You can also click one of the top or bottom corner anchors and drag straight up or straight down to create a vertical perspective. The letters seem to disappear into the distance in a vertical position.

Try This!
When you need to select the Type tool to edit type, double-click the *T* in the type layer thumbnail in the Layers panel. The type on the layer is highlighted, and the Type tool is automatically selected.

More Options!
You can also edit type using the Character panel. Click Window and click Character to open the Character panel. You can then make any type changes directly in the panel.

Make your text
FOLLOW ANY PATH

You can make text move along an angled line or curve and swoop in any direction to create an original design. By creating an angled path with the Pen tool or a curved path with the Freeform Pen tool, you can place the Type tool cursor on the path and type the text. The text flows along the path, starting from the insertion point. Another option is to create a shape using the Shape tool and place the text around the edges of the shape. You can also use any object

in a photograph to create the path. When you add the text, it flows along the edges of the object in the photo, creating a sophisticated design.

You can use any selection tool to select the object. Convert the selection to a complex working path using the options in the Paths panel's pop-up menu. The text remains on a type layer, so you can change or add words or style and color the letters.

1. Click the Quick Select tool.
2. Click the objects to make a selection.

● You can click the Refine Edge button to improve the selection.

3. Click the Paths tab.
4. Click here to open the Paths menu.
5. Click Make Work Path.

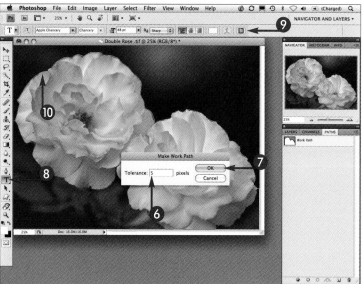

The Make Work Path dialog box appears.

6. Type **5** in the Tolerance field.

Note: For a more detailed path, type a smaller number to have more control points on the path.

7. Click OK.

The dotted selection lines disappear, and a new path appears in the Paths panel.

8. Click the Type tool.
9. Select the font family, style, size, and color.
10. Click the path and type the text.

The text follows the path, and a type path appears in the Paths panel.

⑪ Click the Path Selection tool.

⑫ Press ⌘+spacebar (Ctrl+spacebar) and click the image to zoom in.

⑬ Click the dot at the beginning of the text.

● The cursor changes to an I-beam with a small black arrow.

⑭ Drag along the path to reposition the text.

Note: Optionally, drag the cursor across the path to put the text on the other side of the path.

⑮ Press Option+spacebar (Alt+spacebar) and click the image to zoom out.

⑯ Click the commit button to dismiss the target path and commit the changes.

The type follows the path line on the subject.

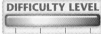
DIFFICULTY LEVEL

TIPS

Did You Know?
When you click the Zoom tool (🔍) to zoom in, you see a small *X* indicating the beginning of the text on a path, and a small *O* indicating the end of the text. If the text is center-aligned, a small diamond shape designates the center.

Try This!
On sharp curves, letters may appear on top of each other. Click Window and then Character to open the Character panel. Select the letters and adjust the tracking in the Character panel or click between the letters and adjust the kerning.

Try This!
To adjust kerning, click between two letters and press Option (Alt) and the right or left arrows. To adjust tracking, select a group of letters and press Option (Alt) and the right or left arrows.

Create a
PHOTO-FILLED TITLE

You can easily create mood-inspiring or memory-evoking titles for a photo or album page by making a photograph fill the letters. Photoshop includes four different Type tools: the Horizontal and Vertical Type tools and the Horizontal and Vertical Type Mask tools. When you use the Type Mask tools, Photoshop automatically creates a selection in the shape of the letters. However, using the regular Type tools to create photo-filled titles gives you more control over the design and makes it easier to see the area of the photo that will be cut out by the letters.

Filling text or any other object with a photograph or other image is one of the many collage and masking techniques in Photoshop. You type text and use a *clipping mask* to *clip* the photograph so that it shows only through the letters and then *mask* the rest of the photo. Because the letters are on an editable type layer, you can change the text even after the letters are filled with the image. You can also add a drop shadow or emboss to the type layer to make the letters stand out.

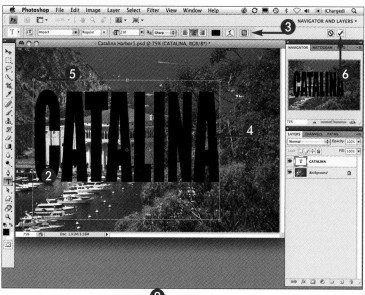

① Open a photograph to use as the base photo.

② Click the Type tool.

③ Select the font family, style, and justification. The size will be readjusted when you transform the text in step 5.

   Note: Thick sans serif fonts work best for this effect.

④ Click in the image and type the text.

⑤ Press ⌘ (Ctrl) and click and drag the transformation anchors to stretch the type.

⑥ Click the commit button.

⑦ Click and drag the Background layer over the New Layer button to duplicate it.

⑧ Click and drag the Background copy layer above the type layer.

⑨ Click Layer.

⑩ Click Create Clipping Mask.

● The Background copy layer is indented with an arrow in the Layers panel, but the image does not change.

⑪ Click the New Layer button to create a new empty layer named Layer 1.

⑫ Click and drag the new empty layer below the type layer.

⑬ Press D to reset the foreground and background colors.

⑭ Press ⌘+Delete (Ctrl+Backspace) to fill the layer with white.

The photo appears to fill the letters on a white background.

⑮ Click the Move tool.

⑯ Click the Background copy layer to select it.

⑰ Click and drag in the image to move the photo into position inside the letters.

The photo is repositioned within the letters, creating an attractive photo title.

● You can click the type layer to select it and click the Layer Styles button to add a drop shadow and Bevel and Emboss layer effect.

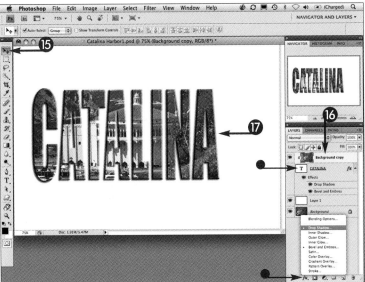

TIPS

More Options!
You can also change the type attributes using the Character panel. Click Window and then Character to open the panel. Position the cursor over any of the settings to activate the scrubby sliders. Move the cursor to change the settings.

Important!
Be sure to highlight the Background copy layer, which must be above the type layer, when you create the clipping mask. Changing the stacking order of the layers after a clipping mask has been applied can remove the clipping mask.

More Options!
You can create a clipping mask using two different keyboard shortcuts. Press Option (Alt) and click between the two layers in the Layers panel or select the layer and press ⌘+Option+G (Ctrl+Alt+G) to clip it to the layer below.

BLEND TEXT
into a photograph creatively

When you type on a photograph, you can reduce the opacity of the type layer to make the letters fade into the image in a uniform manner. For a more interesting effect, use the Blending options in the Layer Style dialog box to give the illusion of the text disappearing behind different elements in the photograph. You can make the letters disappear behind clouds or trees, blend parts of the letters into a mountain, or create a variety of different effects using the colors from the underlying layer and the Blending options for the text layer.

The Layer Style dialog box includes Blending Options sliders for both the active layer and the underlying layer. The sliders determine which pixels appear through the active layer and which are hidden, based on the brightness of the pixels. You can make the text blend even more smoothly with the underlying photo by splitting the sliders and in effect partially blending some of the pixels in the tonal range.

Setting up your workspace first to view the Character and Layers panel makes this task much easier.

① Click Window.

② Click Character to open the Character panel.

③ Repeat step 1 and click Layers if necessary to open the Layers panel.

④ Open an image.

⑤ Arrange the panels to see the image window.

⑥ Click the Type tool.

⑦ Select the font family, style, size, and color.

⑧ Make any other adjustments to the type using the Character panel.

⑨ Click in the image and type the text.

⑩ Press ⌘+Return or Enter on a numeric keypad (Shift+Enter) or click the commit button.

⑪ Click the Layer Style button and select Blending Options.

178

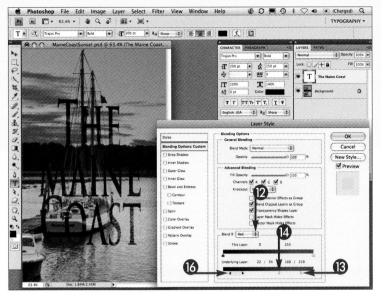

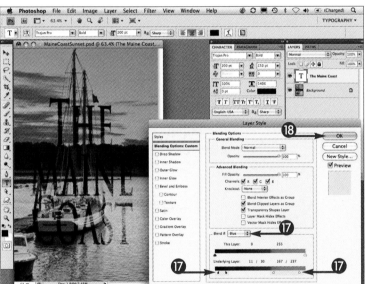

The Layer Style dialog box appears.

⑫ Click here and select Red.

⑬ Click and drag the Underlying Layer white slider slightly to the left to make the lightest values in the underlying photo appear through the text.

⑭ Press Option (Alt) and click and drag the left half more to the left, separating the slider halves.

⑮ Click and drag the slider halves to vary the areas of the photo that blend with the text.

⑯ Repeat steps 12 to 15 using the black slider for the underlying layer and dragging right instead of left to make the darkest values of the underlying photo appear through the text.

⑰ Repeat steps 10 to 14 for Green and Blue until the text blends with the elements in the photograph.

⑱ Click OK.

The text disappears behind some areas in the photo and shows through other parts depending on the color values in the image.

Did You Know?

Splitting the white highlight or the black shadow sliders for the underlying layer defines a range of partially blended or composite pixels and softens the transitions as the text is blended with the background photo.

Try This!

You can also view the Layer Style dialog box by clicking Layer, Layer Style, and then Blending Options or by double-clicking in the empty space next to the layer name in the Layers panel.

More Options!

You can add a bevel and emboss, shadow, or any of the other layer styles to the letters at any time. Open the Layer Style dialog box and click any of the styles to see and apply the effect.

Create an amazing
COLORED SHADOW

When you apply a drop shadow to text using a Layer Style drop shadow, the shadow is gray. Actual shadows of text or other objects are not gray and do not always have the same opacity. Shadows reflect the colors of the objects they cover. If you select another color for the shadow in the Layer Style dialog box, the shadow appears unnatural and uniform in color.

You can apply a drop shadow with the same colors that occur in the real world by using a selection and a Brightness/Contrast adjustment. Then, by linking

the shadow layer to the text layer, you can reposition the text in the image, and the shadow follows, automatically adjusting itself for colors in the image below.

You can use the same technique to add a realistic shadow to text or to any object in an image. Add depth to natural light shadows under a tree or increase the shadow of a person in a sunlit photo. The greater the number of colors and textures affected by the shadow, the more natural your colored shadow appears.

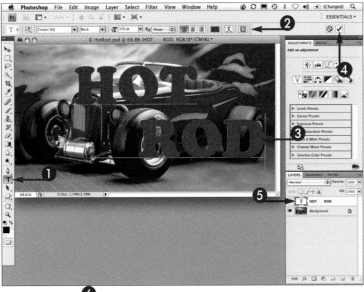

① Click the Type tool.

② Select the font family, style, size, and color.

Note: You can click in the Size field and type the text size.

③ Click in the image and type the text.

④ Click the commit button.

⑤ ⌘+click (Ctrl+click) the type layer thumbnail to select the letters.

⑥ Click Select.

⑦ Click Modify.

⑧ Click Feather.

The Feather Selection dialog box appears.

⑨ Click in the radius field and type a small amount such as **10**.

⑩ Click OK.

⑪ Click the Type tool.

⑫ Press the right arrow key several times and the down arrow key several times.

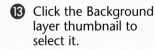

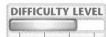

The selection marquee moves down and to the right.

⑬ Click the Background layer thumbnail to select it.

⑭ Click the Brightness/Contrast Adjustment button in the Adjustments panel.

Note: You can also click the New Adjustment Layer button in the Layers panel and click Brightness/Contrast.

DIFFICULTY LEVEL

The Brightness/Contrast adjustments appear in the panel, and the selection marquee is hidden.

⑮ Click and drag the Brightness slider to the left to create the drop shadow.

⑯ ⌘+click (Ctrl+click) both the adjustment layer and the type layer in the Layers panel to select them.

⑰ Click the Link Layers button.

The type and its shadow are now linked.

⑱ Click the Move tool.

⑲ Click and drag the text around on the photo.

The shadow follows the text, and the shadow's colors automatically adjust to the colors in the area of the photo below.

More Options!

You can also keep the type and its shadow separate by not linking them as in steps 16 and 17. You can then move the type and its shadow independently to view the shadow in a new position for a different effect.

Did You Know?

You can quickly change the alignment of type using keyboard shortcuts. Click in the type and press Shift+⌘+L (Shift+Ctrl+L) to align left; press Shift+⌘+R (Shift+Ctrl+R) to align right; and press Shift+⌘+C (Shift+Ctrl+C) to align center.

Did You Know?

The size of the feather radius (see step 9) sets the width of the feathered edge of the selection and ranges from 0 to 250 pixels. A small feather radius in a very large image may not be visible and a large feather radius in a smaller image can spread too far away from the selection.

WEAVE TEXT AND GRAPHICS
for intriguing designs

You can create a design using type as the central element by changing the letter styles and size, adding layer effects, warping the text, or adding perspective. You can also make the individual letters interweave and interact with each other to add more interest to any project. By converting type layers to shapes and overlapping them, you can make some of the areas transparent to the background, creating new design elements. Add a shape to the text, make the letters intertwine with the shape, and you can create eye-catching logos or page titles.

When you convert a type layer to a shape, the text is no longer editable. However, you can still move individual letters. You can transform, warp, and resize one letter at a time or a group of letters. You can also add layer styles to the grouped design elements and change the look completely. Because the letters and shapes are all on one layer, the color and any layer styles that you use are applied to all the elements on the layer. Flatten the layers as a final step in creating the design.

① In a new blank document, click the Type tool.

② Select the font, size, and color.

③ Click in the document and type the text.

④ Click the commit button or press ⌘+Return (Shift+Enter) or Enter on the numeric keypad to commit the type.

⑤ Click Layer, Type, and then Convert to Shape.

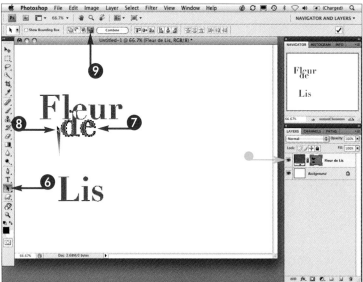

● The type layer changes to a fill layer and a vector mask.

⑥ Click the Path Selection tool.

⑦ Click and drag over the middle line of text to select it.

⑧ Click and drag the line up to overlap the first line of text.

⑨ Click the Exclude Overlapping Shape Areas button.

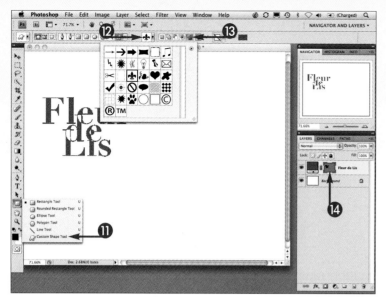

The areas of text that overlap are reversed out.

⑩ Repeat steps 7 to 9 for other lines of text.

⑪ Click and hold the Rectangle tool and click the Custom Shape tool.

⑫ Click here and click a shape to select it.

⑬ Click the Exclude Overlapping Shape Areas button.

⑭ Make sure that the vector mask thumbnail in the Layers panel is selected.

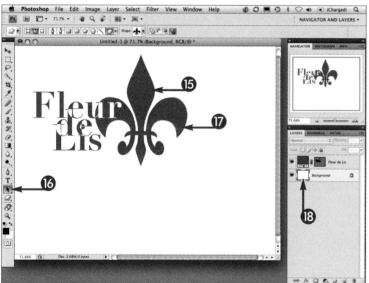

⑮ Click and drag the shape over the letters.

The areas of the shape and text that overlap are reversed out.

⑯ Click the Path Selection tool.

⑰ Click the shape and drag it to reposition it in the design if necessary.

The shape interacts differently with the type as it overlaps different areas.

⑱ Click the Background layer to view the design.

TIPS

More Options!

You can apply a layer style to the shapes and letters. Try adding a Bevel and Emboss layer style. Click Texture and select a pattern for the Texture Elements. The pattern is applied to all the colored areas.

Important!

Whenever you use the Path Selection tool ( ) to move letters or the shape, you must target the vector mask layer thumbnail in the Layers panel and click the Exclude Overlapping Shape Areas button (▣) on the Options bar to select it.

Did You Know?

You can use the Path Selection tool to move individual letters or the shape separately. Click one letter and move it to create a different look. To undo the move, click the previous state in the History panel.

Creating Digital Artwork from Photographs

You can use Photoshop to replicate traditional art materials and techniques and see immediate results on your screen. If you have spent years in art school working with traditional materials, you can find a whole new source of creativity as you experiment with different techniques. Even if you have never tried art in any form or claim you cannot even draw a straight line, you can use Photoshop to draw line art, sketch a person or a building, create a painted portrait, or paint with oils and watercolors. You can experiment and try all sorts of projects without wasting any paper products or paints. You can vary colors, mix media, copy, trace, or draw freehand, and even erase the results before anyone else can see your attempts!

The key to creating digital artwork is to combine different layers, effects, smart filters, masks, and blend modes. The results vary with the methods used, and the style of photograph and the subject matter both affect the overall look of the finished piece. You can vary methods to make your work more efficient and at the same time expand your creative horizons. With so many options and choices, artistic experimentation with Photoshop can be very addictive. You may spend a lot more time with the art projects than you ever thought you would.

The tasks and techniques described in this chapter are only a taste of what is possible.

Top 100

Make any photo appear
SKETCHED ON THE PAPER

You can make a photo appear to be sketched onto the page, giving a traditional photograph an entirely new look. You can create a title page for an album or a Web gallery or use the technique as the final touch to a painted image. The image appears to be applied to the paper using charcoal, soft pencils, or a paintbrush, leaving the edges and brush marks visible. Starting with any image, you add a new layer filled with white. You then use the Eraser tool to erase through the white to reveal areas of the image

on the underlying layer. Using this technique even on a slightly grainy photo intensifies the effect. You can configure the Eraser tool with any of Photoshop's brush settings and change them as you continue sketching the photo onto the page. The greater the number and opacity of the brush strokes, the more of your photograph appears on the white layer. By selecting rough-edged brushes and varying the style of the strokes you use, your photo takes on the characteristics of a sketched image.

① Click the New Layer button in the Layers panel.

② Click Edit.

③ Click Fill.

The Fill dialog box appears.

④ Click here and select White.

⑤ Click OK.

A white layer covers the photo.

⑥ Click the word *Opacity* to activate the scrubby slider and drag to the left just enough to see the image underneath.

⑦ Click the Eraser tool.

⑧ Click here to open the brush picker.

⑨ Click a brush with a rough-looking edge.

⑩ Click and drag the Master Diameter slider to a large brush size.

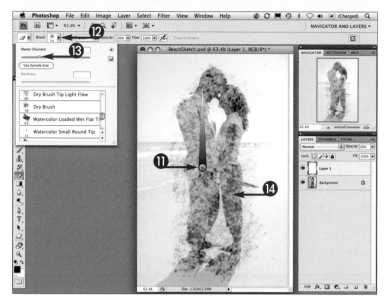

80

DIFFICULTY LEVEL

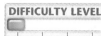

⓫ Click and drag across the image using several broad strokes.

⓬ Click here to open the brush picker.

⓭ Click and drag the Master Diameter slider to a smaller brush size.

⓮ Click and drag across the image to add more brush strokes.

⓯ Click the word *Opacity* and drag the slider for the layer back to 100%.

⓰ Continue applying just enough strokes until the image looks sketched-in.

The image appears to be brushed or sketched on a page.

TIPS

More Options!

You can add more brushes to the brush picker. Click the Brush drop-down arrow in the Options bar to open the brush picker. Click the flyout arrow (or pop-up menu) to open the Brush Picker menu. Click a brush set from the bottom section, such as Dry Media Brushes. Click Append in the dialog box that appears to add the brushes to the existing list.

Customize It!

You can view brushes by name instead of by the stroke thumbnail. Click the Brush drop-down arrow in the Options bar to open the brush picker. Click the flyout arrow (or pop-up menu) to open the Brush Picker menu. Click Small List or Large List. You can return to the default brush set by selecting Reset Brushes from the same list.

ADD YOUR OWN SIGNATURE
to any artwork

Fine art prints are almost always signed by the artist. You can sign your digital projects one at a time after they are printed, or you can apply a digital signature from within Photoshop. You can create a large custom signature brush and save it in your brush picker. You can then quickly apply your signature digitally to all your projects.

You can change the Diameter slider in the Brush options to add a signature to your images with any size signature brush, and you can use any color by selecting the color as the foreground color before applying the brush.

You should put your signature on projects using a separate layer to preserve the layer transparency. You can then add layer styles and easily change the color of the signature or even create a blind embossed signature effect.

Creating your own signature brush is best accomplished using a pen tablet because signing your name with a mouse can be very difficult.

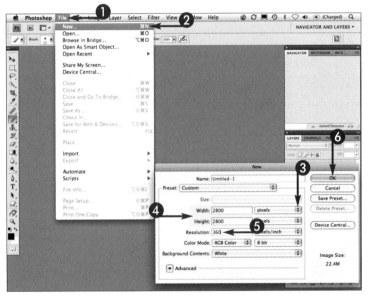

① Click File.

② Click New.

The New dialog box appears.

③ Click here and select pixels.

④ Click in the fields for the size and width and type **2800**.

⑤ Click in the field for the resolution and type **360**.

Note: Starting with a file 2800 × 2800 pixels at 360 ppi gives you the space to make a brush at the largest brush size of 2500 × 2500 pixels. You can then easily resize the brush to fit many different images.

⑥ Click OK.

Note: Make sure Background Contents is set to White, the default.

A new empty document appears.

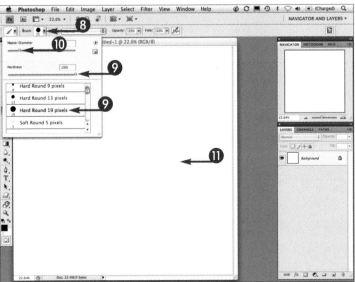

⑦ Press B to select the Brush tool.

⑧ Click here to open the brush picker.

⑨ Select a hard-edged brush.

⑩ Click and drag the Diameter slider to make the brush 35 to 40 pixels.

Note: You can pick any hard-edged brush for your signature. The numbers here are just guidelines.

⑪ Click in the white image and click and drag with the brush to sign your name.

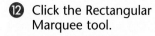

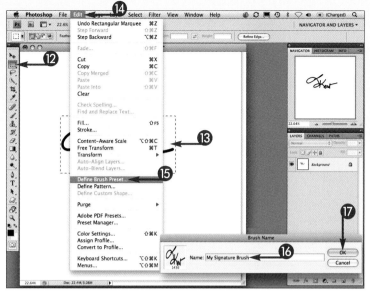

Your signature appears on the white image.

⑫ Click the Rectangular Marquee tool.

⑬ Click and drag just around your signature.

⑭ Click Edit.

⑮ Click Define Brush Preset.

The Brush Name dialog box appears.

⑯ Type a name for your signature, such as **My Signature Brush**.

⑰ Click OK to save the signature brush.

81

DIFFICULTY LEVEL

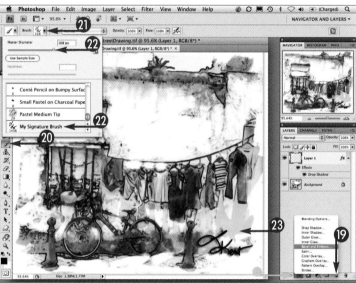

⑱ Open an image to which to add the signature.

⑲ Click the New Layer button to add an empty layer.

⑳ Click the Brush tool.

㉑ Click here to open the brush picker.

㉒ Select your signature brush and click and drag the Master Diameter slider to adjust the size to fit the image.

㉓ Click once in the image.

Your signature appears.

● You can click the Add a Layer Style button to add a drop shadow or bevel.

TIPS

Did You Know?

You can create a custom brush from any signature or any other image up to 2500 × 2500 pixels in size. Signature brushes work best if they are created with a brush with the hardness set at 100%.

Attention!

If you create your original signature in color, the custom brush is still created in grayscale. You can change the signature color by changing the foreground color before applying the signature brush or after it is applied to the image on a separate layer.

Try This!

Add a drop shadow and bevel to the signature layer using the Layer Styles dialog box. Then lower the Fill opacity of the layer to 0 to give your signature a blind embossed look.

Create a digital
PEN-AND-INK DRAWING

You can create the look of a pen-and-ink drawing from a photograph using a variety of methods in Photoshop. Often the method you use depends on the subject matter of the original. Photoshop includes many filters such as Find Edges, which finds areas of contrast and outlines these; however, the filter applies the colors in the image to the edges. By changing a duplicated layer to high-contrast grayscale first and then applying the Smart Blur filter in the Edges Only mode, you get a black image with

white lines. You can then invert the image to get black lines on a white background. Depending on the look that you want, you can apply a filter such as Minimum with a 1-pixel radius to thicken the lines.

Often, the artistic effects do not appear strong enough in a large image. If your art project is still too photographic, you can click File and select Revert, and then click Image and select Image Size to reduce the image size before applying Photoshop filters to achieve artistic-looking results.

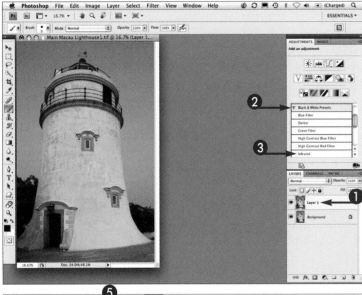

1 Press ⌘+J (Ctrl+J) to duplicate the Background layer.

2 Click the Black and White Presets in the Adjustments panel.

The panel expands.

3 Click a Black and White preset such as Infrared to get a high-contrast grayscale image.

The image appears black and white.

4 Press ⌘+E (Ctrl+E) to merge the adjustment layer with Layer 1.

5 Click Filter.

6 Click Blur.

7 Click Smart Blur.

The Smart Blur dialog box appears.

8 Type **35** in the Radius field and **35** in the Threshold field.

Note: The numbers in step 6 are a guide and will vary with the image and the look that you want.

9 Click here and select High.

10 Click here and select Edge Only.

11 Click OK.

190

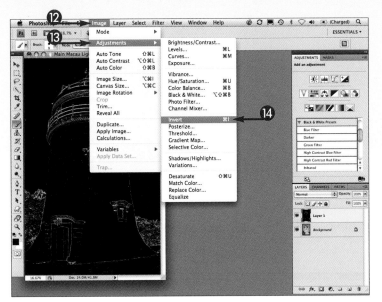

The Smart Blur filter is applied, and the image turns black with white outlines.

⑫ Click **Image**.

⑬ Click **Adjustments**.

⑭ Click **Invert**.

DIFFICULTY LEVEL

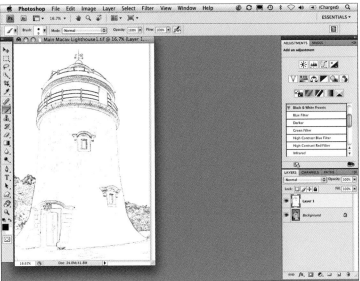

The drawing appears as black lines on a white background.

TIPS

Did You Know?

You can make the lines thicker and darker by clicking Filter, Other, and then Minimum. Set the Radius to 1 pixel. For heavier lines, try clicking Filter, Artistic, and then Smudge Stick, reducing the stroke length to 0.

More Options!

You can get better results by increasing the contrast in the original image. After the grayscale conversion, click Image, Adjustments, and then Levels. Move both sliders slightly toward the center to increase the contrast.

More Options!

You can put the black lines on a separate layer. Click a white area using the Magic Wand tool ( ). Click Select and then Similar to select all white areas. Click Select and then Inverse. Then press ⌘+J (Ctrl+J) and copy all the lines onto a new empty layer.

Give a photograph a
WOODCUT LOOK

A traditional *woodcut* is an engraving made by cutting areas into a block of wood using gouges (types of wood chisels) and knives. The surface is then inked and printed on paper or another material. The uncut areas are raised to receive the ink in a process similar to that of a rubber stamp. A woodcut often has thicker black lines than other types of engravings, depending on the style and skill of the artist. Sometimes the areas that are not inked on the paper let the color of the paper show through, and other times those areas are painted or inked as well.

You can give a photograph a woodcut look using Photoshop to add a unique creative element to any design. Using a combination of filters and adjustments, you create a grayscale image and turn the grayscale layer into a very high-contrast black and white. Then using the layer blend modes, you allow only the black lines to show through on the background image. By changing the Background layer to a smart object, you can change the finished image and customize the settings.

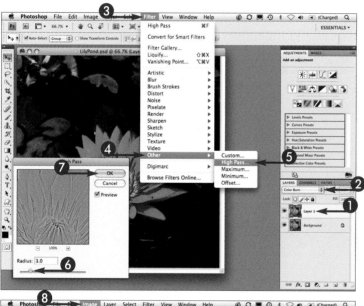

① Press ⌘+J (Ctrl+J) to duplicate the Background layer.

② With the top layer selected, click here and change the layer blend mode to Color Burn.

③ Click Filter.

④ Click Other.

⑤ Click High Pass.

The High Pass dialog box appears.

⑥ Click and drag the Radius slider until you just start to see the image.

⑦ Click OK.

⑧ Click Image.

⑨ Click Adjustments.

⑩ Click Threshold.

The Threshold dialog box appears.

⑪ Click and drag the Threshold Level slider between 123 and 128 to see the outlines of the woodcut.

⑫ Click OK.

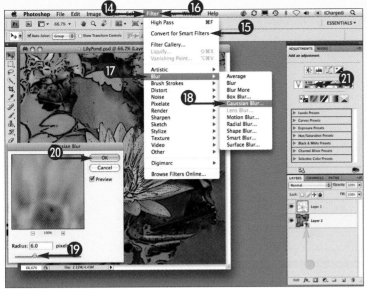

⑬ Click the Background layer to select it.

⑭ Click Filter.

⑮ Click Convert for Smart Filters.

● The Background layer icon changes to a smart object icon and the Background layer is renamed, in this case to Layer 2.

⑯ Click Filter.

⑰ Click Blur.

⑱ Click Gaussian Blur.

The Gaussian Blur dialog box appears.

⑲ Click and drag the slider to blur the main image.

⑳ Click OK.

㉑ Click the Hue/Saturation button in the Adjustments panel.

㉒ Click and drag the Saturation slider to the left to adjust the look.

The photo looks like a woodcut with a painted or inked background.

TIPS

Change It!

You can click the Hue/Saturation adjustment layer to edit the settings. You can double-click the words *Gaussian Blur* in the Layers panel to edit the smart filter and change the amount of blur.

More Options!

The High Pass filter retains edge details wherever there are sharp color contrasts and reduces the rest of the image to a flat grayscale. You can create a woodcut with less detail by lowering the setting of the High Pass filter.

Did You Know?

The Threshold command changes images to high-contrast black and white, in which pixels with gray values above 128 turn white and pixels below 128 turn black. Setting the threshold below 128 reduces the strength of the woodcut lines.

CONVERT A PHOTO
to a high contrast stylized image

An absolute black-and-white image is often used in many designs. You can easily transform any photograph into such a high contrast black-and-white image using an adjustment layer. You can determine the areas to turn black and the areas to change to white, and visually control the maximum contrast in your photo. You can stylize the image even more by adding a solid color or a colored gradient and using a blend mode to combine the effects.

You can start with either a color or a grayscale image and add a Threshold adjustment layer to convert the

image to a high contrast black and white. By adding another adjustment layer with a color or a gradient fill and then setting the top layer to either the Lighter Color or Darker Color blend mode, you can give the design a completely different look. All the changes you make are applied using adjustment layers so the image remains completely editable, enabling you to experiment and try different colors and gradients until you find the best design for your project.

① With an image open, click the Threshold button in the Adjustments panel.

The color information in the photo is changed to either black or white.

● The Threshold slider and histogram appear in the Adjustments panel.

② Click and drag the slider to the right to make more tonal values shift to black or to the left to change more tones to white.

③ Click the New Adjustment Layer button.

④ Click Gradient.

Note: Clicking Solid Color produces a two-tone stylized effect with only one color and either white or black.

194

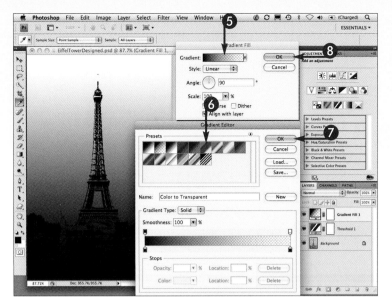

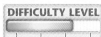

The Gradient Fill dialog box appears.

5 Click in the color bar to open the Gradient Editor.

The Gradient Editor appears.

6 Click a different preset.

7 Click OK to close the Gradient Editor dialog box.

8 Click OK to close the Gradient Fill dialog box.

The gradient is applied as a separate adjustment layer covering the image.

9 Click here and select Lighter Color to make the gradient cover only the black areas in the image, leaving the other areas white.

The gradient layer blends with the high contrast of the image.

TIPS

More Options!

You can create your own custom gradient in the Gradient Editor. Double-click in each of the lower color stops under the gradient to open the color picker and select a new color.

Try It!

Instead of Lighter Color, click the blend mode in the Layers panel and select Darker Color. The image changes, applying the gradient blend to the previously white areas in the image.

Did You Know?

The Darker Color mode displays only the lowest color value from both the blend and base layer; conversely, Lighter Color shows only the highest value color. For example, with the gradient layer in Lighter Color blend mode, only the lightest color value in the image layer below — white in this case — appears through the gradient layer.

Turn a photo into a
COLORED-PENCIL ILLUSTRATION

Colored-pencil illustrations are found in exhibitions and galleries everywhere. Once thought of as an elementary medium, perfect for children, many artists today are working with colored pencils as a medium in and of itself, and not just for texture studies, before using another medium such as watercolor or oils.

You can transform a photograph into a colored-pencil illustration in Photoshop in many ways. Generally, you will get a more traditional colored-pencil effect by reducing the image size before you apply the filters. As with most of the Photoshop filters, simply clicking a filter in the Filter Gallery rarely renders the sought-after effect. By simplifying the colors in the image with the Median filter and then applying several filters, the image more closely resembles a traditional colored-pencil drawing. Start by opening the file as a smart object. You can then easily edit the filters after applying them.

① Open the photo as a smart object by clicking File and then Open As Smart Object.

② Press ⌘+J (Ctrl+J) to duplicate the original smart object layer.

③ Click Filter.

④ Click Noise.

⑤ Click Median to open the Median dialog box.

⑥ Click and drag the slider to about 4 to flatten the colors in the image and soften the edges.

Note: *The amount depends on the image size and the amount of detail in the image.*

⑦ Click OK.

⑧ Click Filter, Brush Strokes, and then Sprayed Strokes to open the Filter Gallery dialog box.

⑨ Click and drag the Stroke Length slider to the maximum and the Spray Radius slider to a number in the first third of the slider.

Note: *The amounts depend on the image size and the artistic look you want to achieve.*

⑩ Click the New Effect Layer button to duplicate the Artistic layer.

⑪ Click Crosshatch, and the filter options change.

⑫ Click and drag the Stroke Length slider and the Sharpness slider to lower numbers and increase the Strength slider.

⑬ Click the New Effect Layer button to duplicate the Artistic layer again.

⑭ Click Artistic to display the available Artistic filters and select Colored Pencil.

The filter options change.

⑮ Click and drag the Pencil Width slider to a lower value such as 3, and the Stroke Pressure slider to about 10 or just above the middle value. Click and drag the Paper Brightness slider to the maximum so the paper underneath appears white.

⑯ Click OK.

The Filter Gallery closes.

⑰ Double-click the Zoom tool to see the drawing at 100%.

⑱ Click here and select Hard Light.

⑲ Press ⌘+J (Ctrl+J) to duplicate the top layer.

⑳ Click here and select Overlay for the top layer's blend mode.

The resulting image looks like a colored pencil drawing.

● You can double-click the Filter Gallery name in the Layers panel to reopen the Filter Gallery and change any settings.

#85

DIFFICULTY LEVEL

TIPS

Did You Know?

You can turn a colored-pencil illustration into a graphite pencil sketch by clicking the Black & White button (◨) in the Adjustments panel or selecting any of the Black-and-White presets to fit your image.

More Options!

To see the document in full on the screen, double-click the Hand tool (✋) in the toolbox or click Fit Screen on the Options bar. To zoom to 100%, double-click the Zoom tool (🔍) in the toolbox.

Attention!

Any of the blend modes in the Lighten and Overlay sections will enhance the colored-pencil sketch. You can also click the bottom layer in the Layers panel and drag the Fill slider to the left for a different look.

POSTERIZE A PHOTO
for a Warhol-style image

Photoshop includes a Posterize command in the Image ⇨ Adjustments menu that automatically posterizes an image by mapping the Red, Green, and Blue channels to the number of tonal levels that you set. However, to create a posterized image reminiscent of the Andy Warhol style of the 1960s and 70s, you can use three adjustment layers in succession instead. Use a Black & White adjustment layer to convert the photo to a grayscale image. Then apply a Posterize adjustment layer, specifying the levels that correspond to the number of colors

you want in the final image. A lower the number of levels limits the number of colors that will be included, making the image more stylized. Finally, use a Gradient Map adjustment layer to map a color to each of the levels of gray. You can edit any of the adjustment layers to change the colors or levels until you get the look that you want. For the best result, select a photo with a main subject on a plain background or extract the subject and place it on a black background.

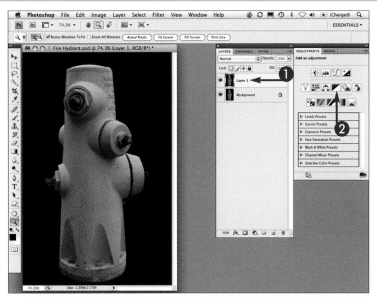

1 Press ⌘+J (Ctrl+J) to duplicate the Background layer.

2 Click the Black & White button in the Adjustments panel.

The image turns to grayscale and the options in the Adjustments panel change.

3 Click Auto to see if the contrast improves.

4 Move the color sliders to enhance the contrast.

5 Click the arrow to return to the Adjustments panel list.

6 Click the Posterize button () in the Adjustments panel.

The options in the Adjustments panel change.

7 Type a low number such as **4** in the Levels data field.

Note: *Use a low number to limit the color gradations when creating a posterized effect.*

8 Click the arrow to return to the Adjustments panel list.

9 Click the Gradient Map button (▣) in the Adjustments panel.

The options in the Adjustments panel change.

10 Click in the gradient.

TIPS

Attention!
You get better results if you match the number of gray levels with the number of color stops in the gradient. To add more gray levels, double-click the Posterize thumbnail in the Layers panel and increase the number of levels. Then double-click the Gradient Map thumbnail and add more color stops.

Try This!
If you want a more realistically colored image, fill the color stops on the right in the Gradient Editor with the lightest colors that you want in the image and the color stops on the left with the darkest colors. The greater the number of color stops and the more colors you use, the wilder the image appears.

Important!
The Poster Edges filter, located in the Artistic filters in the Filter Gallery, creates a completely different look, more like an etching than a posterized print.

POSTERIZE A PHOTO
for a Warhol-style image

After posterizing the first photo by following all twenty-one steps in this task, you can create four copies of the posterized image using different colors and place them in a new document to replicate the Andy Warhol-like layouts with four posterized and juxtaposed images.

To create the second copy, open your posterized image and click File and then Save As to give the copy another name. Click the Gradient Map thumbnail in the Layers panel to reopen the Gradient Map pane of the Adjustments panel. Click in the

gradient to open the Gradient Editor again. Change the colors for each of the four color stops, always selecting the darkest colors for the leftmost color stops and the lightest colors for the rightmost color stops. Click OK to close the Gradient Editor. Click File and then click Save, saving the second version with all the layers. Repeat this process until you have four different versions of the image.

To finish the project, create a new empty document and click File and then Place to place each of the four images on the page.

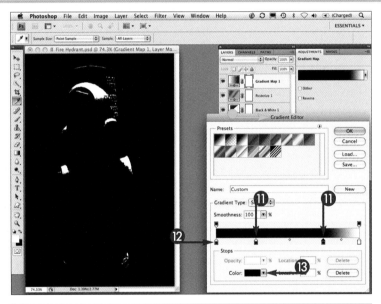

The Gradient Editor appears.

⑪ Click two areas below the gradient bar to add two more color stops.

Note: *The number of color stops should match the levels of posterization that you entered in step 7.*

⑫ Click the leftmost color stop to select it.

⑬ Click the Color thumbnail.

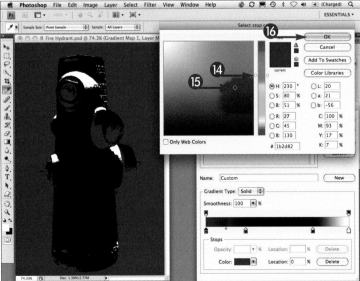

The Select stop color dialog box appears.

⑭ Click and drag the color slider.

⑮ Click in the color selector to select the darkest of the four colors you will use.

Note: *If the warning triangle appears, the color is out of gamut for printing and will not print as you see it. Click the small square below the warning triangle to select the closest in-gamut or printable color.*

⑯ Click OK to close the Select stop color dialog box.

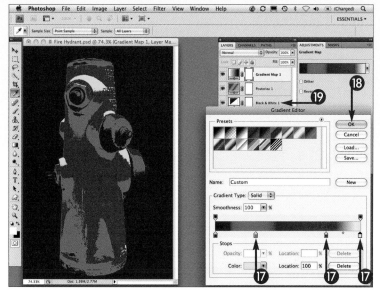

⑰ Repeat steps 12 to 16, selecting each of the other three color stops to change the color.

⑱ Click OK to close the Gradient Editor.

⑲ Click the Black and White adjustment layer.

The Black and White options appear in the Adjustments panel.

⑳ Click and drag the color sliders to change the amount and areas of posterized colors.

㉑ Press ⌘+S (Ctrl+S) to save the file with all the layers so you can readjust it later.

The final image looks like a posterized and stylized print design from another era.

TIPS

Customize It!

Use the Dodge and Burn tools to change individual areas. Click the Background copy layer and click the Dodge tool ( ). Click and drag in the image to make some areas lighter. Click the Burn tool ( ) and click and drag other areas to make them darker. You can lower the Exposure setting in the Options bar to lessen the change.

More Options!

Instead of using a Gradient Map, you can merge the Background copy with the Black and White and the Posterize adjustment layers. Then add colors individually to gray areas. Select the first gray area using the Magic Wand ( ) with a tolerance of 0. Click the foreground color and select a new color. Press Option+Delete (Alt+Backspace) to fill the selection.

Change a photograph into a
PEN-AND-COLORED-WASH DRAWING

You can transform a photograph into a pen-line-and-colored-wash drawing by applying different filters and adjustments to multiple layers. Traditional artists sometimes use India ink and a diluted ink wash to visualize the light and shadow areas before beginning a painting. The technique is also often used in figure studies to create expressive drawings. When applied to a landscape or cityscape, the pen-line-and-diluted-ink wash produces an image with a unique look.

Pen-and-ink-wash drawings are similar to and yet different from traditional watercolors, which generally do not use black lines.

You start with multiple duplicates of the original Background layer and an added layer filled with white. You transform one of the duplicated layers into a layer of simplified outlines from the edges in the photograph using combinations of adjustment layers and filters before using the Brush tool to paint in the washes.

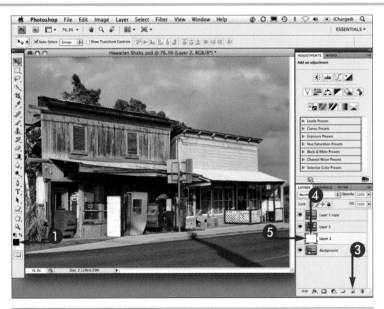

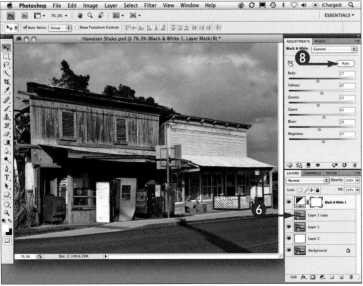

① Press D to reset the foreground and background colors to the default.

② Press ⌘+J (Ctrl+J) twice to create two duplicates of the Background layer, named Layer 1 and Layer 1 copy.

③ Click the New Layer button to create a new empty layer.

④ Press ⌘+Delete (Ctrl+Backspace) to fill the empty layer with white.

⑤ Click and drag the white layer below both Layer 1 and Layer 1 copy.

⑥ Click the top layer, named Layer 1 copy, to select it.

⑦ Click the Black & White button (⬛) in the Adjustments panel.

The image changes to a grayscale image and the Black and White options appear in the Adjustments panel.

⑧ Click Auto to increase the contrast.

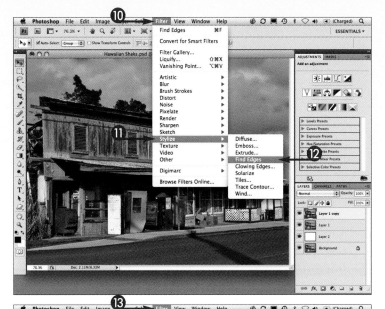

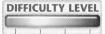
9 Press ⌘+E (Ctrl+E) to merge the Black and White adjustment layer with the layer below.

10 Click Filter.

11 Click Stylize.

12 Click Find Edges.

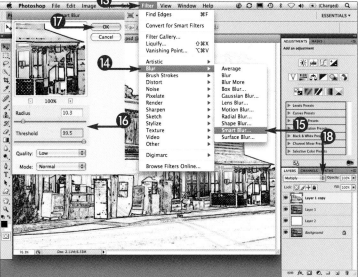

The image changes to resemble a shaded drawing.

13 Click Filter.

14 Click Blur.

15 Click Smart Blur.

The Smart Blur dialog box appears.

16 Click and drag the Radius and Threshold sliders to soften the edges.

17 Click OK.

The amount of detail is reduced. The edges of the lines are softened.

18 Click here and select Multiply for the blend mode.

TIPS

Important!
For more artistic results, start by reducing the size of the image. Click Image and then Image Size. Set one of the Pixel Dimensions in the top section of the Image Size dialog box to about 1000 pixels. The filters are more effective on this size image, and the brush strokes appear more like traditional brush strokes on paper.

Change It!
Change the brush tip shape before you paint with white on the black mask in step 32. With the Brush tool selected, click the Brushes ▼ in the Options bar to open the brushes panel. Click Brush Tip Shape and change any of the attributes.

Customize It!
You can also create a dual brush to change the brush strokes even more. Before step 32, click the Brushes ▼ to open the Brushes panel. Click Dual Brush and click a different brush sample box. Click and drag the sliders to alter the brush style.

Change a photograph into a
PEN-AND-COLORED-WASH DRAWING

The other duplicated layer provides the base for the colors. You first reduce the details in that duplicated layer using the Noise filter to give it a less photographic appearance. Then you paint on a layer mask to make the colored washes appear. For this digital technique, as with a traditional watercolor painting, you add the washes using large, lighter opacity brushes first, then increase the opacity for the next sets of washes, and finally work with

smaller, more opaque brushes to define the details. You can modify the brush sizes and brush tip shapes for each different wash to add variety and make the result appear less digitally created.

You can use any photo to create the pen and colored wash drawing; however, the results look more like a traditional pen and ink wash when the steps are applied to a low-resolution image.

The colored photo shows through the line drawing.

⑲ Click Layer 1, the second layer down in the Layers panel, to select it.

⑳ Click Filter.

㉑ Click Noise.

㉒ Click Median.

The Median dialog box appears.

㉓ Click and drag the Radius slider to blur the image and colors.

㉔ Click OK.

㉕ Press Option (Alt) and click the Layer Mask button to add a black layer mask to the Background copy layer.

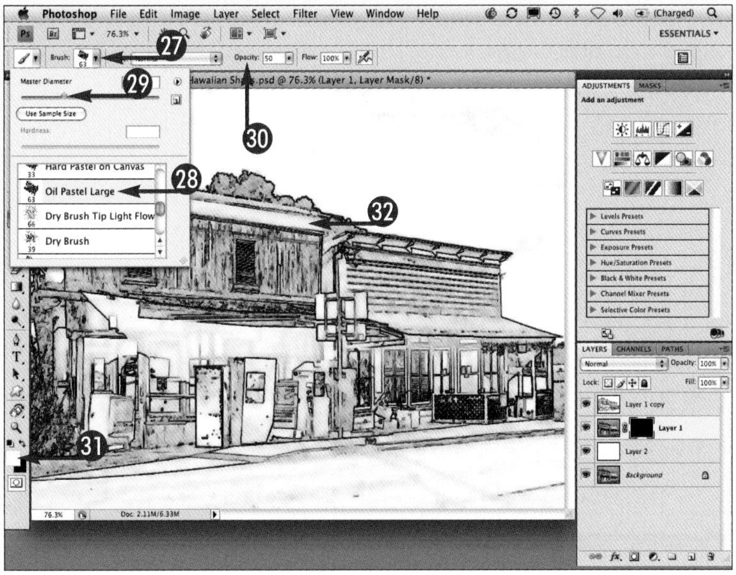

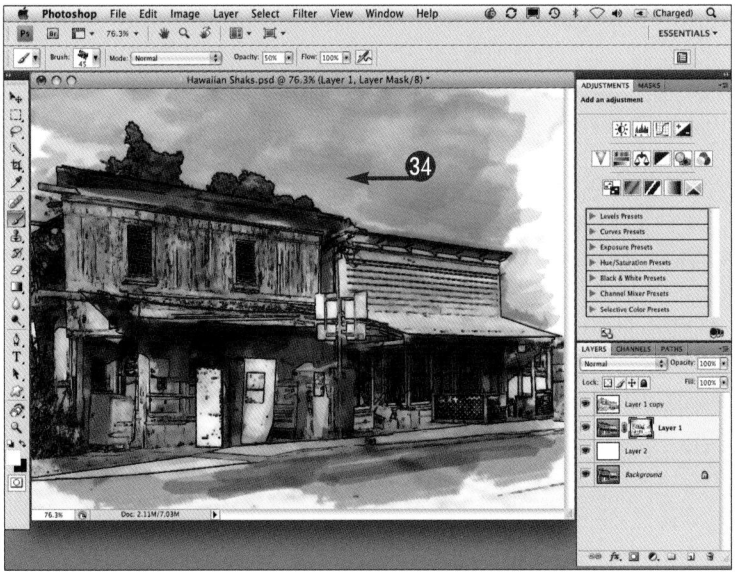

#87 CONTINUED

The black layer mask hides the colored Layer 1 and only the outlines are visible in the image window.

26. Press B to select the Brush tool.
27. Click here to open the brush picker.
28. Select a large ragged-edge brush.
29. Click and drag the slider to increase the brush size if necessary.
30. Click the word *Opacity* and drag to the left to reduce the brush opacity to 50%.
31. Click here if necessary to make sure the foreground color is white.
32. Click and drag in the image painting with white on the mask to bring in the colored wash.

    The colors begin to appear in the drawing as large washes.
33. Press the left bracket key several times to reduce the brush size.
34. Click and drag in the image to paint over the details and increase the look of the wash.

    Note: *Use brush strokes in the direction that fits the objects in the image.*

    The colored wash appears on the image.

TIPS

Did You Know?

You can make the drawing appear to have multiple layers of washes by starting with a very low brush opacity in the Options bar for the first set of brush strokes and then increasing the opacity as you brush a second and third time.

Change It!

You can change the blend mode of the top layer after you finish painting in step 34 to change the final look of the pen-and-wash drawing. Try Hard Light or Darken instead of Multiply for totally different looks.

Attention!

To make the washes appear as though they were painted by hand on white paper, be sure to leave some areas around the edges unpainted, letting the white layer show through.

Compose a
PHOTO COLLAGE

Artists and photographers have long been blending separate images into one combined finished piece. Artists may glue disparate items onto a background, hence the word *collage* from the French for gluing. Photographers may combine exposures on one piece of film or combine several images in the darkroom in a *photo montage,* a term taken from the French for mounting or assembling. Photoshop adds many new and easier techniques for creating such artistic composites. Instead of worrying about image registrations or unexpected interactions of shapes

and forms, you can now visually combine multiple images into one by blending pixels. Starting with a basic Photoshop collage technique, you can apply so many variations that the piece can be used for everything from advertising to fine art.

You start with one image as the background and drag other photographs and artwork onto it in separate layers. Then you resize and adjust the position of each layer and add masks to blend the images together. You can add gradients and paint on the masks, or even add masks to masks for more variations.

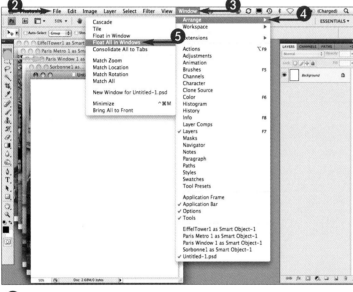

① Create a new empty document the size that you want your collage to be.

② Click File and then Open As Smart Object to open all the images for the collage as shown in Task #21.

③ Click Window.

④ Click Arrange.

⑤ Click Float All in Windows to have each image in its own window.

● The images appear in separate windows cascading on the screen.

⑥ Click the empty untitled document to bring it forward.

⑦ Double-click the Hand tool to make the image fit the screen.

⑧ Click the Move tool and click and drag the first image onto the empty document.

⑨ Click here to close the first image.

⑩ Press ⌘+T (Ctrl+T).

The transformation anchors appear on the image.

⑪ Press Shift and click and drag the corner anchors to resize the image.

⑫ Click the commit button.

13 Press D to reset the foreground and background colors.

14 Click the Layer Mask button.

● A layer mask is added to the image layer.

15 Click the Gradient tool.

16 Click a gradient style.

17 Click and drag the Gradient tool across the image.

The first image blends into the Background layer.

18 Repeat steps 8 to 17 until all the images are layers in the collage.

19 Click each layer to adjust the placement of the image.

20 Click each layer mask thumbnail and click and drag with the Gradient tool to change the look.

The images blend into one another, creating an artistic photo collage.

TIPS

Important!
Make sure that all your photos for the collage are set to the same color space or convert them to Adobe RGB as you place them. Also check the bit depth and resolution of the images and change these as needed.

Did You Know?
Opening the images as smart objects lets you adjust the size of the photos in the composite without losing image quality.

Caution!
The number of additional layers, effects, and layer sets that you can add to an image is limited by your computer's memory. Close any unnecessary files and applications to make as much RAM available as possible for Photoshop to process the collage.

Turn a photo into a
HAND-PAINTED OIL PAINTING

You can use the Filter Gallery and various Photoshop filters to change any photograph into an image that looks like an oil painting. However, because filters are applied evenly to the active layer of an image, the results most often appear to be computer generated rather than hand painted. By applying a filter to a layer and then using brush strokes of varied size to paint the filtered image onto a new layer, you can create an oil painting that appears to be painted one stroke at a time. This technique uses the Pattern

Stamp tool and the entire image as a pattern. The Pattern Stamp tool's Impressionist option makes the brush strokes appear even more traditionally painted. You can then brush the pattern onto a new empty layer so the image appears to be painted rather than digitally generated with a filter.

As with other digitally rendered paintings, this technique works best on a smaller image without too much detail. You can reduce the image size as a first step.

1 Open an image and expand the canvas to create a white border around the photo.

Note: To expand the canvas, use the reverse-crop technique described in Task #25.

A white border appears around the image.

2 Press ⌘+J (Ctrl+J) to duplicate the Background layer.

3 Click Filter.

4 Click Artistic.

5 Click Dry Brush.

The Filter Gallery appears with the Dry Brush filter applied in the Preview window.

6 Click and drag the sliders to adjust the Dry Brush appearance for your photo.

Note: *The larger the Brush Size number and the smaller the Brush Detail number, the less photographic the image appears.*

7 Click OK.

The filter is applied to the image.

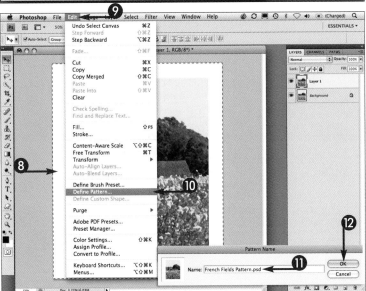

8 Press ⌘+A (Ctrl+A) to select the entire image.

9 Click Edit.

10 Click Define Pattern.

The Pattern Name dialog box appears.

11 Type a new name for the pattern.

12 Click OK.

13 Press ⌘+D (Ctrl+D) to deselect the image.

89

DIFFICULTY LEVEL

 TIPS

Caution!

Take your time to make the image appear hand painted. Change the brush size often. Start with large brushes and make them smaller as you paint in details, deselecting the Impressionist option to emphasize the finest details.

More Options!

If you have a digitizing tablet, you can choose a larger brush and set the Shape Dynamics option of the brush to Pen Pressure. Press lightly with the stylus to produce small strokes and press harder to produce larger strokes.

Attention!

When you first start painting in step 21 using a large brush, click the brush instead of dragging it like a true paintbrush. The effect appears more natural because clicking the brush spreads the paint unevenly.

Turn a photo into a
HAND-PAINTED OIL PAINTING

When trying to replicate a traditionally painted image, you should start with a large brush and paint in more open areas of the photograph. Then reduce the brush size and continue painting in the details. To emphasize a few edges and capture some finer detail, you can deselect the Impressionist option and continue to paint with the Pattern Stamp tool. You can compare your painting and the image as you work by clicking the visibility button on the Background layer off and on.

You can cover the new layer to create a completely separate painting or use the newly painted layer in combination with the underlying Dry Brush filtered layer, depending on the look that you want. And you can add a Texturizer filter using a canvas texture over the painted image as a final touch. You can even add a canvas-colored layer as a background to fill in around the edges for a more realistic look.

⑭ Click the New Layer button to add a new empty layer.

⑮ Click the Pattern Stamp tool.

⑯ Click the Pattern thumbnail in the Options bar.

   The pattern picker opens.

⑰ Click the pattern that you just created of the photo.

⑱ Click Impressionist (☐ changes to ☑).

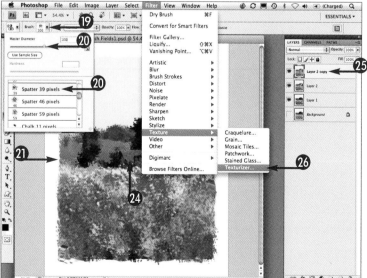

⑲ Click here to open the brush picker.

⑳ Select a rough-edged brush and adjust the diameter to fit your image.

㉑ Click in the layer multiple times to paint the image, covering every area.

㉒ Repeat steps 19 to 21, reducing the brush size or changing the brush shape to paint detailed areas.

㉓ Click Impressionist to deselect it (☑ changes to ☐).

㉔ Click in the image to bring back a few photographic details as needed.

㉕ Press ⌘+J (Ctrl+J) to duplicate the painted layer.

㉖ Click Filter, Texture, and then Texturizer.

The Filter Gallery Texturizer dialog box appears.

27 Click here and select Canvas.

28 Click and drag the sliders to increase the Scaling and Relief.

Note: The preview image shows the details at 100%.

29 Click OK.

The Canvas texture is applied to the finished painting.

TIP

Try This!

You can add a canvas-colored layer as a background to fill in around the edges for a realistic look. After step 25, click the New Layer button (🖾) in the Layers panel to create a new layer. Drag the new empty layer underneath the top painted layer. Click Edit and then Fill. Click the Contents Use arrow and click Color. When the color picker appears, select a color for the canvas, such as Red 248, Green 242, and Blue 224, which appears as a natural canvas color. Click OK to close the color picker and again to close the Fill dialog box and fill the layer. Click the top painted layer to select it. Then continue with step 26 to apply the Texturizer filter with a canvas texture to the whole image as a final touch.

Paint a
DIGITAL WATERCOLOR

You can create a digital watercolor from a photograph and make it appear like a traditionally painted image on watercolor paper using a series of filters from the Filter Gallery on separate layers.

Traditional watercolor paintings have loosely defined shapes without black outlines, transparent colors, and minimal transitions of color tones. To make your painting appear hand painted you can apply the Reduce Noise or the Median filter to the photo before starting the painting. These filters, found in the Filter menu under Noise, eliminate some of the color

changes and sharp edges that make a photograph look like a photograph.

As with many digital art techniques, duplicating the Background layer is the first step. You then start applying filters. When you apply the Dry Brush filter on an image with a limited color palette, the photo already appears more like a painting than a photograph. You duplicate that layer and apply a blur filter to soften the edges and blend the colors even more. Then add an empty layer over the other layers and fill it with a translucent white.

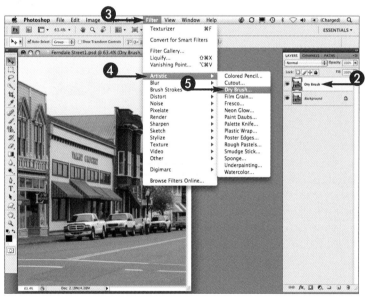

① Open a photo and press ⌘+J (Ctrl+J) to duplicate it.

② Double-click the layer name and type **Dry Brush**.

③ Click Filter.

④ Click Artistic.

⑤ Click Dry Brush.

The Filter Gallery appears with the Dry Brush filter applied in the Preview window.

⑥ Click and drag the sliders to adjust the Dry Brush style.

⑦ Click OK.

The filter is applied to the layer.

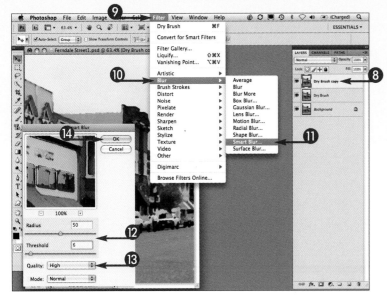

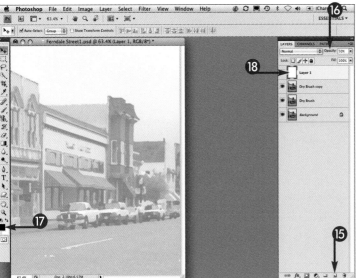

8 With the Dry Brush layer still selected, press ⌘+J (Ctrl+J) to duplicate it.

9 Click Filter.

10 Click Blur.

11 Click Smart Blur.

The Smart Blur dialog box appears.

12 Click and drag the Radius and Threshold sliders to adjust the blur.

Note: The Radius slider determines how much blur is applied and the Threshold slider controls the number of tonal values that are blurred.

13 Click here and select High.

14 Click OK.

15 Click the New Layer button to create a new empty layer.

16 Click the word *Opacity* in the Layers panel and drag to the left to lower the opacity to 50%.

17 Press D to reset the default foreground and background colors.

18 Press ⌘+Delete (Ctrl+Backspace) to fill the layer with white.

The top layer fills with a translucent white.

TIP

Try This!

You can make the paper look more like watercolor paper by using an off-white color to fill the top layer. After creating a new empty layer in step 15, click Edit and then Fill. The Fill dialog box opens. Click the Use 🔽 and click Color to make the color picker appear. Type **250** for the Red data field, **246** for the Green data field, and **239** for the Blue data field to select an off-white color for the watercolor paper. Click OK to close the color picker and click OK again to close the Fill dialog box. Erase carefully over just the objects that you want to show as painted on the image. Areas left blank show through as the watercolor paper.

Paint a
DIGITAL WATERCOLOR

The white layer becomes a background for the painting. Using the eraser set to a chalk-styled brush, you erase through the white layer, revealing parts of the filtered layer below. The strokes appear more realistic if you click and drag in the document using short strokes, and paint vertical objects with vertical strokes and horizontal items with horizontal strokes. You can also vary the opacity of the Eraser tool as you paint so that the colors appear to be painted in washes.

Traditional watercolor paintings often leave rough edges around the borders and even some blank areas in the painting, allowing the surface of the watercolor paper to show through the paint. You can simulate this effect by not erasing some areas completely, in effect making those areas appear unpainted.

Finish the painting by merging the two top layers and duplicating the merged layer. Then apply a Texture filter to create the look of rough watercolor paper. The final step is to lighten the image by setting the layer blend mode to Screen to brighten the watercolor paints.

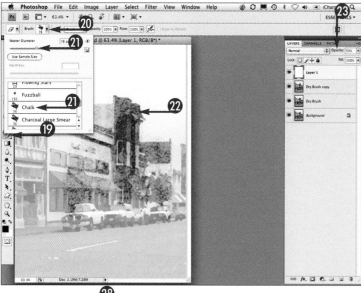

⑲ Click the Eraser tool.

⑳ Click here to open the brush picker.

㉑ Click a large chalk-style brush and adjust its diameter as necessary using the slider.

㉒ Click and drag in the document using short irregular strokes until the painting is visible.

㉓ Click the word *Opacity* and drag to the right to increase the opacity to 100%.

㉔ Press the left bracket key several times to reduce the brush size.

㉕ Continue clicking and dragging in the image to complete the painting.

㉖ Press ⌘+E (Ctrl+E) to merge the two top layers.

㉗ Press ⌘+J (Ctrl+J) to duplicate the new merged layer.

㉘ Click Filter.

㉙ Click Texture.

㉚ Click Texturizer.

The Filter Gallery appears with the Texturizer filter selected.

#90 CONTINUED

③① Click here and select Sandstone.

③② Click and drag the Scaling and Relief sliders to look like rough watercolor paper.

③③ Click OK.

The filter is applied to the top layer.

③④ Click here and select Screen.

The painting is lightened and looks more like a traditional watercolor.

TIPS

Did You Know?
Photoshop actually includes a Watercolor filter in the Filter Gallery. This filter adds too much black to replicate a traditional watercolor and also dulls the colors. A true watercolor palette includes only gray and no black paint at all.

Change It!
With the Eraser tool selected, click the Toggle the Brushes Panel button (▣) on the far right of the Options bar to open the brushes panel. Click the word *Texture* in the brush presets to highlight it. Make changes to the scale, depth, or pattern to add texture to your brush.

Important!
Photoshop's Artistic filters are applied at a fixed size and work best on files smaller than 5MB. Always view your photo at 100% to see the effect and wait for the effect to process when changing adjustment sliders.

Chapter 9

Giving Your Images a Professional Presentation

Presentation is so important that most photos or designs can be improved when properly displayed or framed. For professional designers, a powerful presentation can help keep an art director happy. For photographers, an elegant display can make all the difference in securing a new client or keeping a current one. From displaying family snapshots to presenting your portfolio, Photoshop makes it easy to show your images in a professional manner.

You can add frames to enhance any image with minimal effort using the one-click frame actions included with Photoshop. You can also create your own frames, change the frame colors and borders, and add a matte to the photo. Photoshop can also help you apply an artistic edge to a photo using a sequence of filters from the Filter Gallery, or you can brush an artistic edge onto any images by hand using the Brush tool. You can create custom backgrounds to display your images or, for a novel effect, place your images into a traditional slide template. You can create a contact sheet as a visual index of all the photos in one client folder or on one CD or DVD. You can prepare a custom slide show with professional transitions, burn it to external media, or save it as a PDF document and send it to friends or clients as an e-mail attachment. You can even use Photoshop to design and upload your own photo gallery to a Web site. With Photoshop CS4, you can display all your images with a professional touch.

Top 100

Frame a photo with PHOTO CORNERS

DIFFICULTY LEVEL

You can add interest and give a finished look to your photographs by adding a digital frame to your images. You can apply a variety of designed frames such as photo corners easily and quickly using an action from the Actions panel in Photoshop.

An *action* is a prerecorded set of commands that are automatically performed in the same sequence when you click the Play button.

Photoshop enables you to record your own actions and also provides a number of predefined actions that are installed with the application. When you first open Photoshop and click the Actions panel tab, you find a folder called Default Actions. Clicking the fly-out arrow on the Actions panel opens a menu with other Actions folders. To create photo corners or any other frames, you must first load the Frames Actions and then play the Photo Corners action. You can use the same steps to apply a wood frame or any of the other frames included in the now loaded actions.

Actions are stored as *.atn* files in the Photoshop Actions folder in the Presets folder.

① Open a photo or image.

② Press Option+F9 (Alt+F9) to open the Actions panel.

Note: *Optionally, click Window and click Actions to open the Actions panel.*

③ Click the menu button on the Actions panel.

④ Click Frames.

The Frames actions are automatically loaded.

⑤ Click Photo Corners.

⑥ Click the Play button.

Photoshop plays the action and places photo corners on the image.

MAKE A LINE FRAME
from within a photo

You may have a photo with a larger background area than necessary. Rather than crop the photo, you can transform the excess background into a frame to help focus the attention on the main subject. Making a line frame from the photograph itself is a quick way to give a classic and finished look to any image. You make a selection in the photo as if you were going to crop it. You then invert the selection to create the frame. You can even vary the frame shape by using the Elliptical Marquee tool to select the area with an oval frame. To create any style of line frame from within the photograph, place the frame area on

its own layer above the Background layer and change the blend mode to Screen to lighten the area that will become the frame.

DIFFICULTY LEVEL

To separate the frame from the photo even more, stroke the borders of the new frame layer by applying a layer style. The Layer Style dialog box includes a stroke option with red as the default color; however, you can change it to any color that fits your image. As a final touch, add a drop shadow and an inner shadow, and even a bevel and emboss look.

1 Click the Rectangular Marquee tool.

2 Click and drag a large rectangle in the photo to select the main subject.

3 Click Select.

4 Click Inverse.

5 Press ⌘+J (Ctrl+J) to place the selection on its own layer.

6 Click here and select Screen.

7 Click the Layer Style button.

8 Click Stroke.

The Layer Style dialog box appears.

9 Click the Color thumbnail.

10 When the color picker appears, set the color to white and click OK.

11 Click and drag the Size slider to increase the stroke thickness.

12 Click any of the other layer styles such as Drop Shadow, Inner Shadow, and Bevel and Emboss to give the frame a finished look.

13 Click OK.

The layer style gives the appearance of a realistic frame.

Apply a filter to give a photo
AN ARTISTIC EDGE

You can give any photo an artistic look by adding an irregular edge using the Filter Gallery and the Brush Strokes filters. By duplicating the Background layer and adding a new empty layer filled with white below the top layer, you can create a unique artistic edge. The Filter Gallery enables you to combine the filters in different ways and use the same technique to create a variety of different edges to fit each different image. Make a selection on the top layer just inside the edge of the photo and then add a

layer mask to delineate the borders of the photo. The artistic edge starts from the selected area. Open the Filter Gallery and start adding different layers of Brush Strokes filters. The Preview window of the Filter Gallery shows the edge effect in reverse. The white areas represent the photo area, and the black areas represent what will be cut away. Every time you change the various sliders for the Brush Strokes filters, your edge effect changes in the Preview window of the Filter Gallery.

1 Press ⌘+J (Ctrl+J) to duplicate the Background layer.

2 Click the New Layer button.

3 Click the new empty layer and drag it between the Background layer and Layer 1.

4 Press D to reset the default colors.

5 Press ⌘+Delete (Ctrl+Backspace) to fill the empty layer with white.

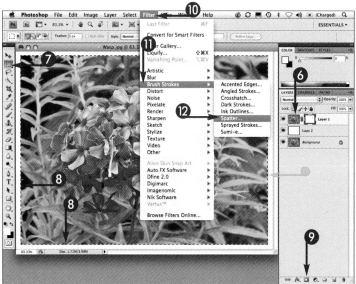

6 Click Layer 1 to select it.

7 Click the Marquee tool.

8 Click and drag a selection just inside the edge of the image.

9 Click the Layer Mask button to add a layer mask to Layer 1.

● The image has a small white border.

10 Click Filter.

11 Click Brush Strokes.

12 Click a filter; this example uses Spatter.

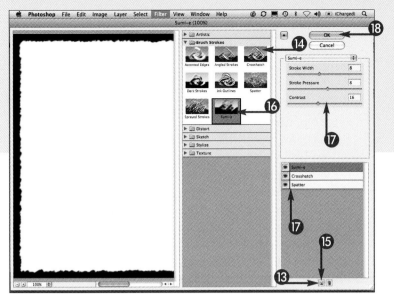

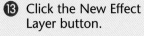

 # 93

The Filter Gallery opens with the Spatter edge applied.

⓭ Click the New Effect Layer button.

⓮ Click another Brush Strokes filter; this example uses Crosshatch.

⓯ Click the New Effect Layer button again.

⓰ Click another Brush Strokes filter; this example uses Sumi-e.

⓱ Click each individual effect layer and adjust the sliders to get the edge that you want.

⓲ Click OK.

The custom edge is applied to the photo.

TIPS

Did You Know?
Add as many Filter Effects layers as your computer's memory allows. Each one you add changes the look of the custom photo edge. Change the order of the layers in the Filter Gallery dialog box, and the overall style of the edge changes as well.

More Options!
For a light-colored image, darken the edge for a stronger effect. Click the Layer Style button (*fx*) in the Layers panel. Click Drop Shadow. Drag the Distance slider to 0. To darken it more, click Inner Shadow also and drag its Distance slider to 0.

Try This!
Click the Layer Style button (*fx*) in the Layers panel. Click Stroke. Click the Color thumbnail and change the default color to black. Click the Position 🔽 and select Inside. Move the Size slider to get the thickness of line that you want.

Create your own
CUSTOM EDGE

You can let a Photoshop filter draw an artistic edge for you as in Task #93, or you can create your own custom edge. You can save your custom edge and apply it to all your images as your personal digital signature. You paint using any rough-edged brush on a separate layer. The default brush set that installs with Photoshop includes various rough-edged brushes; however, you can find many more by clicking the flyout arrow in the brush picker.

To create a custom edge, put the photo on a separate layer and then enlarge the canvas by

selecting the Relative option to add some area evenly around the photo for the frame. Add a transparent layer in between the two photo layers and paint your custom edge on that layer, clicking and dragging around the edges of the photo. You can paint as much or as little of a visible edge as you want as long as the black edges extend underneath the photo. Flatten the image, or save it with the layers so you can reuse your custom edge on other images of the same size.

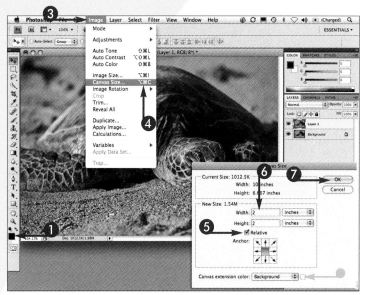

① Press D to reset the foreground and background colors to black and white.

② Press ⌘+J (Ctrl+J) to duplicate the photo layer.

③ Click Image.

④ Click Canvas Size.

The Canvas Size dialog box appears.

⑤ Click Relative (changes to ☑).

Note: *Selecting Relative adds the exact typed amount of width and height to the existing image.*

⑥ Type **2** in the Width and Height fields to add 2 inches to the canvas in each direction.

● You can click in the white color box to select a different color for the Canvas extension.

⑦ Click OK.

A white border appears around the photo.

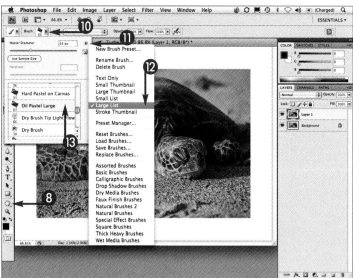

⑧ Double-click the Hand tool to fit the image to the screen.

⑨ Press B to select the Brush tool.

⑩ Click here to open the brush picker.

⑪ Click here to open the brush menu.

⑫ Click Large List.

The brush presets change to labeled thumbnails.

⑬ Click a rough-edged brush such as Oil Pastel Large.

⑭ Click the New Layer button to add a new empty layer.

⑮ Click and drag the empty layer between the other two layers.

⑯ Using the Brush tool, click and drag to paint on the empty layer along the visible edge of the photo.

Note: Make sure to paint partially over the edge of the photo. The overlap will not be visible because the photo layer is above the painting layer.

⑰ Click the Brush thumbnail.

⑱ Click another brush such as Hard Pastel on Canvas.

⑲ Continue painting brush strokes around the edge of the photo to add variety to the edge.

The photo appears with a custom border, giving it a unique look.

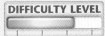

TIPS

Did You Know?

You can change the brush angles by clicking the Toggle the Brushes Panel button (▣) in the Options bar and clicking Brush Tip Shape in the Brushes panel. Click and drag on the Brush Angle and Roundness thumbnail to narrow the circle. Change the Brush Tip Shape for each side.

More Options!

You can gradually blend the photo into the custom edge by making a rectangular selection on the top photo layer just inside the edge of the photo, and then clicking Select and Inverse. Click Select, Modify, and then Feather. Type a number such as **10** pixels for the Feather Radius and click OK. Press Delete to soften the edge of the photo and blend it into the custom border.

Try This!

Save your custom edge as a separate file. Click the Background layer, press ⌘+A (Ctrl+A), ⌘+C (Ctrl+C), and then ⌘+N (Ctrl+N) to create a new same-size document. Click back on the original image. Press Shift as you click and drag the edge layer onto the new document so it fits in the same exact position. Click File and click Save to name and save the new custom edge file.

Create a
CUSTOM SLIDE TEMPLATE

You can create a template that looks like a traditional photographic slide mount and use it to feature your photos when you print them, or even use the photos mounted as slides in a PDF slide show. After you create the custom slide template, you can use it over and over again with any image.

You can create a slide with any color or use a gray or off-white color similar to a traditional slide mount.

You use the Rounded Rectangle tool to create the basic shape and the Rectangular Marquee tool to cut out the photo-viewing area. You apply a drop shadow to add depth, giving the illusion of a traditional slide mount on the photo. Save the template with both a white Background layer and the slide layer so that you can sandwich an image between them for the final slide.

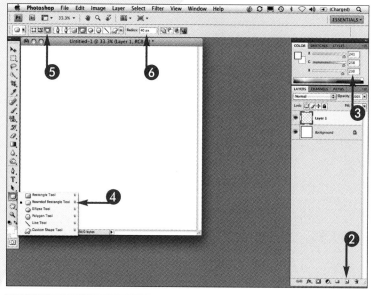

① Press ⌘+N (Ctrl+N) and create a new RGB file at 300 ppi, setting both the width and height to 5 inches.

② Click the New Layer button to add a new empty layer.

③ Click the Color panel and type **241**, **238**, and **230** in the data fields for a light-gray color.

④ Click and hold the Rectangle tool and select the Rounded Rectangle tool.

⑤ Click the Fill Pixels button.

⑥ Type **40 px** in the Radius data field.

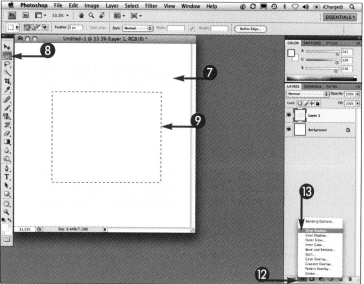

⑦ Press Shift and click and drag a square shape in the layer.

⑧ Click the Rectangular Marquee tool.

⑨ Click and drag a rectangular shape in the center of the slide.

⑩ Press Delete (Backspace) to create the hole in the slide.

⑪ Press ⌘+D (Ctrl+D) to deselect.

⑫ Click the Layer Style button.

⑬ Click Drop Shadow.

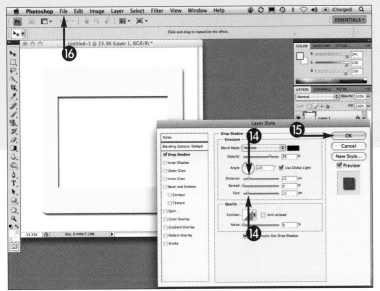

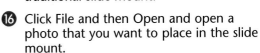

The Layer Style dialog box appears.

⑭ Click and drag the Distance and Size sliders to about 15 to give the slide depth.

⑮ Click OK.

The design resembles a traditional slide mount.

⑯ Click File and then Open and open a photo that you want to place in the slide mount.

Note: Click Window, Arrange, and then Float All in Windows to keep the windows separated.

⑰ Click the Move tool.

⑱ Click and drag the photo on top of the slide template.

⑲ Click the photo layer and move it between the other two layers.

⑳ Press ⌘+T (Ctrl+T) to add transformation anchors.

㉑ Press Shift to maintain the aspect ratio of the image as you click and drag the corner anchors to fit the photo inside the slide.

㉒ Click the commit button to commit the transformation.

The photo appears to be inside a traditional slide mount.

Try This!

To add text to your slide, click the Type tool (T) and type the text above and below the opening in the center. Use all caps in a common font such as Helvetica or Courier for a realistic effect, then lower the opacity of the Type layer to 50% or add an Inner Bevel layer style to the text. Press ⌘+E (Ctrl+E) to merge the type layer with the slide layer.

Customize It!

You can make a customized slide template for each of your clients or friends for a unique presentation by adding the name or project description to each slide.

Apply It!

To use your slide on multiple photos, drag the first photo on top of the slide file. Drag the photo layer between the slide and the Background layer. Adjust the photo using the transformation anchors and flatten the layers. Click File and then Save As to save the filled slide with a new name. Repeat this process for each of the photos.

Create a
CUSTOM COLOR BACKGROUND

You can create any number of different backgrounds for album pages or photo layouts starting with a new white document, adding colors and applying Photoshop filters and effects. The Clouds filter found under the Render filters is particularly useful for creating backgrounds because it changes the look of the image each time it is applied. You can make a white document look like an old piece of parchment by applying the Clouds filter to a white Background layer, using two shades of tan. You can then burn the

edges with the Burn tool to give the paper an aged parchment look. Save the document as a new file and use it as a Background layer for different photographs, a base layer for any number of designs, or as a background for text.

You can create different variegated color backgrounds by using two different shades of any color, or even two different colors, for the foreground and background and then applying the Render filter and selecting Clouds, Difference Clouds, or Fibers.

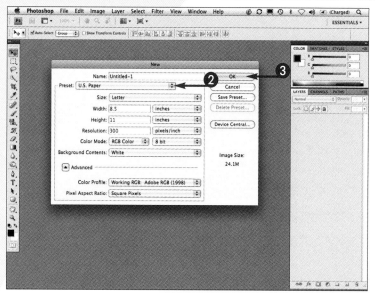

① Press ⌘+N (Ctrl+N) to create a new document.

② Click here and select U.S. Paper to automatically create a new document in RGB color mode at a resolution of 300 pixels/inch.

Note: You can create any size document with a white background in the RGB mode at 300 ppi.

③ Click OK.

④ Press ⌘+J (Ctrl+J) to duplicate the layer.

⑤ Click in each field in the Color panel and type **246**, **236**, **216** to select a light tan for the foreground color.

⑥ Click in the background color swatch in the Color panel and type **207**, **177**, **117** in the fields for a dark tan.

Note: You can use any light and dark color to create a colored background.

⑦ Click Filter.

⑧ Click Render.

⑨ Click Clouds.

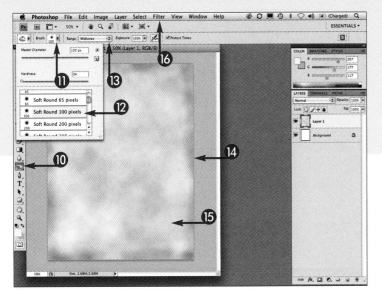

The image fills with a mottled tan color.

⑩ Click the Burn tool.

⑪ Click here to open the brush picker.

⑫ Click a large soft-edged brush.

⑬ Click here and select Midtones.

⑭ Click and drag across the edges of the document.

⑮ Repeat step 14 to darken some areas more.

Note: Click and drag irregularly to create a ragged burned edge.

⑯ Click Filter, Texture, and then Texturizer.

The Filter Gallery opens.

⑰ Click here and select Sandstone.

⑱ Click and drag the Scaling slider and the Relief slider until the surface has enough texture for your project.

⑲ Click OK.

The document looks like an old piece of parchment.

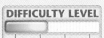

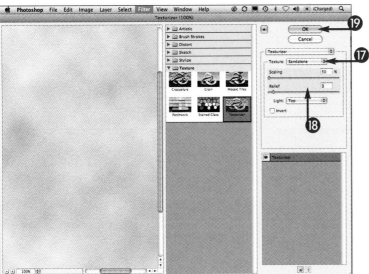

TIPS

Try This!

You can give the parchment some torn edges. Double-click the Background layer name and click OK in the dialog box that appears, changing the name to Layer 0. Click the Lasso tool () and click and drag several small irregular shapes in different areas of the paper edge. Press Delete (Backspace) to cut these areas out of the parchment.

More Options!

If the Background is too dark, press ⌘+J (Ctrl+J) to duplicate the layer. Change the blend mode of the top layer to Screen. If the Background is too light, duplicate the layer and change the blend mode of the top layer to Multiply. Then flatten the layers and save the file with a new name to use it as a background.

Make a photo look like
A GALLERY PRINT

You can give your photograph a professional finish by making it look like a gallery print. This technique is effective for both color and grayscale photographs. Gallery prints generally have wide white, black, or even gray borders depending on the tones in the image. The photo is placed in the top portion of the border or frame area, allowing the name of the gallery, artist, and artwork to fit under the image in stylized type.

After making a selection of the photo and cutting it out onto its own layer, you enlarge the canvas size by about 3 inches using the Relative option to add the space evenly all around the photo. You then add another inch below the photograph, to extend the area for the text. You can add a stroke or even a double stroke around the outside edge of the photo to give a finished look to the gallery print. The strokes can be the same or different colors and each stroke can have a different pixel width.

1. Press D to reset the foreground and background colors to black and white.

2. Press ⌘+A (Ctrl+A) to select the photo.

3. Press ⌘+Shift+J (Ctrl+Shift+J) to cut the photo out of the background and place it onto its own layer.

   Note: *The Background layer fills with white.*

4. Click Image.

5. Click Canvas Size.

The Canvas Size dialog box appears.

6. Click Relative (☐ changes to ☑).

   Note: *Selecting Relative adds the exact typed amount of width and height to the existing image.*

7. Type **3** in both the Width and Height data fields to add 3 inches to the canvas in each direction.

8. Click here and select White.

9. Click OK.

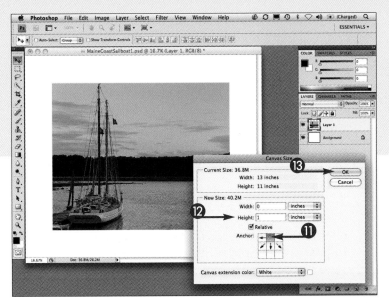

The image is centered in a wide white border.

Note: *Relative remains selected.*

⑩ Repeat steps 4 and 5 to open the Canvas Size dialog box again.

⑪ Click the top center square of the Anchor grid.

⑫ Click in the Height data field and type **1** to add 1 inch to the bottom of the white border.

⑬ Click OK.

97

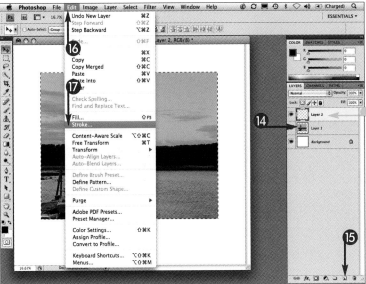

The photo is offset in the white border.

⑭ ⌘+click (Ctrl+click) the photo thumbnail in the Layers panel to select the photo.

⑮ Click the New Layer button to add a new empty layer.

● The new layer is automatically selected.

⑯ Click Edit.

⑰ Click Stroke.

TIPS

Try This!
For a realistic look, type a print number or the words **artist's proof** on the left side under the border using black for the color and a script styled font. You can then make the stylized letters appear to be written in pencil by lowering the opacity of the Type layer.

Change It!
Set the canvas color to black in the Canvas Size dialog box for a dramatic effect. Use white for the inside border stroke color and gray for the outside border stroke color and type the text using white or gray.

Chapter 9: Giving Your Images a Professional Presentation **229**

Make a photo look like
A GALLERY PRINT

By placing the strokes on separate layers, you can adjust the opacity of each stroke individually and change the look of the gallery print. You ⌘+click (Ctrl+click) the photo layer to have an active selection the exact size of the photo. You add a new empty layer above the photo layer and, with the selection active, apply a stroke on the new layer. The stroke makes the photo stand out. With the selection still active, you make the selected area slightly wider and higher, add another empty layer, and then apply a stroke on the second empty layer.

Gallery prints often have the name of the gallery set in a serif-styled font in all capital letters. Type a gallery name and click Window and then Character to open the Character panel. Use the tracking options to increase the space between the letters for a more realistic look. You can also type your name, your studio, or even the name of the image in the open area below the photo. Select a script font to sign your work under the outside stroke and add a print number to complete the gallery print look.

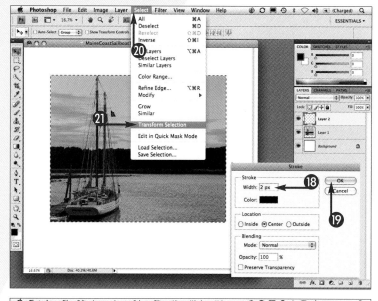

The Stroke dialog box appears.

⓲ Type **2 px** in the Width data field.

Note: Leave the default color as black and the location set to Center.

⓳ Click OK.

A thin, black stroke is applied to the image on the top layer.

⓴ Click Select.

㉑ Click Transform Selection.

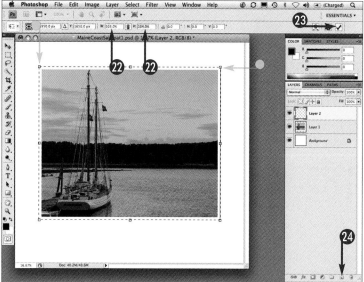

● Anchor points are added to the selection.

㉒ Type **103.0%** in the W data field and **104.0%** in the H data field.

㉓ Click the commit button to commit the transformation.

㉔ Click the New Layer button.

㉕ Repeat steps 16 to 19 to add a black stroke outside the border of the photo on the new layer.

㉖ Press ⌘+D (Ctrl+D) to deselect the border.

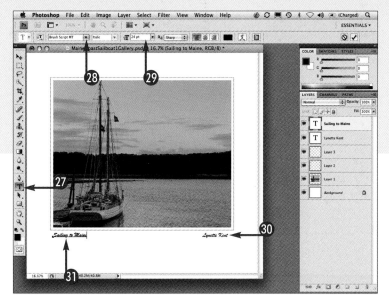

27 Click the Type tool.

28 Click here and select a font that looks like handwriting.

29 Type a font size in the data field.

30 Type your name, and press Enter (Ctrl+Enter) or click the commit button.

31 Type a name for the image, and press Enter (Ctrl+Enter) or click the commit button.

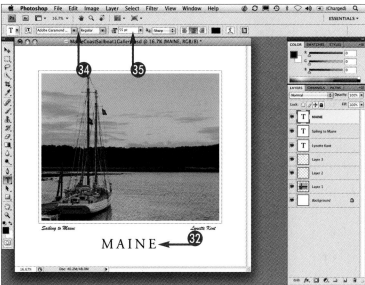

32 Click in the center of the gallery frame and type the name of the photo studio, gallery, or print series.

33 Press Enter (Ctrl+Enter).

34 Select a serif font such as Adobe Garamond and a font style such as Regular.

35 Type a font size in the data field.

36 Press Enter (Ctrl+Enter) to commit the font changes.

The image now appears like a traditional gallery print.

97
CONTINUED

TIP

More Options!

The size of the stroke that you apply to the borders depends on the size and resolution of the image. Use a thicker stroke for both the border of the photo and the outside border if the image is large or if you want to give the photo more of a framed look. You can also use different colors for the stroke for different effects. If the photo is light in color, try using a shade of gray to stroke the inner border instead of black. Because each stroke border is on its own layer, you can also lower the opacity of the layer if the color of the stroke appears too bold.

MAKE A CONTACT SHEET
of your photos

Your digital files are like digital negatives. Whether these are photos from a digital camera or scans of traditional prints and negatives, the first file downloaded or scanned is the original. You should always keep a duplicate set of the photos on another hard drive or burn a CD or DVD of the originals before you enhance them or use them in projects. You can create a contact sheet using the Output module in Bridge CS4, which is included with Photoshop CS4. The contact sheet helps you identify and keep track of the images on the external drive or

other removable media. You can also create a photo index of all the images in one project folder using the same steps.

Use the Output button in Bridge to open the appropriate options on the right panel. Select a contact sheet template, define the layout of the images and spacing you prefer, and select the font, size, and color of the text captions, or *overlays*, for each photo on the sheet. Bridge CS4 builds the contact sheet as an Acrobat PDF file that you can save or print as a visual reference.

① In Photoshop, open Bridge by clicking the Bridge button (Br) on the Application bar or by clicking File and then Browse in Bridge.

Bridge launches.

② Click Folders.

③ Navigate to the folder of images to use for the contact sheet.

④ Click Output.

The interface and options change.

⑤ Click PDF.

⑥ In the Output section, click here to select a contact sheet template, such as 4*5 Contact Sheet.

⑦ In the Document section, click here and select U.S. Paper.

Note: Optionally, select International Paper.

⑧ Click here and scroll to view the next sections.

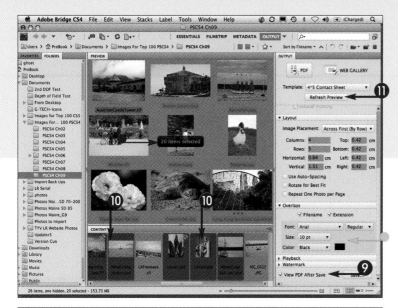

- In the Overlays section, you can change the font, size, and color for the file names and extensions that will print on the contact sheet.

#98

9 Click View PDF After Save (☐ changes to ☑).

10 ⌘+click (Ctrl+click) the photos in the content pane to use on the contact sheet.

- The number of items selected is updated and the thumbnails appear in the Output Preview pane.

11 Click Refresh Preview to view the contact sheet.

The Output Preview pane displays the contact sheet as it will print.

12 Click Save.

The Save As dialog box appears.

13 Type a name for the contact sheet.

14 Click Save.

Bridge builds the contact sheet, saves it as a PDF, and launches Acrobat or Acrobat Reader to display it.

DIFFICULTY LEVEL

TIPS

Did You Know?

The size of the thumbnails is constrained by the number of rows and columns. More columns and rows result in smaller thumbnail images. You can generally select Low Quality in the Document section for printing a contact sheet because a higher resolution does not make a noticeable improvement.

More Options!

To make a contact sheet fit a CD/DVD jewel case, use these settings:

In the Document section, type **4.688** inches in both the width and height fields. The page Preset changes to Custom.

In the Layout section, type **5** in both the Columns and Rows fields. Select Use Auto-Spacing.

In the Overlays section, click the Size down arrow and select 6-point type to fit the text under the thumbnail.

CREATE A SLIDE SHOW
presentation

If you want to e-mail photos to friends, send your portfolio to a prospective employer, or send a client some images for review, you can use Photoshop and Bridge CS4 to help create a slide show and save it as a PDF presentation. You can then attach the PDF slide show to an e-mail or burn it to a CD or DVD. You can use any images from Bridge to create the slide show. You determine the layout of the images, and you can add a watermark or copyright to each

image. You can select a complete folder to use as the source images or individually select the images to include in the slide show. You determine the amount of time that each slide appears on-screen and decide if the slide show should stop after the last image or continue in a loop. You can even select from a number of slide transitions to give your presentation a professional look.

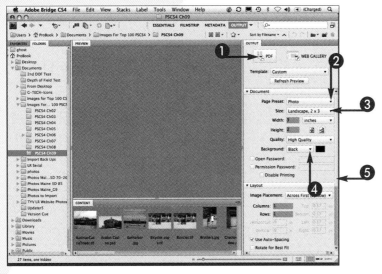

1. Repeat steps 1 to 5 in Task #98 to open the PDF Output options for Bridge.

2. In the Document section, click here and select Photo.

3. Click here and select Landscape 2 x 3 for a small slide show to attach to e-mail.

   Note: Clicking a larger page size such as 5 x 7 or 8 x 10 creates a larger PDF file.

4. Click here and select Black.

5. Scroll to view the next sections.

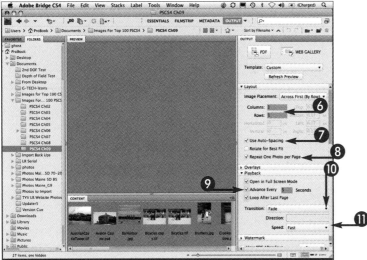

6. Click in both the Columns and Rows fields and type **1**.

7. In the Layout section, click Use Auto-Spacing (☐ changes to ☑).

8. Click Repeat One Photo per Page (☐ changes to ☑).

   Note: Deselect Rotate for Best Fit if necessary.

9. In the Playback section, select all three check boxes.

10. Click here and select a transition style, such as Fade.

11. Scroll to view the next sections.

⑫ ⌘+click (Ctrl+click) the photos in the content pane to use in the slide show.

● The thumbnails of the selected images appear in the Output Preview pane.

⑬ Click Refresh Preview.

The Output Preview pane displays the first slide of the slide show.

⑭ Click View PDF After Save (☐ changes to ☑).

⑮ Click Save.

The Save As dialog box appears.

⑯ Type a name for the slide show.

⑰ Click Save.

Bridge builds the slide show, saves it as a PDF, and launches Acrobat or Acrobat Reader to display it.

⑱ When Acrobat's Full Screen dialog box appears, click Yes to have the slide show fill the screen.

⑲ You can press Esc in Acrobat to end the slide show.

Customize It!

You can change the transition style from the Fade transition to any of the other transition options in the drop-down menu, such as Dissolve or Blinds. Some of the slide transitions, such as Zoom In or Zoom Out, allow you to determine the direction and speed of the transition's effect. You can also change how many seconds each image appears on the screen by typing the number of seconds in the Advance data field in the Playback section. If you want the presentation to repeat in a continuous loop, click Loop After Last Page.

Did You Know?

To protect the images from being printed without permission, click Permission Password (☐ changes to ☑) in the Document section. Type the password in the data field and click Disable Printing (☐ changes to ☑).

Create a
WEB PHOTO GALLERY

In addition to PDF slide shows and contact sheets, you can build a Web gallery using Bridge CS4. You can easily create a Web site home page with your images displayed both as thumbnails and full-sized images. You can select from a variety of Web gallery styles and personalize your Web page. Bridge CS4 includes many different templates, including Flash and HTML galleries. The steps to creating a Web photo gallery are similar to those for creating a contact sheet or a PDF slide-show presentation. You

select the images in Bridge CS4, determine a template and a style, and add a gallery name, your name, your e-mail, and whether or not to display the file names as image titles. You can select your own set of colors to use on the Web gallery to customize your site's appearance even more. You can preview your Web gallery inside Bridge as you create it and also preview how it will appear in a Web browser. You can even upload your Web gallery directly to an FTP server from within the Bridge CS4 application.

CREATE A WEB GALLERY

① Repeat steps 1 to 4 in Task #98 to open the Output options for Bridge.

② Enlarge the Preview pane by clicking and dragging the separator bar to the left.

③ In the Output pane, click Web Gallery.

④ ⌘+click (Ctrl+click) some images in the Content pane to select them.

The images appear in the Preview pane.

⑤ Click Refresh Preview.

Bridge builds a Web gallery and displays it in the Output Preview pane.

⑥ Click here and select a different template such as Left Filmstrip.

⑦ Click here and select a style such as Large Thumbnail.

⑧ In the Site Info section, click in each text field and type all the information for your gallery.

⑨ Type your name.

⑩ Type your e-mail address.

⑪ Click Refresh Preview.

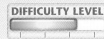

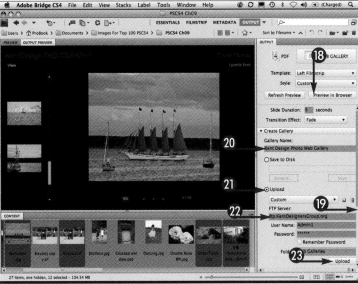

Bridge builds the Web gallery in the selected style and displays it in the Output Preview pane.

● You can click the Play button in the Output Preview pane to view the Web gallery slide show.

⑫ Scroll to view more options.

⑬ In the Color Palette pane, click a color box, such as the Text color box under Title.

The Colors dialog box appears.

⑭ Click another color in the Colors box.

⑮ Click OK.

⑯ Click Refresh Preview to view the color changes.

⑰ Repeat steps 13 to 16 for any other color to change.

⑱ Click Preview in Browser to see how your Web gallery will appear in the default Web browser on your computer.

UPLOAD YOUR WEB GALLERY TO AN FTP SITE

⑲ Scroll to view more options.

⑳ Type your Gallery Name.

㉑ Click Upload (○ changes to ⊙).

㉒ Type your FTP server, User Name, Password, and a Folder name.

㉓ Click Upload.

Bridge CS4 creates the Web gallery and uploads it to your FTP site.

Try This!

You can design your Web gallery and click Save to Disk (○ changes to ⊙) in the Create Gallery section to save it to your hard drive or removable media such as a DVD. You can then upload it to an FTP site or publish it to a WebDAV server such as Apple's MobileMe when you have a good Internet connection or when it is more convenient.

Did You Know?

You can include your contact information in the Site Info section, so that when a viewer clicks on your name on the Web gallery site, his e-mail client automatically launches and opens a new mail message with your e-mail address in the address field.

Plugging in to Photoshop CS4

Although Photoshop CS4 includes a variety of different brushes, shapes, and filters and comes with the Bridge application for organizing and viewing images, third-party plug-ins can help you improve your images more easily, augmenting Photoshop's functionality and often offering even more editing power than using the application alone.

Plug-ins exist for nearly every project and for every user level. With the imaginative layouts, brush sets, frames, backgrounds, ornaments, and edges from Graphic Authority, you can quickly give a finished look to your images. Alien Skin's Blow Up plug-in enables you to resize images while maintaining the highest image quality, and Alien Skin's Snap Art helps you quickly turn any image into traditional-looking art. Akvis Coloriage enables you to accurately colorize black-and-white photos.

Vertus Fluid Mask, a powerful masking tool, helps you make difficult selections. Using Nik Software's Sharpener Pro and Dfine to sharpen and reduce noise removes the guesswork from Photoshop's filters. Nik Software's Color Efex Pro, Viveza, and Silver Efex Pro help you visually adjust the colors and tones in your photos better than using Photoshop's tools alone. Kubota Image Tools offer sophisticated actions you can run to enhance and give a finished look to all your images. AutoFX plug-ins help you selectively paint colors and tones into your photos. Extensis Portfolio 8.5 can help you organize, categorize, archive, and find your digital images from the time you first upload them to the computer through storing them on external media.

Third-party plug-ins can enhance the way everyone uses Photoshop.

Top 100

Embellish a photo effortlessly with
GRAPHIC AUTHORITY

You can easily frame a photo or create a complete page layout using design elements from GraphicAuthority.com. Graphic Authority products are not actually plug-ins, but rather multilayered templates for page layouts, creative custom brushes, and professionally designed backgrounds, papers, edges, frames, and vector ornaments, which all work with any version of Photoshop. You can place your photos into pre-designed album pages or an assortment of different frames, or simply add vector ornaments to embellish the edges of an image for a unique look.

You can select a Graphic Authority template or an individual edge and a background, such as an antique paper, as the base layer. Adjust the size of these elements to fit the photo's dimensions and your design. With all the parts open and resized, you simply click and drag the photo onto the Graphic Authority document, adjust the placement of the layers, and modify the overall appearance by turning off the visibility of any of the layers. You can customize any design more by adding decorative vector ornaments. At www.graphicauthority.com, you will find a variety of products and tutorials.

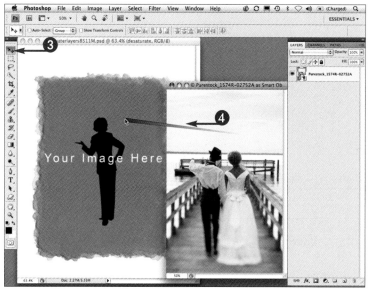

① Open both the photo file and a Graphic Authority layout or frame.

② Set the desired dimensions of both files using the Image Size command as in Task #32.

③ Click the Move tool.

④ Click and drag the photo onto the frame image.

Note: *You can open or place the photo as a smart object to preserve the image's source content.*

⑤ Click and drag the photo layer below the Your Image Here layer.

⑥ Click the visibility button to hide the Your Image Here layer.

⑦ Close the photo file.

● With Graphic Authority's multilayered designs, you can click other visibility buttons to hide other layers and alter the look.

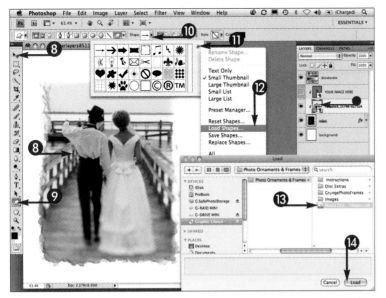

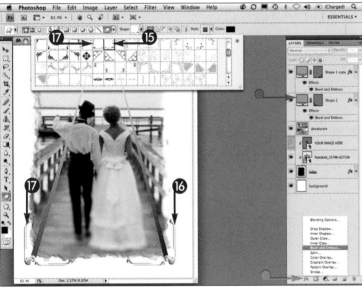

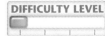
- The photo layer appears recessed in the Layers panel.

⑧ Use the Move tool to adjust the photo in the frame.

⑨ Click the Custom Shape tool.

⑩ Click here to open the custom shape picker.

⑪ Click here to open the menu.

⑫ Click Load Shapes.

⑬ When the Load dialog box appears, navigate to the Graphic Authority DVD and click the Photo Ornaments Custom Shapes.csh file.

⑭ Click Load.

Graphic Authority's photo ornaments now appear in the Custom Shape Presets.

⑮ Click a Custom shape.

⑯ Click and drag in the photo frame file to add the ornament.

⑰ Repeat steps 15 and 16 if desired.

- You can click the Shape layer thumbnail to change the color of the ornament to match a color in the image.

- You can click the Layer Style button to add a layer style such as a Bevel and Emboss effect.

The photo is now framed with an ornamental edge.

TIPS

More Options!

Copy the custom shapes and brushes from the Graphic Authority DVD to your computer and load them from the copied file. If you upgrade or reinstall Photoshop later, you can reload the shapes more quickly from a location on your hard drive than from the DVD.

Did You Know?

With Graphic Authority's products, you will not have to pay to upgrade a plug-in when you upgrade your version of Photoshop. Graphic Authority's backgrounds, edges, and frames are multilayered Photoshop files, and the brushes and ornaments can be used with any version of Photoshop CS.

Try This!

Adjust the edges layer even with the clipping mask applied by clicking the layer and pressing ⌘+T (Ctrl+T). Press ⌘+0 (Ctrl+0) to see the anchors. Click and drag the anchor points until the edges look the way you want.

ENLARGE IMAGES
with maximum quality with Alien Skin Blow Up 2

To change image size in Photoshop, you select an interpolation method such as Bicubic Smoother or Bicubic Sharper for resampling the pixels. Resized images often lose image quality, most noticeably when enlarged. They can display a stair step or halo around some edges, often referred to as *fringe artifacts*. Alien Skin's Blow Up 2 is a plug-in for enlarging images using an interpolation method which increases the size of the image while maintaining smooth, sharp edges.

You can enlarge 8-, 16-, and 32-bit images in almost any color space, including CMYK and Lab, making

this plug-in perfect for both amateur and professional photographers as well as graphic designers.

You can automatically create a duplicate of the image before resizing and even control the amount of photo grain that appears in the enlarged image. Blow Up 2 includes over 100 presets for preparing photos for print, saving you time and numerous calculations of the dpi and aspect ratio involved in resizing images for print. You can download a demo version at www.alienskin.com.

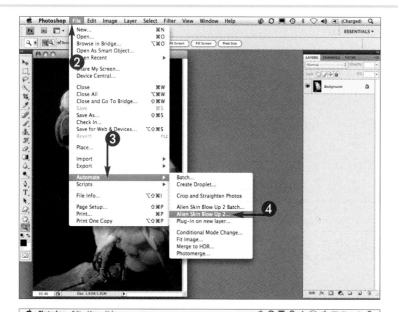

① Open the photo to enlarge.

② Click File.

③ Click Automate.

④ Click Alien Skin Blow Up 2.

The Alien Skin Blow Up dialog box appears.

⑤ Click the Settings tab.

The list of presets for resizing images for specific sizes and output destinations appears.

⑥ Click the arrow by an output size, such as Large Photo Paper.

A set of paper sizes and types appears.

⑦ Click an output size and paper type such as 16x20 (300 dpi), Inkjet Luster.

A crop rectangle appears on the photo.

Note: *Blow Up 2 attempts to center the subject inside the crop rectangle.*

102

DIFFICULTY LEVEL

8 Click and drag inside the crop rectangle to frame the photo if necessary.

9 Click the Controls tab.

The Controls options appear.

10 Click Duplicate Image Before Resizing (☐ changes to ☑).

11 Click OK.

A progress bar appears.

● Blow Up enlarges a duplicate of the image and assigns the same name as the original but with the word *copy*.

TIPS

Attention!

Use Blow Up's Sharpen Edges slider carefully to avoid making the enlarged photo appear too smooth. You can also sharpen the original first with Photoshop's Sharpen filters.

More Options!

You can use Blow Up's Add Grain slider to visually restore overly smooth details by applying artificial film grain. For extreme enlargements, however, you may need to use Alien Skin's more powerful Exposure plug-in to add the correct amount of grain.

More Options!

Blow Up 2 also includes a batch processing function which enables you to resize multiple images from a source folder and place the resized images into a destination folder with one click.

CHANGE YOUR PHOTOS INTO ART
with Alien Skin Snap Art

Turning a photograph into a fine art piece such as a painting or sketch using Photoshop's actions and brushes can be fun but time-consuming. By using the Snap Art plug-in from Alien Skin Software, you can transform a photograph into art that looks as though it was done with traditional art tools with just a few clicks. You can apply the Snap Art filter settings and then move the various sliders and controls and view your painting or sketch as it builds in the large preview window.

The Snap Art dialog box includes several split screen previews so that you can see both your photo as a reference and the effects as you apply them. By applying different types of art media filters on multiple layers and changing the blending modes, you can completely alter the results and make your artwork unique. The Alien Skin Web site (www.alienshin.com) includes more downloadable settings you can apply to increase the amount of detail in your finished art.

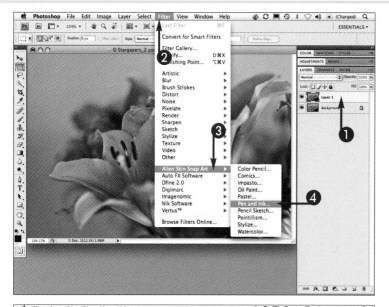

CREATE A PEN-AND-INK DRAWING

① Press ⌘+J (Ctrl+J) to duplicate the Background layer.

② Click Filter.

③ Click Alien Skin Snap Art.

④ Click a filter such as Pen and Ink.

The Alien Skin Snap Art dialog box for that media appears.

⑤ Click the Basic tab.

⑥ Click here to apply the filter to a separate layer (☐ changes to ☑).

⑦ In the small preview window, click and drag the red box over the main subject.

⑧ Click here and select a preview split.

⑨ Click and drag any of the sliders to adjust the look.

A progress bar appears briefly, and the large preview image displays the results.

⑩ Click OK.

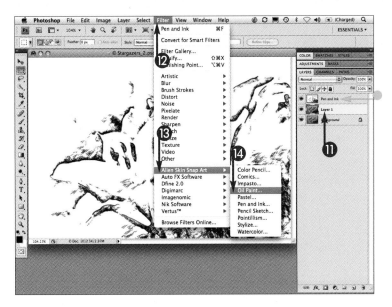

- The filter is applied to a new layer named for the type of filter, Pen and Ink in this example.

CHANGE THE LOOK BY ADDING ANOTHER FILTER

⑪ Click Layer 1 to select it.

⑫ Click Filter.

⑬ Click Alien Skin Snap Art.

⑭ Click another filter such as Oil Paint.

⑮ Repeat steps 5 to 10 to apply the other art media filter on a separate layer.

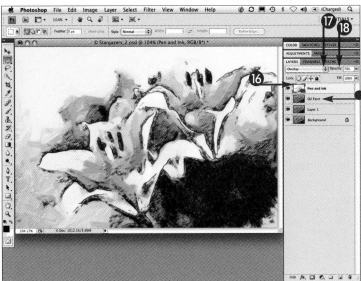

- The filter is applied to a new layer named for the type of filter, Oil Paint in this example.

⑯ Click the top layer to select it.

⑰ Click here and select a layer blend mode such as Overlay.

⑱ Click the layer opacity and drag slightly to the left.

Note: Optionally, to vary the effect more, repeat steps 11 to 18 using different Alien Skin Snap Art filters in step 14.

The final image looks more like artwork than a photograph.

Did You Know?

Snap Art uses edge detection to outline the objects in the photo. It uses this outline to place the natural media strokes and fill areas with colors. Snap Art uses an advanced paint engine to transform your photo into an artistic composition, preserving enough detail while giving the piece a loose and artistic appearance.

Try This!

Each filter in Snap Art has many sliders and options. Move a slider to try a different look. To undo a change, press ⌘+Z (Ctrl+Z) or, to redo the change, press ⌘+Y (Ctrl+Y). You can return to the default settings anytime by clicking the Settings tab in the Snap Art dialog box and clicking Factory Default or by pressing ⌘+R (F5) to reset the filter to the original settings.

COLORIZE A BLACK-AND-WHITE
photo with AKVIS Coloriage

You can add color to a grayscale photo in Photoshop using adjustment layers, masks, and brushes; however, the Coloriage plug-in from AKVIS makes colorizing a black-and-white photograph quick and automatic. You can easily add color to a variety of images from antique photos to hand-drawn sketches and cartoons and still maintain a very natural look. You can even use Coloriage to replace the colors in a color image.

Your image must be in RGB mode for the Coloriage filters to be applied. Click Image in the menu, and then click Mode and RGB before selecting AKVIS Coloriage from the Photoshop filters.

You can colorize an image with Coloriage by clicking different colors from the Colors palette or using the Color Library for difficult colors such as skin, hair, and lips. Paint over the areas in the photo with loose brush strokes. When you click the green forward button, the software determines the borders of the various areas and applies the color based on the grayscale values.

You can find Coloriage along with other AKVIS filters at http://akvis.com.

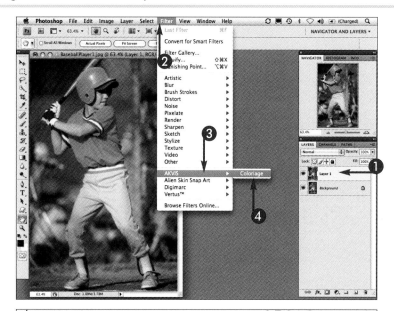

1 Press ⌘+J (Ctrl+J) to duplicate the Background layer.

2 Click Filter.

3 Click AKVIS.

4 Click Coloriage.

The Coloriage dialog box appears.

5 Click and drag the slider to reduce or enlarge your preview.

6 Click a color you want to apply to one area, such as the skin in this example.

7 Click the Pencil tool to make the size slider appear.

8 Click and drag the slider to adjust the pencil size.

9 Click and drag to draw in the image with the first color.

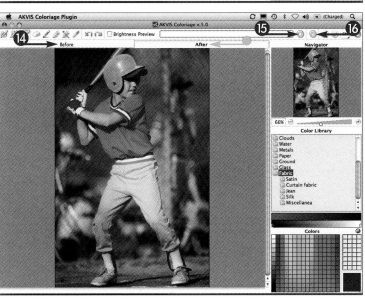

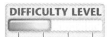

104

DIFFICULTY LEVEL

⑩ Repeat steps 5 to 9 to set all the colors to be used.

⑪ Click the Eraser tool.

⑫ Click and drag to correct any stray marks.

⑬ Click the Run button to see a preliminary colorization.

● AKVIS determines the blends, and the colorized image appears in the After tab.

⑭ Click the Before tab and repeat steps 6 to 12 to change any colors as needed.

⑮ Click the Run button again to view the corrections.

⑯ Click the Apply button.

The final colorization is applied to the image.

Note: If the colors are too vibrant in the Background copy layer, you can lower the opacity of the layer.

TIPS

Did You Know?

If you want to change one particular color in a color image and not alter the rest of the colors, use the Pencil tool and draw on the object. Then use the Keep-Color Pencil tool and draw a closed outline around the object.

Try This!

When you colorize a black-and-white photograph, select the less saturated colors in the Colors palette to make the colorization appear more natural. The less saturated colors are at the bottom of the palette.

More Options!

You can save the color strokes to edit colors later or vary different colorization schemes. Click the Save button after drawing all the strokes but before applying them and closing the dialog box.

MAKE A SELECTION
and remove the background with Vertus Fluid Mask

Making selections so that you can cut out or replace backgrounds in Photoshop can be difficult and is often incomplete, especially when selecting hair, fur, or trees. Using Photoshop's selection tools and Refine Edge command may work on some photographs but not all, and not always easily. You can make selections or masks more effectively with a tool from Vertus Tech called Fluid Mask. This plug-in uses highly advanced technology that mimics the way the eye and brain look at objects.

Fluid Mask automatically detects edges in the image and outlines them in blue. Depending on the complexity of your photo, you can increase or reduce the number of objects Fluid Mask outlines by increasing or decreasing the edge sensitivity. You paint over the objects to be removed with the Delete Local mask brushes and fill areas to keep with Keep mask brushes or the Keep mask auto fill command. You can preview your work using the Test Render tool.

You can even find easy-to-follow tutorials and samples online at www.vertustech.com.

1 In Photoshop, click Filter, Vertus, and then Fluid Mask.

The Fluid Mask dialog box fills the screen, and Fluid Mask automatically places blue outlines, dividing the image based on areas of contrasting values.

2 Click the Delete Local brush.

3 Click and drag in the image over areas to remove.

The areas turn red.

4 Click and drag the slider to adjust the brush size.

5 Click the Delete Exact brush.

6 Click and drag to paint over detailed areas to be removed.

7 Click the Keep Local brush.

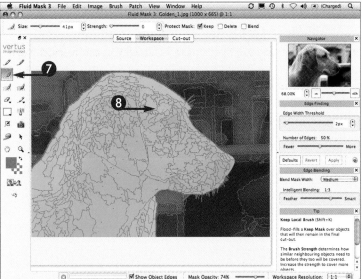

8 Click and drag in the image over areas to keep.

The areas turn green.

Note: You can also click Image and then Auto-Fill with Keep to fill the keep areas with green.

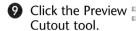
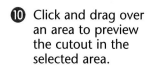
⑨ Click the Preview Cutout tool.

⑩ Click and drag over an area to preview the cutout in the selected area.

The selected area in the Preview area displays the kept object(s) against a blue background.

Note: You can change the background color by clicking the color patch in the Vertus toolbar.

⑪ Click the Create Cut-out button to create the cutout.

Fluid Mask replaces the background with the preview color in the color box.

⑫ Click File and then Save and Apply to remove the background from the photo on the duplicated layer.

Vertus Fluid Mask removes the background and leaves the extracted foreground on a transparent layer in Photoshop.

Did You Know?

You can click the Zoom tool and click in the image to enlarge delicate edge areas. Then paint with the Delete Exact brush and double-click the Hand tool to return to the full view. You can also use the Blend Exact brush, the fourth brush down, to paint over areas with complex edges such as hair to further refine the selection.

More Options!

You can save the extracted area so you can reselect it quickly later by storing it as an *alpha channel*. An alpha channel in Photoshop is a black-and-white channel in which the white areas represent the selection. ⌘+click (Ctrl+click) the extracted layer thumbnail in the Layers panel to select it. Click Select and then Save Selection. Give the channel a name in the Save Selection dialog box and click OK. The layer is saved as a new alpha channel. You can then reload the alpha channel at any time by clicking Select and then Load Selection and selecting the alpha channel.

CONTROL DIGITAL NOISE
with Nik Dfine

Digital noise is inherent in digital photographs. Noise can appear as bright, colored specks called *chrominance noise* or as dark spots called *luminance noise*. Various factors can affect or create noise, including the light, length of exposure, and temperature when the photo is taken, as well as the peculiarities of individual cameras and sensors. You may also see more noise in photos taken using high ISO speeds and in low-light situations. Although you can reduce digital noise in a general manner with the built-in filters in Photoshop CS4, using Nik Dfine

enables you to control how you reduce the noise and optimize the detail. Dfine reduces luminance noise, chrominance noise, and JPEG artifacts; improves contrast; and adjusts colorcasts while taking into account the effects of the noise reduction. You can reduce the noise for the whole image, for specific color ranges, or by setting control points. The large preview screen enables you to see the improvements as you try them. You can try Nik Dfine on your own images by downloading the trial software from www.niksoftware.com.

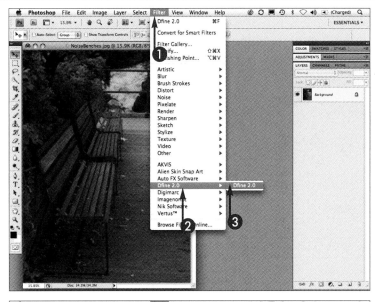

① Click Filter.

② Click Dfine 2.0.

③ Click Dfine 2.0.

The Dfine dialog box appears.

④ Press ⌘+Option+0 (Ctrl+Alt+0) to view the image at 100%.

⑤ Click and drag the resize corner if necessary, to get the most screen space.

⑥ Click the Pan tool.

⑦ Click and drag in the image to view different areas.

● You can click and drag the red navigator box over different areas to view the noise.

⑧ Click one of the two Split preview buttons to view a split preview either horizontally or vertically.

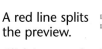

- A red line splits the preview.
- ⑨ Click here and select Automatic.
- ⑩ Click Measure Noise.

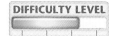

DIFFICULTY LEVEL

Nik Dfine 2.0 automatically measures the noise in the image, creates a profile for it, and reduces the noise in the preview.

Note: In the figure shown here, the bottom split displays the results of applying the Nik Dfine filter.

⑪ Click OK.

A progress bar appears as Nik Dfine 2 creates a new layer and applies the noise reduction filter.

More Options!

Instead of clicking OK in step 11, click Brush. The Dfine dialog box disappears, and a layer mask is added to the Dfine layer. Click Paint in the Dfine palette. Click the Brush tool and paint in your image to selectively reduce noise. Use a pressure-sensitive pen tablet for the most control with Dfine Selective.

Did You Know?

Noise reduction is more effective when applied early in the image-editing workflow. Apply Dfine right after importing or converting from the RAW format. Because in-camera sharpening increases noise structures in images, you can more precisely reduce noise and preserve details with Nik Dfine by turning off noise reduction and sharpening on your camera.

SHARPEN PHOTOS
with finesse using Nik Sharpener Pro

Sharpening is an essential step in digital imaging. Photoshop's built-in filters apply the sharpening based on the screen image. The various output methods and devices, such as displays and different types of printers and papers, require specific kinds of sharpening. Using Nik Sharpener Pro, you can sharpen your images for all types of output. Sharpener Pro analyzes the image and sharpens according to the type of detail in the image and the output device.

You can sharpen the whole image or apply sharpening to specific areas using Nik's Selective tool and a Photoshop brush to paint over areas or using Nik's U Point technology. With U Point technology,

you place points called *control points* directly on an area you want to edit. Then you click and drag the points to change specific sharpening attributes that Nik calls output sharpening strength, structure, local contrast, or focus sharpening.

You can also use Nik Sharpener Pro for a creative effect. For example, you can use a Nik control point and increase the Focus sharpening amount to slightly sharpen a particular area and draw the viewer's eye to that point.

You can find tutorials and trial software at www.niksoftware.com.

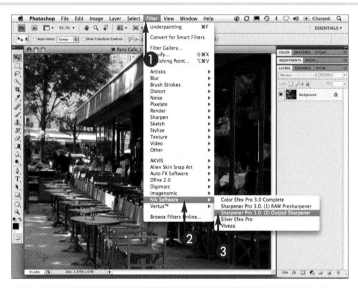

1 Click Filter.

2 Click Nik Software.

3 Click Sharpener Pro 3.0 (2) Output Sharpener.

The Sharpener Pro dialog box appears.

4 Press ⌘+Option+0 (Ctrl+Alt+0) to view the image at 100%.

APPLY GENERAL OUTPUT SHARPENING

5 Click here and select a type of output, such as Inkjet.

6 Click here and select Auto.

7 Click here and select a paper, such as Glossy.

8 Click here and select the resolution of your printer, such as 2400 x 2400.

9 Scroll down.

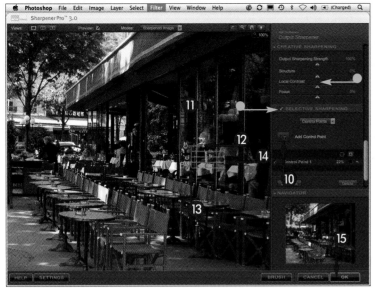

APPLY CREATIVE SHARPENING

⑩ Click Add Control Point.

⑪ Click an area in the image.

A control point is added.

⑫ Click and drag the top line to control the size.

⑬ Click the triangle to expand the controls.

⑭ Click and drag each of the control point lines to change the type of sharpening.

Note: Structure sharpens areas of texture under the control point. Local Contrast sharpens small edges or details under the control point. Focus adapts to sharpen areas that are out of focus more than the areas in focus under the control point.

● You can also deselect Selective Sharpening and move the Creative Sharpening sliders to sharpen the overall image.

⑮ Click OK.

● Nik Sharpener Pro adds a layer with the specific type of sharpening applied.

● In this image, the woman looking through the window is highlighted by the creative sharpening.

TIPS

Important!

The order in which you apply image enhancements affects the quality of the final print. Apply noise reduction first, adjust the image for tone and color, and then resize the image. Output sharpening should be the final step in the editing process to avoid introducing unwanted details in the image.

Did You Know?

Although JPEG and TIFF images have some sharpening applied automatically when the camera processes the capture, RAW files do not. Sharpener Pro includes a RAW Presharpening filter to sharpen RAW image files at the beginning of the editing process, without increasing noise or introducing artifacts. Be sure to turn off any sharpening in the camera's settings and in the Camera Raw processing software. Apply Nik's RAW Presharpener so you can better view your photos on your monitor.

APPLY PHOTO FILTERS
digitally using Nik Color Efex Pro

Professional photographers often carry a selection of lens filters and light reflectors to take advantage of every lighting condition they might encounter. You can achieve similar effects using Color Efex Pro from Nik Software. Nik filters can help you enhance images better than using Photoshop alone. Based on photographic filter technology, these filters calculate the existing color and light in an image and apply the effect accordingly. The filters can adapt to any previous adjustments in the photo, so you can apply multiple filters in a different order and achieve more natural-looking photographic enhancements. Color

Efex Pro can also be applied to a smart object photo layer so you can readjust images even after the effects have been applied. You can even save your settings to apply them to a range of photos for a consistent workflow and increased productivity.

The Sunshine filter shown in this task is just one of the many traditional-styled filters. It transforms the grayed colors from a photo shot on an overcast day into a bright colorful scene, yet in a very natural way. You can see samples of the many Color Efex Pro filters at www.niksoftware.com.

① Click Color Efex Pro 3.0 Complete in the Selective palette.

Note: *If the Selective palette is not open, click File, Automate, and then Nik Selective Tool.*

② Click the L-S tab.

③ Click Sunshine.

Note: *Optionally, you can click Filter, Nik Software, and then Color Efex Pro 3.0 to open the Nik Color Efex Pro dialog box.*

The Sunshine filter dialog box appears.

④ Click the Lock Loupe Position button to lock the position of the loupe.

⑤ Click and drag the Saturation Correction slider to control the intensity of the colors.

⑥ Click and drag the Cool Color Reduction slider to manipulate the blue colors.

⑦ Click the Light thumbnail and select the type of sunlight to add.

⑧ Click either the Split preview button or the Side-by-side preview button to select a before and after preview.

⑨ Click and drag the Light Intensity slider to control the amount of added light.

⑩ Click and drag the Radius slider to control the increased detail smoothing.

108

DIFFICULTY LEVEL

⑪ Click the Select Prefilter thumbnail and select a color contrast filter to enhance different colors and objects.

⑫ Click and drag the Prefilter Strength slider to change the amount of the prefilter added to the image.

⑬ Click OK.

Color Efex Pro applies the filter to a separate layer.

⑭ Click the visibility button for the Background copy layer on and off to compare the results with the original.

TIPS

Try This!
You can click Brush instead of OK in step 13 and paint any filter into your image using a brush to easily control the location and amount of the effect. The filter is automatically applied to a layer with a layer mask so you can paint the effect directly on the photo. Use a pen tablet for even greater control.

More Options!
In addition to applying the filter to the entire image, you can also click Brush in the Color Efex Pro dialog box after selecting the settings and paint the filter effect onto specific areas using Photoshop's Brush tool. For even more control, you can apply the filters to specific areas using Nik's patented U Point technology, as in Task #107.

Did You Know?
Nik Color Efex Pro complete has 52 filters, including conventional film emulation filters, as well as special effects filters and retouching tools. Other editions include either 15 filters or 35 filters.

ENHANCE COLORS AND LIGHT
selectively with Nik Viveza

You can edit the color and light in your images using Photoshop's filters; however, to do so to specific areas requires selections, feathering, layer masks, and an in-depth knowledge of the tools in Photoshop. You can easily enhance the color and light in your images and do so with greater control using Nik Software's Viveza plug-in. You can darken the background and lighten the main subject, or modify the tones in specific areas visually using interactive sliders. Like other Nik plug-ins, Viveza includes the U Point technology so you can create multiple control points in the image and change how the filter is

applied to each area individually. As you move the point sliders to control the brightness, contrast, and saturation, Viveza edits the colors of the objects under the points and automatically blends the tonal changes as it applies them. You can also choose to paint the edits directly on the image using the Brush option in the dialog box.

If you apply Viveza to a smart object layer, you can fine-tune any edits after they have been applied. You can find many examples, tutorials, and download a trial version at www.niksoftware.com.

① Click Filter.

② Click Convert for Smart Filters.

● The Background layer is changed to a smart object layer.

Note: The Brush option is deactivated when using a smart object layer.

③ Click Viveza in the Selective palette.

Note: If the Selective palette is not open, click File, Automate, and then Nik Selective Tool.

Note: Optionally, you can click Filter, Nik Software, and then Color Efex Pro 3.0 to open the Nik Color Efex Pro dialog box.

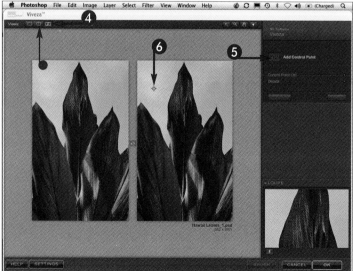

The Viveza dialog box appears.

④ Click the Side-by-side preview button to select a before and after preview.

● You can also click the Split preview button to display a split preview.

⑤ Click Add Control Point.

⑥ Click an area to adjust in the photo.

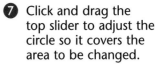
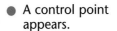

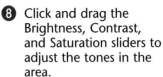

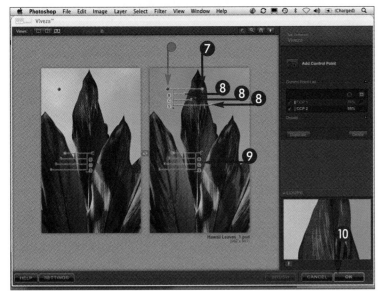

- A control point appears.

7 Click and drag the top slider to adjust the circle so it covers the area to be changed.

8 Click and drag the Brightness, Contrast, and Saturation sliders to adjust the tones in the area.

9 Repeat steps 5 to 8 to add more adjustment points.

10 Click OK.

109

DIFFICULTY LEVEL

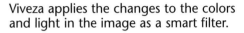

Viveza applies the changes to the colors and light in the image as a smart filter.

- You can double-click the Viveza smart filter to reopen the dialog box and readjust the sliders.

TIPS

Did You Know?

When you view the full image in the preview window, the Loupe tool shows the image at 100%. When you click the Zoom tool to preview the image at 100%, the Loupe tool shows the whole image and acts as a navigator.

More Options!

You can click the Settings button in the Viveza dialog box to set how the interface functions. You can select the default zoom size, change the default preview style, change the control point size and the types of sliders, and choose to always have the filter applied to a separate layer.

Try This!

Add a control point and click the arrow below the fourth slider. More lines are added to the control point so you can individually adjust the hue, red, green, blue, and warmth of the selected area.

CREATE A DYNAMIC
black-and-white image with Nik Silver Efex Pro

Photoshop CS4's Adjustments panel includes many presets and adjustments for converting a color photo to black and white non-destructively. Nik Software's Silver Efex Pro is a sophisticated and easy-to-use tool for converting color images to grayscale and re-creating the different techniques for traditional darkroom photographic film processing. As with other Nik plug-ins, Silver Efex Pro enables you to selectively control the tones and contrast in the image with the U Point technology. Silver Efex Pro conversions have the look of traditional film black-and-white images because the Nik plug-in re-creates

the film grain from the pixels in the photo, instead of overlaying a grain pattern as with other digital conversions. You can also select a black-and-white film type so your final image more closely emulates the look of a grayscale photo shot with film.

Silver Efex Pro includes a number of presets, such as tints and toners, so you can vary the resulting conversion in numerous ways. You can add a vignette or burned-in edges, and you can even save your own settings as presets. You can download a trial version to use with your images at www.niksoftware.com.

① Click Silver Efex Pro in the Selective palette.

Note: If the Selective palette is not open, click File, Automate, and then Nik Selective Tool.

Note: Optionally, you can click Filter, Nik Software, and then Color Efex Pro 3.0 to open the Nik Color Efex Pro dialog box.

The Silver Efex Pro dialog box appears.

② Click and drag the resize corner so the dialog box fills the screen.

③ Click any of the preset styles in the left panel to view the preset conversion in the main preview window.

④ Click and drag any of the sliders to adjust the overall tones in the image.

Note: Increasing the Brightness slider increases the lightness of the image. Increasing the Contrast slider increases the contrast in the image. Increasing the Structure slider makes finer details more noticeable. Decreasing the structure slider gives the area a smoother appearance.

● You can click Add Control Point; click in the image to add a control point and drag the sliders as in steps 7 and 8 of Task #109 to adjust the tones in a specific area.

⑤ Click the Show Image Only button to hide the style browser and make the image in the preview area larger.

⑥ Click a color filter, such as the red filter.

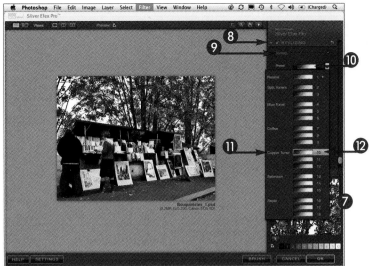

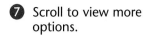

The preview enlarges and the color filter changes the grayscale composition.

7 Scroll to view more options.

8 Click Stylizing.

9 Click Toning.

10 Click here to view the presets.

11 Move the cursor over each preset to view the results.

12 Click a preset to apply it.

13 Click Vignette.

The Vignette options appear.

14 Scroll to view the sliders.

15 Click and drag the Amount and Size sliders to adjust the vignette.

16 Click and drag the slider under Rectangle to create a rectangular vignette as in this example, or under Circle for a circular vignette effect.

17 Click OK.

The black and white filter is applied to the image as a separate layer.

 TIPS

Did You Know?
You can select a different location for the center of the vignette by clicking the Place Center button in the Vignette pane and then clicking the image in the area you want for the center.

More Options!
Stylize a black-and-white image by clicking one of the presets, such as the Copper Toner as in step 12. Then move the Strength, Balance, and Paper Toning sliders to customize the look.

Try This!
Click Burn Edges at the bottom of the Stylizing pane. Click one of the four edge buttons to adjust the left, top, right, or bottom edge. Then click and drag the Strength, Size, and Transition sliders to digitally burn one edge of your image for a unique look.

TRANSFORM AN IMAGE
with an action from Kubota Image Tools

Kubota Image Tools designs image enhancing tools to help photographers process images quickly. The various tool packs include an assortment of Photoshop actions you can use to change an image with one click. You can increase the strength of the colors, add overall contrast, or even add an ethereal glow to an image without working through the steps in Photoshop. Kubota Image Tools also includes easy-to-apply standard frames so you can quickly give any image a finished look. Because actions are a series of prerecorded steps, some actions stop and ask you to

adjust a selection for your photo or enter values in a dialog box before the transformation is complete.

Installing actions differs from the installation of plug-ins. Once copied to the hard drive, you load the actions using Photoshop's Actions panel. To apply a Kubota Image Tools enhancement you can then click the desired action in the Actions panel and click the Play button. You can process multiple images with a single action using the batch command in Photoshop to increase your productivity. You can view the results of many of Kubota Image Tools actions at www.kubotaimagetools.com.

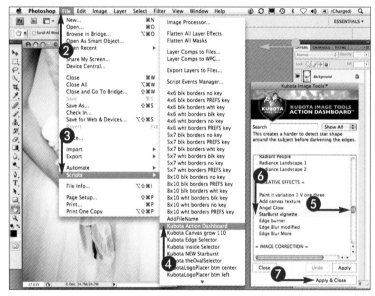

APPLY A STARBURST VIGNETTE WITH AN ACTION

① Load the Kubota actions following the step-by-step instructions on the DVD.

② In Photoshop, click File.

③ Click Scripts.

④ Click Kubota Action Dashboard to bring up the Dashboard.

⑤ Scroll to view the action choices.

⑥ Click an action such as StarBurst vignette.

⑦ Click Apply & Close.

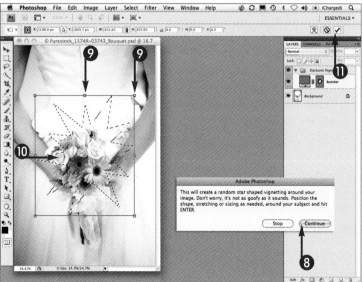

⑧ Click Continue in the dialog box describing the action.

The action creates a custom shape layer and stops so you can adjust the starburst shape to fit your photo.

⑨ Click and drag the anchors to adjust the shape.

⑩ Click and drag the shape into position over the main subject, if necessary.

⑪ Press ⌘+Return (Ctrl+Enter) or click the commit button.

- The action applies a blended starburst vignette-shaped layer and mask to the photo.

APPLY A BORDER WITH AN ACTION

⑫ Repeat steps 2 to 5 to open and view the actions in the Kubota Action Dashboard.

⑬ Type a word, such as **Border**, into the search field.

The corresponding actions are listed in the menu.

⑭ Click a border, such as Border Black with White vertical.

⑮ Click Apply.

- The action applies a new layer with a black frame and a white keyline on the photo.

- Depending on the action selected, a dialog box may appear with more instructions. Close the dialog box by clicking Stop.

⑯ Click Close to close the Kubota Image Tools Action Dashboard.

⑰ Click Layer and then Flatten Image to finish the enhancement.

111

DIFFICULTY LEVEL

TIPS

Important!
Kubota's Action Paks include the Action Dashboard utility. The instructions on the DVD show you how to create a keyboard shortcut to bring up the Action Dashboard.

Did You Know?
Kubota actions create snapshots of your image before applying complex sets of layers. You can easily click Undo on the Dashboard or use the History panel to restore the previous image.

More Options!
The Production Tools Pak includes actions for resizing images to standard photographic sizes, creating black or white borders, and automatically placing your logo on your photos.

EXPLORE COLORS VISUALLY
with AutoFX Software

The colors in your images can express moods and messages that transcend the subject matter. Although you can change the colors and tones in Photoshop, using software plug-in filters such as Mystical Tint, Tone, and Color from AutoFX Software can help you explore color tones and reinterpret your images in an artistic way. Mystical Tint, Tone, and Color includes 38 different visual effects with over 400 presets. You can make overall changes to your images or brush over the specific areas of colors and tones you want to change. You can try the layer

presets from a visual gallery or explore the results with any number of the individual special effects, experiment with various settings, and watch the results in a large display. You can also combine multiple effects and still control the settings for each one. When you see the results you want, you apply the filters to the image. The following task uses only two of the effects to enhance the photograph.

You can find other visual imaging solutions for creative effects on the gallery pages at www.AutoFx.com.

① Press ⌘+J (Ctrl+J) to duplicate the Background layer.

② Click Filter.

③ Click AutoFX Software.

④ Click Mystical Tint • Tone • Color.

The Mystical interface fills the screen.

⑤ Click Special Effects.

⑥ Click Soft Saturation.

● The Soft Saturation controls appear.

7 Click and drag the Saturation slider to the right to increase the saturation.

8 Click Special Effects again.

9 Click Over Exposed.

● The Over Exposed controls appear.

Note: The image temporarily appears overexposed.

10 Click and drag the Exposure slider to lighten the overall image.

11 Click the Mode pull-down menu.

12 Click Brush On.

The overall effect reverts to the previous look.

13 Click the Brush button.

14 Click the Brush Size controls and drag the bottom slider to increase the brush size.

15 Click and drag in the image over dark areas to lighten them.

16 Click OK to apply the filters.

The Mystical dialog box closes and the image reopens in Photoshop with the filter applied to Layer 1.

TIPS

Did You Know?
You can add multiple effects on various layers by clicking Special Effects and selecting different filters each time. You can use the floating layers palette in the Mystical dialog box to delete effect layers or even to add others.

Try This!
Apply an effect in the Global mode. Click the Eraser tool. Change the Size, Feathering, and Opacity using the sliders in the thumbnail below the Eraser. Click and drag in the image to remove the effect in specific areas.

More Options!
Click the View pull-down arrow in the Mystical dialog box and click Fit in Window. You can also use the Zoom tool to view specific areas as you add the effects. Press Option (Alt) and click the Zoom tool to zoom out.

ENHANCE YOUR PORTRAITS
with Imagenomic Portraiture

Retouching portraits in Photoshop involves many different tools and techniques. Softening the skin can involve multiple masks and many tedious steps. You have to make detailed selections of areas such as hair and eyelashes to protect them when you apply softening effects to the skin. You can use Imagenomic's Portraiture plug-in to smooth skin and remove imperfections without making selections or manually creating masks.

Portraiture's algorithms work differently compared to standard Photoshop tools. The plug-in includes an Auto Mask feature that automatically selects only the range of skin tones in the image so you can build an effective mask without selecting the hair, eyelashes, or other detailed areas. You can adjust the auto mask and then select from different tones to give your particular image the most natural-looking results.

Portraiture includes presets you can apply or use as a starting point. You can refine the corrections using the Enhancement sliders. You can also tailor any preset and save the modified version as your own custom preset to fit your photos and speed up your processing time. You can download a trial version from www.imagenomic.com.

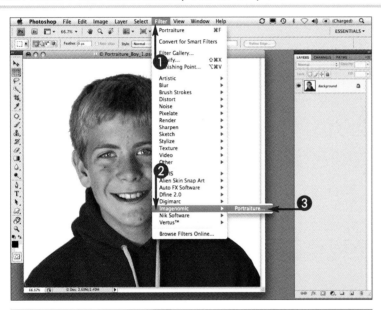

❶ Click Filter.

❷ Click Imagenomic.

❸ Click Portraiture.

The Portraiture interface fills the screen and the default smoothing is applied.

● Imagenomics remembers the last settings you applied. You may need to click here and select Auto if it is not selected.

❹ Click a Split Preview Window button to see a before and after preview.

❺ Click here and select 100%.

❻ Click Accurate to see the most accurate preview.

❼ Click here and select New Layer.

❽ Click Create Transparency Mask to apply the adjustments on a transparent layer.

❾ Click and drag the Detail Smoothing sliders to increase or decrease the effect.

● You can click here to select another preset, such as Smoothing: Normal.

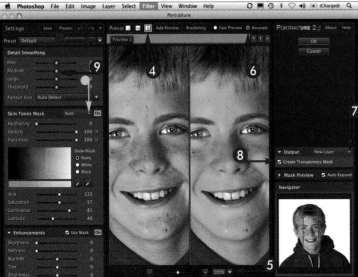

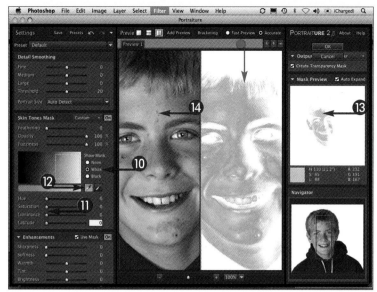

10 Click White to see the current Auto Mask.

11 Click and drag the Hue, Saturation, Luminance, and Latitude sliders completely to the left.

12 Click the left eyedropper.

13 Move the cursor over the skin tones to see the mask selections in the Mask Preview window.

14 Click the most representative area of skin in the image.

● A new mask appears in the after view.

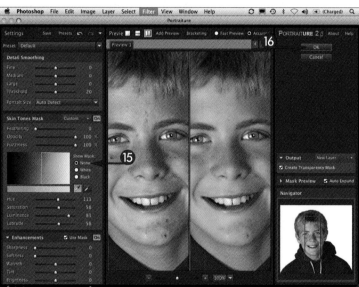

15 Click None to hide the mask and show the preview of the smoothed image.

16 Click OK.

The smoothing appears on a separate layer above the Background layer in Photoshop.

 TIPS

Try This!
You can apply Portraiture's auto mask even when batch-processing images. The masks are built based on each image's unique skin tone range, so even in a group of photos every skin type is handled individually.

More Options!
You can add a glamour effect to a portrait quickly by using the sliders under Enhancements to change the sharpness, softness, warmth, brightness, and contrast for a different effect.

Did You Know?
The area on the forehead between the two eyebrows is generally a good representation of the overall skin tone in the portrait and a good area to select from with Portraiture's eyedropper tool.

TRAVEL BEYOND BRIDGE
with Extensis Portfolio

Extensis Portfolio is a unique tool for organizing and managing all kinds of digital files. Portfolio enables you to categorize and store files in a variety of ways, including creating searchable CDs or DVDs. You can quickly find a specific file whether it is stored on your computer or on any external drive, CD, or DVD. Because of its added functionality, Portfolio goes beyond the capabilities of Bridge and many other applications for managing digital assets. Use Portfolio to download your photos to your computer, rename

the files, and include any EXIF, XMP, or catalog data you want. Portfolio adds thumbnails and screen previews to the database. You can burn a CD or DVD from within Portfolio's dialog box and include not only the original images but also Portfolio's read-only browser application. This browser allows you to quickly search through the CD/DVD media when inserted into any computer. Portfolio's powerful database tracks your files and gives you a visual preview of any image wherever it is stored.

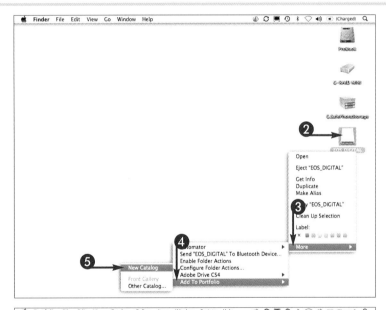

CREATE A CATALOG OF IMAGES

1 Insert a digital media card into your card reader.

2 Control+click (right-click) the digital media icon on the desktop.

3 Click More.

4 Click Add To Portfolio.

5 Click New Catalog.

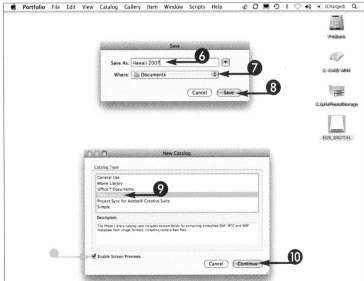

Portfolio opens a Save dialog box for the new catalog.

6 Type a name for the catalog.

7 Click here and select the location to save your catalog.

8 Click Save.

● The New Catalog dialog box appears with Enable Screen Previews selected by default.

9 Click a Catalog Type such as Photo Library.

10 Click Continue.

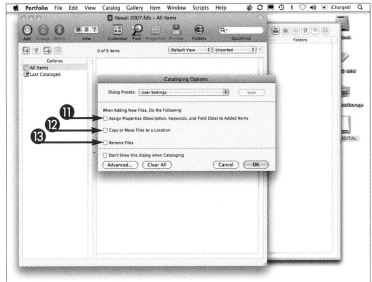

SET THE CATALOG OPTIONS

114

A new catalog and the Cataloging Options dialog box appear.

⑪ Click Assign Properties (☐ changes to ☑).

DIFFICULTY LEVEL

The Cataloging Options dialog box expands.

⑫ Click Copy or Move Files to a Location (☐ changes to ☑).

The dialog box expands again.

⑬ Click Rename Files (☐ changes to ☑).

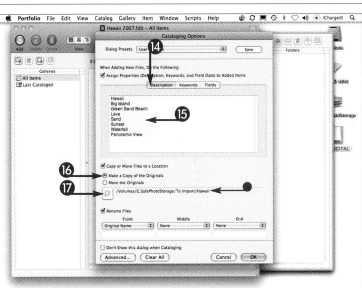

The dialog box expands again.

⑭ Click the Description tab.

⑮ Type descriptive words for your images in the field.

⑯ Click Make a Copy of the Originals (○ changes to ⊙).

⑰ Click the Folder button.

⑱ Navigate to the location for the catalog in the dialog box that appears and click Choose.

● The location appears in the field.

TIP

Try This!

Burn a DVD of the original images. From the menu, click Gallery and then click Burn to Disc. Type a name for the disc in the Volume Name field. Click Original Files and click Link Paths in Catalog to Files Burned to Disc. You can now search the Portfolio catalog on your computer and identify the specific DVD that includes those photo files. Type a folder name for the original files or previews and click Organize Files into Matching Folder Hierarchy. Click Create a Catalog and type a catalog name. Click Include the Macintosh (Windows) Browser Application and click Burn. Portfolio copies the files, prepares the catalog, and automatically launches the disc-burning application on your computer.

TRAVEL BEYOND BRIDGE
with Extensis Portfolio

Portfolio can catalog almost any type of digital file. You can add individual files, folders, or complete volumes such as a DVD or a hard drive by simply dragging the file, folder, or disk icon into an open catalog window. However, using the Instant Cataloging feature described in this task offers more options and control over the way Portfolio stores the information. By entering descriptions, keywords, or information in the custom fields, you can organize your files more easily. You can then customize

Portfolio to display images in galleries and to view images as thumbnails, lists, or individual items with all the stored data. To find a particular file, you can search with Portfolio's Quick Find, located on the toolbar, using any words or phrase you entered when cataloging the file. You can also search using the Find command and search for specific criteria associated with the file.

You can learn more about Portfolio and download a trial version at www.extensis.com.

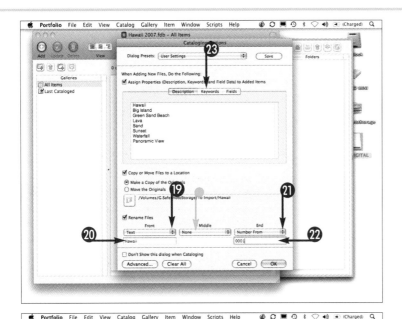

⑲ Click here and select Text.

⑳ Type a name in the data field.

● You can repeat steps 19 and 20 to set the middle part of the file names.

㉑ Click here and select Number From.

㉒ Type a starting number for the images in this catalog.

㉓ Click the Keywords tab.

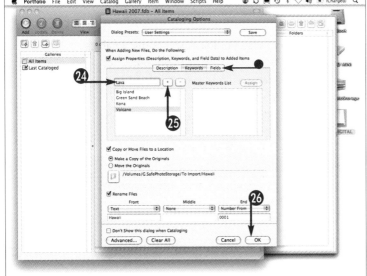

The Keywords pane of the dialog box appears.

㉔ Type a keyword here.

㉕ Click the plus sign to add the keyword to the list below.

● You can click the Fields tab and select the data to edit.

㉖ Click OK.

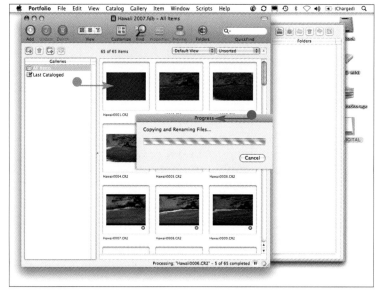

- A progress bar appears.

Note: *The time required to copy, catalog, and rename your files depends on the number and size of the files, as well as the speed and type of connection of the card reader.*

- Portfolio displays a partial catalog as it completes the process.

VIEW AN IMAGE AND ITS PROPERTIES

㉗ Click an image thumbnail.

㉘ Click the Preview button.

- Portfolio displays a larger preview of the photo.

㉙ Click the Properties button.

- Portfolio displays the details of the image data.

CUSTOMIZE THE CATALOG

㉚ Click the Customize button.

㉛ In the dialog box that appears, select the type of information to display with the thumbnails, such as the file name and camera model. You can also change the size of the thumbnails and the font size for the field names.

㉜ Click Apply to apply the changes and then Done to close the dialog box.

TIP

Did You Know?

Portfolio includes a separate application called Portfolio Express that enables you to find cataloged files without launching the complete application. After you launch Portfolio Express, you can keep it running in the background and hide or show the palette using a hot key. The compact Portfolio Express palette floats above other document windows. Use the QuickFind feature from the palette to find a particular image and double-click a thumbnail in the Portfolio Express palette to edit the original image. You can also drag and drop the thumbnail onto an alias (shortcut) of Photoshop to open it. You can even drag a thumbnail directly into an e-mail message to send a copy of the original file as an attachment.

Index

Index

Index

Index

Index